In Search of Identity

In Search of Identity

The Ongoing Crisis of Israeli Society

GADI HITMAN

Published by State University of New York Press, Albany

© 2025 State University of New York

All rights reserved

Printed in the United States of America

No part of this book may be used or reproduced in any manner whatsoever without written permission. No part of this book may be stored in a retrieval system or transmitted in any form or by any means including electronic, electrostatic, magnetic tape, mechanical, photocopying, recording, or otherwise without the prior permission in writing of the publisher.

Links to third-party websites are provided as a convenience and for informational purposes only. They do not constitute an endorsement or an approval of any of the products, services, or opinions of the organization, companies, or individuals. SUNY Press bears no responsibility for the accuracy, legality, or content of a URL, the external website, or for that of subsequent websites.

EU GPSR Authorised Representative:
Logos Europe, 9 rue Nicolas Poussin, 17000, La Rochelle, France
contact@logoseurope.eu

For information, contact State University of New York Press, Albany, NY
www.sunypress.edu

Library of Congress Cataloging-in-Publication Data

Name: Hitman, Gadi, author.
Title: In search of identity : the ongoing crisis of Israeli society / Gadi Hitman.
Description: Albany : State University of New York Press, [2025]. | Includes bibliographical references and index.
Identifiers: LCCN 2024053739 | ISBN 9798855803198 (hardcover : alk. paper) | ISBN 9798855803204 (ebook) | ISBN 9798855803211 (pbk. : alk. paper)
Subjects: LCSH: Israel—Population. | Israel—Ethnic relations. | Israelis—Ethnic identity. | Social integration—Israel. | Ethnicity—Israel. | Group identity—Israel. | National characteristics, Israeli. | Jews—Israel—Identity. | Palestinian Arabs—Israel—Ethnic identity.
Classification: LCC DS113.2 .H57 2025 | DDC 305.80095694—dc23/eng/20250121
LC record available at https://lccn.loc.gov/2024053739

Contents

Preface		vii
Chapter 1	Theoretical Dimensions of Identity and Cleavages	1
Chapter 2	The Evolution of Right and Left	15
Chapter 3	Statehood and Religion	41
Chapter 4	The Jewish-Arab Cleavage	73
Chapter 5	The Internal Arab Rift	105
Conclusion		131
Notes		135
Bibliography		149
Index		161

Preface

The internal political turmoil in Israel since November 2018 was the incentive to write this book. I felt that it was not just another case of political instability, but something different, unique, that Israeli society has never experienced before. The opening situation was not the same: a prime minister under police investigation (which later became an indictment); a judicial authority that had to rule whether the same prime minister was able to hold his position or not; new political figures who formed the "change" bloc; and, perhaps most important, the inability of the Israeli public to decide between two political blocs: one that supported a prime minister accused of criminal offenses and another that sought to end what it defined as "political corruption." In practice, these situation also reflects old and new divisions within Israeli society. This is what the book deals with: a snapshot of Israeli society from 2018 until the beginning of 2023.

This book, which is academic in nature, was also written as a service to the public in Israel. I decided to write it for several reasons. Firstly, I am an Israeli and a Jew. Or a Jew and an Israeli. For me, these are combined identities, not opposites. Secondly, my legal status is that of Israeli citizen, and I am watching the changes that Israeli society is going through at the beginning of the twenty-first century with interest (and concern for the future). Thirdly, I have not yet found a book that presents the readers with a comprehensive picture of the situation, one that breaks down Israeli society rift by rift. Finally, I believe that Israel, as a country and as a society, is searching for a new identity.

Previous studies have distinguished between the terms "Jewish state" and "democratic state" or between "right" and "left." I believe some of these terms, used regularly in the media and public discourse, are no longer relevant to Israeli society. The latter's search for a new identity has been going on for a long time and is the result of two profound processes. The first is on the geographical level and includes the establishment of a state, the increase in the area under Israel's control in June 1967 (the West Bank and the Gaza Strip), and the territorial contractions of 1982, 1994–1995, 1998, and 2005. On the other hand, the settlement project in the territories of Judea and Samaria resulted in a demographic change of the first order of magnitude, which calls into question the solution of two states for two peoples (Israelis and Palestinians). However, the subject of the book is not the ongoing Israeli-Palestinian conflict and the fate of the territories. This work goes much deeper than that: It deals with the search for identity within Israeli society, which is partly due to the existence of a non-Jewish population that has been continuously controlled by Israel since 1967. The search for identity is shared by both the Jewish majority in Israel and the non-Jewish minority, commonly called the Arabs in Israel. Generally speaking, the term "Arabs" in Israeli public discourse includes Muslims, Christians, Circassians, Baha'is, and Druze).

The second process is at the security-political level. Israel has experienced two national traumas: the October War in 1973, also known as the Yom Kippur War, and the assassination of Prime Minister Yitzhak Rabin in November 1995. The first trauma manifested in the failure of the intelligence concept, the huge number of war casualties, and the political price the war exacted in the elections of May 1977 from the ruling coalition headed by the Labor Party. The second trauma was embodied in the disbelief that a Jew would assassinate an elected prime minister in a country where the political model is representative democracy.

Since Rabin's murder, Israel has experienced several dramatic national events, such as the harsh clashes between the Arab minority and the security forces in October 2000, the Second Intifada (2000–2005), unilateral disengagement from the Gaza Strip (2005), the Second Lebanon War (2006), and Hamas' takeover of the Gaza Strip (2007), which increased the terror threat on the Israeli home front (however, my understanding is that this does not pose an existential threat to Israel). Following that, Israel and Hamas had four significant military collisions (2008, 2012, 2014, and 2021), plus dozens of low-intensity conflicts. Most recently, Israel has signed historic peace and normalization agreements with Arab countries—the United Arab Emirates, Bahrain, Morocco, and Sudan (2020)—but without solving the Palestinian question. And after all this, it must of course be remembered that Israel and Hamas have been at war since October 2023.

These events, composed of political, diplomatic, and security issues, are just part of the mosaic of change in Israeli society. In the Israeli internal arena, a term for describing the Israeli society, it seems that the polarization between various groups is becoming more extreme, far beyond the tribal speech of the former president, Reuven Rivlin, back in 2015. Such cleavages still exist between the center and the periphery, veterans and new immigrants, Jews and non-Jews, Ashkenazim and Mizrahim, and within the Arab society (see chapter 5). I have also noticed that various politicians and public figures are calling, time and again, for "unity in Israeli society." In this short preface, I suggest that people stop using this term because Israeli society is not unified. It seeks an identity, which is not necessarily uniform, and seeks to impose that identity on all the citizens who are members—Jews, Muslims, Christians, and others—of the same political community: the State of Israel.

Israeli society's lack of unity (and statehood—see chapter 3) is also reflected in its politics. Since Avigdor Lieberman resigned as minister of defense in November 2018, Israel has been subject to political instability, with five elections in less than four years. The political tumult into which Israeli society has fallen is not only the result of the inability of any candidate to form a majority in the House of Representatives (Knesset), the supreme state body in Israel's representative democracy—it has also been accompanied by violent (both verbal and physical) public discourse, and it paralyzed many public systems until mid-2021 due to inability of the Israeli Parliament (the Knesset) to pass an annual state budget. Perhaps it is this discourse, above all, that emphasizes the multiple cleavages of identity that exist in Israeli society between Jews and Arabs, between Jews and Jews, and between Arabs and Arabs.

Two crucial terms, which serve as an academic link connecting each chapter, are "identity" and "cleavage." Since its foundation, Israel has had optimal conditions to be a divided society: a heterogeneous demographic, a democratic regime that allows freedom of ideas and speech, a translation of these ideas into practice, a national conflict between Israel and its neighbors that affects the non-Jewish minority in Israel (most of them Muslims), and a built-in tension between the terms "Jewish" and "democratic." This book focuses on four major divisions in Israeli society, each impacting its search for identity and, possibly, making it difficult to find a common identity that the founding fathers of the State of Israel dreamed of.

Chapter 1 undertakes a theoretical review of the two basic and abstract terms "cleavage" and "identity." This will help the reader create a clear distinction between different groups that together form a heterogeneous demographic mosaic. Cleavage and identity are two terms intertwined in numerous research fields, such as sociology, psychology, political science, and history. Chapter 1's theoretical framework is necessary not only for scientific needs but also to frame the discussion and create a uniform language. In this way, when the topic is "right" versus "left," for example, the reader can associate it with a collective or personal identity, in addition to understanding the component of the division this study attempts to present.

Chapter 2 analyzes the left-right cleavage, considering the terms "right" and "left" in the global and Israeli context and offering a new analytical framework. From the many conversations I have had with Israelis in recent years and from analyzing countless press materials (written and electronic media), including news articles, comments on websites, Facebook posts, and WhatsApp messages, it has become clear to me that most Israelis are not fully aware of the left-right issue (what the ideological right is, what the ideological left is, what the roots and sources of these two terms are), which has divided Israeli society since the June 1967 war, if not earlier. Phrases such as "extreme rightist" or "traitorous leftist" have become commonplace for many Israelis who do not understand the essence of that extremism, if it exists. Additionally, the term "traitor" is being used for people who fought for the establishment of the state and defended it with body and soul.

Chapter 3 deals with the split between the national and religious camps. The national camp requires respect for the law, the policies of the executive authority, and the decisions of the judicial authority. This camp also unites liberals, conservatives, and religious, traditional, and secular people, for whom Israel must be not only sovereign over the land but also capable of governing. The religious camp includes ultra-Orthodox (about 12.5 percent of the population, 1.2 million souls at the end of 2020), religious, traditional, and conservative secular people, who are the smallest group in it (details of the demographic segmentation will be presented in chapter 3). Various communities within this camp choose Torah law over state law. This position undermines the state's ability to govern (see, e.g., the behavior of the ultra-Orthodox public during the coronavirus epidemic in 2020–2021) and demands the sanctity of the land for the Jewish people. From this perspective, political positions are derived that affect not only the legislative and executive authorities but also the entire Israeli public.

The third cleavage is the national one, which divides Jews and non-Jews. This is often characterized as the most severe split in Israeli society. At first glance it appears to be true that this is indeed the most significant rift in Israeli society, at least in 1967 and after the attempt to resolve the conflict between Israel and the Palestinians in the Oslo Accords (1993). However, it seems that this argument lost its power after Israel and the Arab states signed a series of accords between 1979 and 2020. Moreover, the Jewish public, which constitutes the majority in Israel, treats Arabs—not always correctly—as a unified community, without discerning between the Palestinians living in the Gaza Strip under the rule of Hamas since 2007, the Palestinians in Judea and Samaria under the rule of the Palestinian Authority, and the Arab citizens of Israel. Chapter 4 thus offers an orderly distinction between the various groups that receive the collective name "Arabs" and analyzes the relationship of each such group with the State of Israel.

Chapter 5 deals with the rift within the Arab minority society in Israel. This internal conflict is not just an outcome of political rivalry. Its roots go back to the fact that the non-Jewish minority in Israel is heterogeneous and has different sociopolitical ideas (national, religious, civic). Arab liberals and conservatives are fighting for a modern versus traditional lifestyle, and, perhaps most significantly, in recent years there has been enmity between those who seek integration into Israeli society (and politics) and those who prefer separatist approaches. The manifestations of this divide are diverse and include positions on political participation, the use of violence and harming innocents, self-esteem, and personal promotion versus collective identity and minority groups' interests. These divisions are reflected in internal public discourse about issues such as enlisting in the army or police or for national service, which are all ways to gain legitimacy for integration into Israeli society.

This book is the product of long conversations with numerous Israelis to whom I am indebted. I thank them for their comments, clarifications, remarks, questions, solutions, and suggestions. They are Israelis who label themselves as Jews (in the religious-national meaning), Zionists, Israeli Arabs, ultra-Orthodox, and Druze, as well as Israelis who do not have an ethnic-religious affiliation. This book uses language intended to be accessible to all souls, although I realize its contents will not necessarily be pleasant for parts of the Israeli public. It is not my goal to antagonize such readers. The goal is to present to the reader a society and country that has long been searching for identity, not only geographically but also in terms of moral values, ethics, and integrity.

Gadi Hitman
December 2024

Chapter 1

Theoretical Dimensions of Identity and Cleavages

We are all born with both personal and collective identity. Our personal identity is gendered and associated with race and ethnicity. Our collective identity is family, class, and sometimes also sectarian, tribal, and national. But how do we define the term identity? The Jewish poet Shaul Tchernichovsky once wrote "Man is nothing but a pattern of his native landscape."[1] If we accept this definition, which is, of course, a line from a poem and is not based on scientific research, then anyone born in a territory subject to the sovereignty of a regime automatically has the identity of that country. This is without defining whether it is a civil identity (i.e., a citizen has an identity card and a passport) or a national identity in the sense of belongingness. Everyone born in Israel, for instance, has a civil identity, but some challenge this term and explain that citizenship is a legal status, not an identity.[2]

We are not just born with an identity; we are all also looking for identity because it defines the individual, as we perceive ourselves and as society perceives us. In some cases, the individual and society see the same lines of identity, but in others, this is not necessarily true. What we think about ourselves is not automatically reflected outward, whether to family, tribe, community, or society. This perceptual gap meets us in every social contact in the family, school, army, university, workplace, or recreation arena. We are all also characterized by multiple identities. For example, on special occasions when every family member is sitting around the same table, four generations can sit next to each other: great-grandfather, grandfather, son, and grandson. In this case, the grandfather carries three family identities:

He is simultaneously a son, a father, and a grandfather. In the interactions that develop, he switches identities automatically. Yet there is more to this point. What about identifying with the school that each family member attended? They can identify themselves as part of the same family but not as a part of the same school, university, army unit, or sports team. We can apply this argument to the discussion of political identities and social perceptions, which deserves a central place in a book about Israeli society, which itself is looking for a political identity.

Being accurate when defining identity requires complex efforts. Psychologists and sociologists have suggested different explanations for why everybody is searching for an identity. Concentrating on cognitive reasons, people understand how they identify themselves and what their values, principles, morals, and ethics are after realizing the essence and meaning of these values. But cognition itself is not enough because all human beings have emotions that influence our self-definition. We all possess the basic, human need to be part of a group or community, mainly due to the fear of being ostracized, left out, or taken away. In such situations, subgroups develop with which each person chooses to identify in any given society.[3] We all have multiple identities, some complementary and some conflicting. There are cases where we define ourselves and other cases where the environment instills in us other identification marks, though these are not always correct. There are permanent identities, such as skin color or height, and there are variable identities, such as weight or religion.[4]

We can illustrate this abstract theory with two examples. On the one hand, Tunisia is a country of about eleven million people, the vast majority of whom are Sunni Muslims (over 98 percent). In scientific language, such a country is classified as a homogeneous country. Despite this, the different identities that have developed in Tunisia are not based on religion but rather on gender, class, and ideological backgrounds (religious vs. liberal). Lebanon, on the other hand, has eighteen different communities belonging to three large groups (Christians, Muslims, and Druze). Such a society is heterogeneous, and the possibilities to create multiple identities, some overlapping and some conflicting, are endless. These raise, inter alia, the question of what the national characteristics of Lebanon are. In other words, while there is no collision between different religions in Tunisia, this collision exists in Lebanon and has affected politics in the country since the days of the French Mandate.[5]

Identity, therefore, has individual and collective components. Humans identify themselves according to their born and acquired traits, their interactions with the environment (me vs. the other), and the experiences they have accumulated over their lives (external influences). These include the influence of people perceived by the individual as leaders or mentors who shaped their path, starting with their teacher at school, their instructor in the youth movement, their commander in the army, or their lecturer at university. Even the home in which each of us grew up has a real impact on shaping our personal and sometimes group identity.[6]

Scholars who have tried to define the term "identity" have pointed out its internal (inherent) problematic. Bernd Simon, for instance, advised that identity may be imagined and ambiguous as an analytic fiction and that the endless effort to understand what it is may be futile. He approached the issue from the angle of social psychology and examined the self-identity of the individual vis-à-vis the environment. The model he proposes is based on three stages. In the first stage, the individual receives stimuli from the environment (the input stage). In the second stage, they consolidate their identity (personal and collective), that is, how they see themself, where they aspire to go, and with which values of a community or society they identify. The third stage is the realization stage (the output stage), in which the individual places themself in the social circles they wish to integrate into and within which everyone operates.[7]

Rogers Brubaker and Frederick Cooper argued that the term "identity" is elusive: There are contexts in which it is used excessively, there are situations in which its use is rather weak, and there are cases in which it is vague and incomprehensible.[8] In their article, they examined the use of the term in academia and media in the United States from the early 1960s and discovered that it was overused in various social contexts. According to them, American society—which has experienced significant events such as the 1960s civil rights protests and the Vietnam war, and has been empowered to discuss race, class, gender, immigrants, and social, ethnic, and national movements—has worn out the use of the term "identity," and thus they did not know how to investigate the meaning of each of these topics in depth in the given context.

The famous American sociologist Charles Tilly proposed the following definition of identity: "The experience of the individual who is in a group, relationship, position or organization that has a public representation, which sometimes takes on an element of a shared story." Tilly associates this with the categories of race, gender, class, hand delivery, religion, and national origin.[9]

If we go back to Brubaker and Cooper, as political scientists they see the term "identity" in terms of its use for analyzing political behavior.

And yet, according to them, it is not necessary to analyze such behavior precisely through identity. As an example, they cite the term "nation," which describes a group of people with political claims to sovereignty over a certain territory. These claims do not have to be explained by using identity. At the theoretical level, the analytical model they offer can be considered legitimate—that is, to analyze political behavior (e.g., ideology) regardless of identity. However, in reality, at least in the case of the Jewish-Arab divide in Israel (see chapter 4), it is difficult, if not impossible, to have a serious discussion on the subject without raising arguments about what constitutes identity on a primordial basis.

As part of the theoretical discussion, which is a platform for diagnosing the different identities within Israeli society, Simon suggested some parameters that may be useful to establish what personal and collective identity consists of

a) Personality traits, e.g., shyness or extroversion

b) Abilities, e.g., athleticism, acting or dancing skills, phenomenal memory

c) Physical features, e.g., facial structure, eye color, hair type, thin or broad body

d) Behavioral characteristics, e.g., waking up early or late, eating habits, drinking alcohol or abstaining from it

e) Political ideology, i.e., supporting a party's platform

f) Faith (or lack thereof) in a cultural system, which consists of religion, tradition, customs, and personal and collective historical memory

g) Role or place in society, e.g., leader or follower of public opinion, ability or inability to form social relationships, status in a workplace

h) Language belonging

i) Membership of a social, sports, musical, or cultural club; youth movement; traveling group; or veteran organization.[10]

Anyone who reads these parameters can easily form the elements of their identity. The problem starts when we identify with a certain group and are surprised to discover that it includes people who, until a moment ago, we were sure were not part of the group to which we now belong. Take the example of a sports team in Israel, whose fans include Jews and non-Jews, religious and secular, old and young, women and men, whites and blacks. In this situation, there exists a social structure of intersecting identities. The fans meet in the same stadium, in the same stands, cheering on their favorite team, but as soon as the game ends, they go their separate ways. The collective identity expressed in common sympathy for their favorite sports team (Maccabi Haifa, Maccabi Tel Aviv, etc.) vanishes and clears the spiritual area for a new circle of identities. Here, naturally, there will already be another social network of contextual identity: Religious people will find it in prayer in the church, mosque, or synagogue with other religious people who are not sports fans, while secular people will not attend the holy places and whites and blacks will return to their neighborhoods. In the Israeli case, Jews and non-Jews, despite the same sporting identity, will return to their identity based on nationality-religion.

If we agree that we all have a personal identity and group identity and we all incorporate more than one element into our identity, then quite a few people also have a hybrid identity. The word "hybrid" originates from biology: "In its etymology it meant the offspring of a tame sow and a wild boar, hybrid, and this genetic component provides the first meaning."[11] It means, in fact, a mixture, a cross between two separate races or plants. Despite its biological origin, scholars have used the term over the years to explain new forms of culture, suggesting that people originating from two (or more) ethnic groups have formed something new. Thus, its use became common among nonbiological researchers, such as sociologists, anthropologists, political scientists, and historians who sought to explain new cultures. For example, they proposed the term "hybrid" for people who have a different ethnic or racial background, such as the offspring of a black man and a white woman, the offspring of a religious man and a secular woman, or the offspring of a man and a woman of different religions (or different groups within Islam or Christianity).

Among researchers in the West, the term "hybridity" was often used to refer to the relations between the representatives of the colonial powers (Britain, France, Portugal, Germany, Belgium, the Netherlands) and the indigenous populations whom they met in the continents of Asia, Africa, and America. In these places, cultures grew that merged that of the conquerors with that of the conquered, and the new product was called a "hybrid culture." In the case of Israeli society, hybridity can describe the relationships between Jews from the East and those who came from Western (and Eastern) Europe, first-generation and later-generation immigrants, and Jews and non-Jews.

The Argentinian researcher Néstor García-Canclini claims that the fact that the word "hybrid" is biological in origin means that it does not explain social phenomena. In his understanding, to say that a certain person has a hybrid identity like a hybrid between two plants means, in fact, nothing. The hybrid identity of that person must be tied to history, religion, leaders, language, customs, or values in the sense of traditions that are passed down in a family or community from generation to generation.[12] Nikos Papastergiadis, an art researcher from Australia, examined hybrid identity by looking at paintings and sculptures and found that the artists presented works that connected the past and the present. By observing the artisans at work, he identified two stages in the formation of the new hybrid culture. The first was the understanding and awareness that the culture created was a combination of two different cultures; that is, a third culture was created—the hybrid one. In the second stage, he tested how willing the community is to neutralize the effects of a foreign culture or, alternatively, to adopt these influences.[13] Keri Iyall Smith and Patricia Leavy claim that identities do not change independently but rather that a combination of elements causes the formation of a new, hybrid identity. In their view, the term "hybrid" was used in the past to present an inferior identity due to being a fusion of two pure identities. Here, too, there is a perceptual distortion. This is because there is no pure identity, if only because cultures are influenced by each other.[14]

The discussion of the term "identity" is also relevant to politics, where individuals, groups, and parties seek to realize ideas, goals, and visions that reflect their identity. Since people are different from each other in many aspects, disputes arise that create rifts when they meet in political environments. In the Israeli case, we are dealing with a heterogenous society that has many identities and many (perhaps too many) subdivisions. As part of the theoretical discussion, I wish to distinguish between two terms that represent two completely different populations in the context of the State of Israel. The first is "the sons of Israel" ("Bnei Israel" in Hebrew) and is synonymous with "Jews." This term has religious roots, and since Judaism claims sovereignty over people and territory, it has also adopted national elements. Tangible examples can be found not only in the Jewish holidays that originate in the Jewish holy book, the Torah, but also in three national holidays that the state has established: Holocaust and

Heroism Remembrance Day (Yom HaShoah), Memorial Day for the Fallen Soldiers of the Wars of Israel and Victims of Actions of Terrorism (Yom HaZikaron), and Independence Day (Yom Ha'Atzmaut). Some would also add Jerusalem Day and Hebron Liberation Day. Holocaust and Heroism Remembrance Day begins with the words "The nation of Israel unites with the six million Jews who perished in the Holocaust." There is automatically an overlap between the terms "the nation of Israel" and "Jews." The refrain is almost the same for Memorial Day. The difference is in the mention of the members of the minorities (mostly Druze) who sacrificed their lives in defense of their homeland.

The fact that Druze defended Israel (their homeland) from its enemies serves as a bridge to the second term: "the Israeli people." This refers to all the people who are part of the sociopolitical community who are allowed to participate in the process of electing representatives to the legislature (Knesset). These people can live in Israel or outside of it and may be Jews or non-Jews. Nevertheless, "the Israeli people" is not just a legal term. It also reflects cultural aspects of customs shared by the ethnically, religiously, and linguistically heterogeneous population living in the State of Israel.

The heterogeneity of the population is a constant challenge for any government that seeks to regulate its relationship with minority groups. These can be, for example, national minorities, such as the non-Jewish minority, who are variously called the "Arabs of Israel," the "Arab citizens of Israel," and the "Palestinian citizens of Israel." There may also be a minority within the majority group. In the Israeli case, these include Ethiopian Jews (so-called because of their skin color) and ultra-Orthodox Jews.

The research literature offers four different models for shaping relations between groups with different identities living in the same territory. The first model is nation-building, and its purpose is to unite different groups in society into one nation. Such an attempt has been made, for example, in Canada since the 1960s against the background of cultural differences between English speakers and French speakers. The former believe that decentralizing power from the federal government contributes to shaping Canadian nationalism. The latter believe that this decentralization harms the uniqueness of French Canadian culture, which they seek to preserve.

The second model is egalitarian pluralism, which sees groups' identity differences as an opportunity for the growth of a heterogeneous culture.[15] Each group in such an environment can preserve its unique characteristics and at the same time be part of a nation containing groups (including hybrid groups) with different identities and cultures.[16] A democratic country that uses this model is the United States, where, for example, cultural freedom is given to the Native Americans in the reservations where they live. When they leave the reservation, they can preserve this culture while simultaneously being part of the American nation. This is also the case regarding the preservation of religion, which does not harm the freedom of occupation and equal opportunities at work.

The third model is unequal pluralism. Researchers of Israeli society agree that Israel is one a country that creates unequal pluralism. Sammy Smooha believes Israel is an ethnic democracy in which all citizens have political rights, but the Jewish majority group enjoys structural and essential priorities.[17]

The fourth and final model is separation, where leaders decide to create a nation based on one ethnic group. Such separation between groups with different ethnic and religious identities can be seen, for example, in the establishment of Bosnia and Herzegovina on the understanding that only such separation would allow a daily routine that would not be accompanied by violence and bloodshed.[18]

Cleavages

Multiple identities lead, almost unwittingly, to the construction of barriers between the various groups that make up the population. These barriers can become cleavages that decrease the power and strength of a shared identity. A rift is a tangible or abstract boundary that divides and separates different groups in any given society, between which tension, discord, and hostility exist. Naturally, the chance of identifying divisions (economic, social, class, etc.) is higher in heterogeneous societies such as Israel. In a divided society, there is also the possibility that the rift will become one that cannot be reconciled, as happened, for example, in the struggle between the Hutu and Tutsi tribes to control Rwanda in 1994.[19] A deep rift or rupture threatens the cohesion of a society and its resilience and may also erode its fundamental principles, such as pluralism and tolerance in a society with democratic characteristics.

When we discuss cleavages that separate groups, we are actually referring to the divisions that exist within a given society. In the international arena, such divisions are made, among other things, on issues such as economic left and right, democracy versus authoritarianism, religion versus secularism, and separatism versus integration. There are other divisions as well, all of which are relevant to the analysis of Israeli society that will follow:

a) A gap between a city and a village marks a geographical difference that manifests itself, e.g., in the nature of one's residence, hand delivery, accessibility to places of consumption and recreation, and culture of leisure time.

b) A difference between employer and employee expresses a class and economic gap.

c) A gap between the center and the periphery distinguishes between different cultures and, in many cases, between populations with ethnic differences.

d) A rift between church and state symbolizes a political dispute over the characteristics of the ruling culture.[20]

Such divisions, in the Israeli case, exist between economic and social classes, the educated and uneducated, women and men, religious people and communities and secular ones, whites and blacks, Jews and non-Jews, residents of the center and residents of the periphery, and residents living in Israel and those living in the territories of Judea and Samaria (and, until August 2005, in the Gaza Strip). All these territories were and still are subject to Israeli military control without being legally annexed to the sovereign territory of Israel. All these divisions not only have different types of divisions in their content but different elements of identity can also be identified within these groups, even if, for example, all Jews define themselves as Jews, Israelis, or Zionists.

Seymour Lipset and Stein Rokkan presented their analysis of the formation of political divisions in the 1960s. They claimed that two revolutions, the industrial and the national, affected the voting patterns of voters in democratic elections. They concluded that the industrial revolution that began in the nineteenth century in Western Europe created clear class differences in those countries. These differences deepened an economic-class cleavage that was expressed, among other ways, in the political participation of the voters. Second, the idea of nationalism that took root in the West sharpened differences between groups in terms of their ethnic background, affected political voting patterns, and highlighted different identities.[21]

Identities and cleavages are expressed politically through parties. The word "party" expresses the representation of one part of the population.[22] This is also the political reality in Israel, which is a representative democracy where many parties seek a place in the Knesset. Political divisions change over time for various reasons, including generational changes, events that change public consciousness, the entry of new players (whether individuals or groups/parties) into the political arena, demographics, the economic situation, and so on.

Clem Brooks, Paul Nieuwbeerta, and Jeff Manza, who examined voting patterns in democracies, mapped three structural divisions in society: gender (male-female), class (economic-social), and religion (religious-secular).[23] Theoretically and practically, we can create at least eight types of identities according to this key:

1. Male, low socioeconomic status, religious
2. Male, high socioeconomic status, religious
3. Male, low socioeconomic status, secular
4. Male, high socioeconomic status, secular
5. Female, low socioeconomic status, religious
6. Female, high socioeconomic status, religious
7. Female, low socioeconomic status, secular
8. Female, high socioeconomic status, secular

Now, let us take these divisions into Israeli society. As we have seen, there are eight different identities, without including the subgroups within each of them, that make up Israeli society, which also includes a Jewish majority and a non-Jewish minority, all of whom have heterogeneous identities. Moreover, none of this takes into account personal backgrounds: the experiences we have accumulated over time; the values we have absorbed from our family, education systems, or the army; or, of course, our political tendencies. The resulting conclusion is clear: In Israel, there are countless divisions and identities. They overlap and collide with each other at the same time and cause us all, almost automatically, to wear several identities that we adopt according to the socioeconomic, political, military, cultural, sports, or family context.

Lipset and Rokkan's analysis can be used, at least in part, as a theoretical basis for analyzing the cleavages in Israeli society. The model they propose is appropriate because they claim, for instance, that as soon as a rift is created, it becomes a constant barrier that preserves the identity and ideological and political differences between different individuals, groups, and communities. I suggest focusing on the social and national cleavages and skipping the class divide. Not because it is not important but because it does not directly (and perhaps not even indirectly) affect the process of Israeli society's search for identity. This search causes, apparently unwittingly, changes in the meaning of terms used as cornerstones for defining identity, such as right and left, religious and secular, and nation-state and nationalism.

Israeli Society Data

Israel's population is heterogenous: It has a Jewish majority and a non-Jewish minority. The Jews (74 percent) consist of four subgroups or tribes, as the former president of Israel, Reuven Rivlin, pointed out in 2015: ultra-Orthodox, religious, traditional, and secular. Table 1.1 illustrates the distribution of those aged eighteen and above—that is, those who have the right to vote and influence the political system, according to the data of the Central Bureau of Statistics (August 2021).

Israel has another identity group that cannot be ignored: As of the beginning of the twenty-first century, there is a third generation (and the beginning of a fourth generation) of Jews from countries in the West and the East. There is also a group of about 160,000 Jews who originate from Ethiopia and whose skin color is different from that of most other Jews.[24]

These subgroups—all within the Jewish majority group—produce common and contrasting identities simultaneously. They maintain a traditional identity based on stories passed down from generation to generation (a kind of oral Torah) and, at the same time, adopt modern identities that result from external influences (outside the family circle), starting with the education system, the military, social networks, the media, and global social phenomena.

Table 1.1. The Jewish Majority's Four Subgroups

Total population	Ultra-Orthodox	Religious	Traditional	Secular
4,495,000	456,000	525,000	1,482,000	2,012,000

Source: Israel Central Bureau of Statistics, "Persons Aged 20 and Over, by Religiosity and by Selected Characteristics," December 5, 2021, https://www.cbs.gov.il/he/publications/Lochut-Tlushim/לוחות%20שנתון/st28_06x.pdf.

Table 1.2. The Non-Jewish Minority's Main Subgroups

Total population	Muslims	Christians	Druze	Non-Arab Christians
1,632,000	1,345,000	138,320	149,000	44,000

Source: Israel Central Bureau of Statistics, "The Muslim Population in Israel: Data for Eid al-Adha 2022," July 6, 2022, https://www.cbs.gov.il/he/mediarelease/pages [Hebrew]; Israel Central Bureau of Statistics, "The Christian Population in Israel: Data for Christmas 2021," December 21, 2021, https://www.cbs.gov.il/he/mediarelease/pages/2021/-הנוצרית-האוכלוסייה-חג-נתונים-לרגל בישראל [Hebrew]; Israel Central Bureau of Statistics, "The Druze Population in Israel: Data for Ziyarat al-Nabi Shu'ayb 2022," April 24, 2022, https://www.cbs.gov.il/he/mediarelease/pages/2022/חג-לרגל-נתונים-לקט-בישראל-הדרוזית-האוכלוסייה [Hebrew].

A similarly heterogeneous picture, or perhaps even more complex, exists among the non-Jewish minority group (21 percent), which receives the collective name of Israeli Arabs or the Arab citizens of Israel. According to 2021 data from the Central Bureau of Statistics, this population numbers 1,632,000 citizens (not including Arabs living in East Jerusalem who hold resident status).[25] These include Muslims (including Bedouins), Christians, Druze, Circassians, Baha'is, Ahmadis, and Alawites.

Summary

This opening chapter, mostly theoretical, is intended to serve as a form of orientation for the reader. Global terms such as left and right, state and religion, and Jews and Arabs are all, without exception, part of the public, media, academic, and political discourse in the State of Israel on a daily basis. These terms are often used to label entire groups, without the tagger realizing not only that the label iswrong but that they belong to that group themselves.

This chapter has also presented eight different identities on the basis of gender, class, and religious divisions. By adding other features such as personal qualities, skills, and abilities; held ideas that, naturally, translate into political positions; and the fact that Israel is a heterogeneous society, we can map an even larger number of identities and divisions.

Figure 1.1 illustrates the multitude of identities and divisions that exist in Israeli society. Within Jewish and non-Jewish society, we only distinguish between secular and religious (a concept we attribute to anyone who is ultra-Orthodox, traditional, or religious) to simplify the complexity of the

Figure 1.1. Identities and divisions in Israeli society. *Source:* Created by the author.

Status / Identity	Male, low socio-economic status,	Male, high socio-economic status,	Male, low socio-economic status,	Male, high socio-economic status,	Female, low socio-economic status,	Female, high socio-economic status,	Female, low socio-economic status,	Female, high socio-economic status,
Israeli								
Zionist								
Jew								
Muslim Arab								
Christian Arab								
Palestinian								
Israeli Arab								

issue as much as possible. We also did not include references in the table to minority groups in Israeli society such as Druze or LGBT individuals for the same reason, although it is clear that these identities have an impact, sometimes decisive, on the self- and collective definition of each citizen.

The rest of this book focuses on four central rifts that have a decisive influence on the question of the collective identity (social and national) that Israel seeks in an attempt not only to stabilize the political system but to mark a path in which Israeli society seeks to make its way and formulate a vision. As such, chapter 2 is dedicated to trying to find out what, if anything, divides the right and the left. Chapter 3 discusses the formation of two camps within the Jewish majority group: the religious camp versus the state camp. Chapter 4 analyzes the Jewish-Arab (non-Jewish) rift that has accompanied Israeli society since 1948, and chapter 5 is dedicated to the rift within Arab society in Israel.

Chapter 2

The Evolution of Right and Left

The development of the terms "left" and "right" in the social and political context began in France in the second half of the eighteenth century. In those years, Louis XVI ruled France, and during his reign, the kingdom fell into a severe economic crisis. At that time, France was a class society ruled by the king. He had an heir apparent (and other princes who did not have the status of heir), an aristocracy that enjoyed the benefits of power, a bourgeois class that mainly consisted of merchants, and, at the bottom of the socioeconomic ladder, the workers, or as they are sometimes known, the proletariat.

This social order was preserved for hundreds of years, but at the beginning of the eighteenth century, there were some noblemen, such as Count Henri de Agussino, who secretly discussed a question that until then few, if any, had dared to ask: If all men were born equal in the image of God, why was society class-based? Ever since this question first came up for discussion in 1715 it has been posed regularly in the intellectual airspace. This question was not only about trying to find the correct social order for residents living in France; it also touched on political aspects, the most important of which was who the sovereign is—that is, who makes the decisions on social, economic, security, health and welfare issues, and so on.[1]

The financial crisis in 1780s France forced the king to adopt a policy of raising taxes, and, in the spirit of the time, he was forced to get the consent of all classes in French society and convene an assembly of representatives. This was a significant crack in the ability of the king, until then an all-powerful sovereign, to make decisions unilaterally. From then on, not only did representatives flow into the hall but so did social ideas circulating among intellectuals, which, until that moment, had remained in private rooms. Thereafter, these ideas became part of a discourse in which all of French society participated. The order of seating at that assembly (May 1789) was as follows. The representatives of the aristocracy, the king's loyalists, who enjoyed his proximity, sat on his right. They sought to preserve the existing social order, the status quo, as it served their social and economic interests. Therefore, the aristocracy's position on the right side of the hall created the equation that "right" means "conservative." On the left side of the hall sat the representatives of the lower classes, those who asked for far-reaching reforms that would benefit them. Due to the difficult economic situation in France, there was a chance that these reforms would harm the upper classes. The equation is simple: A paucity of resources and a more equitable distribution will almost certainly hurt those who have previously received more. About three months later, when the representatives of the aristocracy and the representatives of the patriots (the name the change-seekers gave themselves) met in August 1789 to draft a constitution after the revolution that broke out on July 14, the seating order was the same: aristocracy on the right, revolutionaries on the left.[2]

In an extraordinary article published in early 1977, Yehuda Gottholf wrote, "Concepts become confused until a person can no longer distinguish between his right and his left."[3] This confusion has become a stumbling block to communication between people and prevents understanding issues thoroughly and profoundly. If this is indeed the situation, then discussing any topic has no value. In a debate, both parties (sometimes more than two parties) use the same language, but the terms they bring to the discourse, including "right" and "left," often have different meanings and interpretations for each side. In such a reality, not only is it impossible to reach agreements on the outlines of human society (laws, rules, values, regulations, norms), but it is also impossible to promote such a society according to a clear ideology or worldview.

I will argue in this chapter that in Israel, the right has become the left and the left has become the right. For now, to illustrate this argument, let us use the following example. At the end of 2022, a right-wing government based on a coalition of 64 members out of 120 in the Knesset came to power in Israel. The finance portfolio was given to Aryeh Deri, leader of Shas, an ultra-Orthodox party. One of the first decisions made by the new government was doubling the allowance given to ultra-Orthodox students who study in religious seminaries (*yeshivot*) instead of entering the labor market and contributing to the development of the Israeli economy. In the traditional separation between the right's support of a liberal economy and the left's support of a socialist economy, this decision has a clear policy alignment with the left rather than the right. However, this does not prevent Deryi from perceiving himself as a right-wing politician.

Historically, the term "right" had meaning for social (and political) forces seeking to preserve the existing social structure and prevent changes. On the other hand, "left" was a moniker given to anyone who sought to withhold privileges from the upper classes in society, starting with the feudal lords in the Middle Ages, through the aristocracy at the beginning of the modern era, to the upper class and the capitalists in modern times. Even so, the two terms began to lose their original meaning at the beginning of the twentieth century, especially after the First World War. The noble and respectable right became associated with fascism and Nazism, while the left was pejoratively referred to as Stalinism. This was not just because of the Soviet leader's surname but because it symbolized and expressed unlimited and uncontrolled power and the use of violence for political goals. After the First World War, in Russia the peasants asked for land, bread, and peace, and the Germans, who signed, in practice, a surrender agreement at Versailles, asked for the same thing. In Russia, the left trampled the peasants. In Germany, the right did.

If the ordinary people in two different states with completely different ideologies asked the regime to fulfill the same basic needs, what significance, if any, does the regime's character have in the division of right and left? The historical result, seen almost one hundred years later, was that Russia became a totalitarian state, as did Germany. In Russia, the left had the power. In Germany, the right ruled. And, no less importantly, the opposition in both countries was utterly wiped out, the ones who dared to think differently and propose reforms that would improve the existing situation. When there is no valuable social and political discourse between two camps—right and left, as in their original meaning—then these terms are filled with a different meaning that sterilizes the discourse if only because each side calls the other derogatory names or works to exterminate it.

Since the eighteenth century, new meanings have been added to the terms "right" and "left" insofar as they are used to distinguish between two camps with a clear identity, idea, and vision. In other words, if the original idea distinguished between those who wanted to perpetuate an existing social structure (in a monarchical regime) and those who wanted far-reaching reforms (which, in the eighteenth century, were considered revolutionary, such as the right to choose the state's political leader, women's suffrage, and the just distribution of resources and minority rights), then, as the years passed, other issues separated "right" and "left," such as being for or against abortion, for or against divorce, and for or against same-sex marriage.

Socialism and Liberalism: Between Right and Left

Socialism and liberalism are two terms that are regularly mentioned when talking about the distinction between right and left. Using them without understanding their original meaning and the parties' readiness to reach a mutual understanding may lead to a deadlock.

If we reduce the discussion to economic issues, researchers worldwide (and in the Israeli case) would agree with the following diagnosis. On the one hand, socialism is interested in equality between all citizens. This equality is a reform (change) to the aristocratic society that was common until the French Revolution, and economic equality is therefore seen as a position of the left. On the other hand, liberalism allows for free competition in the market, minimal intervention from the state mechanisms in the market, and the possibility for every citizen to earn as much as they can. Such a position has been labeled as the "economic right."

However, if we expand the discussion to other issues, such as the right to vote, freedom of speech, or minority rights, the boundaries between socialism and liberalism blur. The left, being an advocate of equality, supports the right to equal choice for all people and, of course, the freedom of speech that allows opinions to be voiced, even if they are contrary to those of the sovereign. On the other hand, the conservative right is not interested in granting everyone the right to vote, and certainly not in a democratic regime, where every vote matters.[4]

The reason for this confusion stems, among other things, from the view that increasing equality usually requires expanding the state's involvement, while increasing freedom requires reducing the state's involvement. However, this diagnosis can be easily refuted. If the state wants to extend political rights to minorities and has the power to do so, this means that its involvement has increased in a process that is essentially liberal. Hence, the term "liberalism," as originally used in the West, does not reflect the sociopolitical reality in different countries around the world. Liberalism, as a constructivist philosophical idea, seeks to shape society according to new values and favors intellectual freedom of thought, freedom of speech and association, freedom of occupation, and personal freedom in everything related to faith and religion, marital relations, and social relations between the sexes. The inherent paradox is that liberalism is identified with the right, and this association is at most only partially true. The idea of these freedoms, certainly in allowing them to be decisive, is contrary to the worldview of the conservative right, which seeks to perpetuate the sociopolitical status quo.[5]

Liberalism allows intellectual freedom, freedom of speech, association, and civil liberties in general in public life. Regarding one's personal life, liberals support freedom of belief and religion, freedom in lifestyle, and freedom in everything related to sexuality, relationship matters, pornography, and drug use.[6] But these freedoms are not part of the conservative right's ideology. Ed Rooksby, who dismantles the term "liberalism" into its basic components, proposed seeing such a liberal approach as sanctifying individual freedom, but beyond this sanctity it does not really offer the subsystem of enlightened values that the term itself seems to express. In his eyes, a liberal is nothing but an egoist who interacts with others only to satisfy their private interests and preferences. From this analysis, it appears that socialism embodies the idea of self-realization while demonstrating solidarity and reciprocity, while liberalism protects individual property, thus perpetuating class differences.

If liberalism is not fully resolved, then the same is true of equality in the case of socialism. The founding fathers of the Soviet Union—Vladimir Lenin, Joseph Stalin, and Leon Trotsky—drew a clear line between Marxism and socialism on the one hand and liberalism on the other. Trotsky spared no derogatory words for the liberal ideology, which he called "polluted," while Lenin distinguished between the ideologies of the working class and the bourgeoisie, which also had aspects of democracy. In other words, Lenin, who held the views of the economic left, was against democracy, which is a liberal value, if only because he was against allowing subjects/citizens to determine who will lead them. If so, is Lenin a leftist because of his economic stance or a rightist based on his political position? Rooksby claims that of the three (Trotsky, Lenin, and Stalin), Lenin's doctrine is the one that most influenced socialist thought.[7]

Let us move this discussion to Israeli society, where the following question immediately arises. If a citizen supports a free economy (right) yet favors a form of democracy in which there is equality between citizens belonging to subgroups according to criteria of gender, religion, ethnicity, nationalism, and class (left), how shall we define that citizen? Are they right-wing or left-wing? This dilemma becomes even more complicated when examining the issue of Israeli society in the context of the nature of the state (Jewish and religious, Jewish and democratic) and in the context of the conflict between Israel and the Palestinians.

Right and Left in Jewish-Israeli Discourse

Let us turn to the content of the terms "left" and "right" in the Jewish discourse (up to 1948) and in the Jewish-Israeli discourse from 1948 onward. Concretely, we will examine how the public and the leadership in the Diaspora, in the Jewish settlement in the Land of Israel, and, after 1948, in the State of Israel perceived these terms in the social, economic, and, later, security and political contexts.

It seems that the correct starting point for discussing the question of right and left in the Jewish and Israeli context is the appearance of the Zionist idea, which expresses the desire to return to Zion, the ancestral land of the Jews. The reason for starting the discussion at this point is not arbitrary. It corresponds with the evolution of the terms "right" and "left" with the historical closeness of time to the appearance of these terms in the late eighteenth century in Europe. In the Israeli case, the question of right and left refers to two intertwined elements: the human being and land. My argument is that the various currents that developed within Zionism had to address the question of human rights and the right to land before addressing the potential economic or social structure for the country where the Jews would rule. This was required because of the constant deprivation suffered by Jews throughout Europe in the eighteenth and nineteenth centuries. As such, the dispute between right and left begins with questions of nationalism and sovereignty, not just class equality and human rights in a broad sense.

Unlike previous research, I seek to analyze the terms "right" and "left" according to the writing and thinking of the various currents in Zionism. Our analysis is based on a model consisting of four variables: land, religion, the economy, and attitudes toward non-Jews (Arabs were a majority before 1948, while Israeli/Palestinian Arabs were a minority after 1948). These four themes accompany the evolution of the Zionist movement in its various currents. From a historical point of view, within Zionism, different currents were created that offered different solutions to the problems Jews faced in Europe in the nineteenth century (and even before). I suggest a division of Zionism into five internal currents and will analyze each of them to discuss questions (and maybe also answers) regarding the right and the left. Figure 2.1 presents the model and its independent variables.

Figure 2.1. Currents of Zionism and the independent variables. *Source:* Created by the author.

Current / Topic	Spiritual Zionism	Political Zionism	Social Zionism	Religious Zionism	Revisionist Zionism
Land					
Economy					
Religion					
Policy toward non-Jews					

THE SPIRITUAL (CULTURAL) CURRENT

Asher Ginzberg (1856–1927), also known as Ahad Ha'am, is identified with the idea that a Jewish spiritual home should be established in the Land of Israel. Its main goal is to strengthen the connection between the Land of Israel and Judaism and Jews inclined to education. Avraham Levinson, who has analyzed the writings of Ahad Ha'am, says in this regard,

> Nationalism in Ahad Ha'am is the supreme being that encompasses Judaism and humanity. Religion is only one of the manifestations of nationalism and not its full formation. Religion does not create the people, but the people create their religion. The Jew who wants the revival of his people and does not acknowledge God is, in a certain sense, more Jewish than the believer because "the national pride of a believing Jew is a pride of the past . . . and that of the free nationalist in his views is the pride of a free man who knows the power within his soul, looks with contentment on his former great enterprise, and believes in himself as a nation for the future."[8]

This is a foundational text not just because it connects the past and the future and differentiates them but because it discusses the question of Jewish nationalism, which must be brought to the Land of Israel with an emphasis on Jews inclined to education. Hence the questions, will Jews who are not inclined to education not come to the Land of Israel (*Eretz Yisrael*)? Assuming that this is indeed Ha'am's approach, should it be placed on the right (religious-national) or the left (modern education)? Einat Ramon has pointed out the complexity that exists in Ahad Ha'am's thought, which constantly oscillates between national-religious conservatism and releasing the burden of mitzvahs.[9]

If this is so, then it can be said that Ahad Ha'am was a Zionist Jew, well-versed in matters of religion and nationality, who created his own order of priorities regarding the immigration of Jews to the Land of Israel. During the period in which he was active (Ahad Ha'am visited the Land of Israel in 1891 as a reporter for the *Shiloah* newspaper), it was widely believed that although most of the land was unpopulated, it would not be possible to house all the Jews. If a person believes that Jews cannot be settled in a desert land, is such a position expressive of the left or right? Our answer is that such a position does not express one side or the other. It reflects a realistic-pragmatic assessment of the situation that asks for a solution to the situation of the Jews in Europe, provided that this solution is feasible.

The discussion on Ahad Ha'am's thought has not yet offered a real answer to the question, was Ahad Ha'am right-wing or left-wing? In order to try and answer it, we must consider another central component in his writing: national morality. Ahad Ha'am does not see national morality and religion as synonymous. His explanation was that religion does not change but national morality does. It expands and takes on content and meaning according to the spirit of the time and is also related to universal morality—the one that distinguishes, for example, between good and evil. Thus, he writes that actions that were moral in the past are no longer so in modern times. Ahad Ha'am's national morality is intertwined with the national redemption of the people of Israel; as Levinson notes, it is messianism. That is, next to the messianic perception, he advocates for national morality connected to universal morality. During his visit to the Land of Israel in 1891, in an article entitled "Truth from the Land of Israel," Ahad Ha'am wrote about the immoral behavior of Jews toward the local non-Jews: "Slaves were in the land of their exile, and suddenly they find themselves with unlimited freedom, wild freedom, as always happens to a slave when he rules, and they walk among the Arabs with enmity and cruelty and reach their limit without justice."[10] At the same time, Ahad Ha'am held Jewish ethnocentric beliefs (he refused to allow his family members to marry Christians) and supported redemption in the style of the coming of the Messiah. He wrote, "Israel's salvation will come not from diplomats but from prophets." Is a person who holds such beliefs a rightist or a leftist?

The Political Current (Political Zionism)

The political current, or political Zionism, is commonly thought to have been founded by Benjamin Ze'ev Herzl and sought diplomatic ways to establish a national home for the Jewish people. This current began with Rabbi Dr. Yehuda Aryeh Leon Bivas (1782–1852), who was one of the first to call for the establishment of a Jewish state in the Land of Israel. Bivas also combined conservative and progressive thought. Yael Weiler Israel wrote that Bivas saw the verses of the Bible as a tool for understanding the national and political reality. His interpretation of these verses led him to declare that the Jews must change their curriculum and add a science curriculum to the sacred studies. He also spoke about the necessity for a sufficiently strong and sophisticated Jewish military force that would be able to eradicate the Ottoman authorities ruling the country.[11] This position does not allow Bivas to be placed on an axis between right and left in relation to the topics I proposed. Like those who came after him, he called for initiatives, the establishment of a protective force, and the integration of traditional and modern studies.

Although the original idea was Bivas's, it was realized by Herzl, who initiated the Zionist Congress and established a series of Jewish institutions through which he sought to promote a national home for Jews. Herzl preferred that this national home be in the Land of Israel. From 1896 to 1898, he tried to get a concession from the Ottoman Empire for Jewish settlement in the Land of Israel, and he met the Ottoman sultan for this purpose. In 1898, Herzl met the emperor of Germany in Jerusalem and proposed that the Jews be responsible for improving the financial situation of the Ottoman Empire in exchange for the sultan's relinquishment of his rule in the Land of Israel and his consent to the establishment of an independent Jewish state. Under these circumstances, Herzl was willing to compromise on a colony in Africa (Sixth Zionist Congress, 1903) as a temporary default. During that gathering, Herzl announced that the British proposal/agreement to allocate territory to the Jews in East Africa did not change the ultimate goal of settlement in the Land of Israel. A commotion broke out in the hall, especially among the delegates from Russia, who saw this as treason in the Land of Israel. Herzl declared that he would not for a single moment stop his efforts to realize the Land of Israel, and it was and will always be the goal of Zionism.[12] Yehuda Reinhart distinguished between two approaches in Herzl's philosophy, specifically about Judaism as a religion and socialism as an idea for society and the economy. Herzl believed that the realization of Zionism—that is, immigration to the Land of Israel—would allow socialists to realize their ideas of an egalitarian society. At the same time, he believed that although religion has no place in the affairs of the state, it is proper to respect the traditions of Israel, and perhaps there would be a place to help the rabbis when necessary.[13]

Herzl's conception of the Land of Israel and the place of religion in it, as well as his political activity for the realization of the Zionist idea, almost automatically raise the question, Was Herzl right-wing or left-wing? In the spirit of the times in which he worked, he did not compromise on his vision to bring about Jewish settlement in the Land of Israel. Many (probably most) Jews worldwide shared the same vision. Is the willingness to compromise with Great Britain and accept an estate in East Africa a compromise of a right-wing person, a left-wing person, or a statesman who is aware of his inferiority vis-à-vis the powers and is ready to accept any piece of land, provided that he can give the Jews a sovereignty that will free them from the tyranny of the regimes in Europe?

Let us go one step further and analyze Herzl's position regarding the Arabs. In 1898, Herzl wrote,

> In the settlement areas that will be assigned to us, we will gradually hand over private property. We will try to move the poor population across the border without them noticing by creating jobs in the transit countries but preventing them from getting any work in our own country. Wealthy residents will move to us. The purchase operations, like taking them beyond the border of the poor, must be done gently and with a soft hand. The owners of the real estate properties must believe that they are piling us up, that they are selling us at a high price. But we don't sell anything back.[14]

Here, too, it is difficult to determine whether Herzl had a distinctly left-wing or right-wing attitude. Derek Penslar, an expert on the issue, cites scholars with a revisionist view who claim that Herzl conceived of the transfer by seeking to settle the poor population (mainly peasants) beyond the borders of the Jewish state. It is possible that Herzl's position is rooted in his childhood: He grew up in a wealthy home with wealthy parents and, as an adult, moved around the circles of high society. Therefore, it is natural that he wanted to keep wealthy Arabs in the territory of the future Jewish state. In the Israeli discourse, support for the transfer represented the positions of right-wing parties in the second half of the twentieth century. On the other hand, Herzl supported wealthy Arabs remaining in the territories of the Jewish state and their integration into its institutions, just as Ze'ev Jabotinsky proposed later. If this is so, why is Jabotinsky seen as distinctly right-wing and Herzl is not?

The Socialist Current

In the second half of the nineteenth century, there was a need to respond to social and economic changes occurring in Europe, including increasing secularism, capitalism, modernization, and anti-Semitism. The basic idea was to create an egalitarian society that would allow the Jews, who were a minority religious group in Europe, to find their place and receive rights as Jews or equal citizens before the law. Zionists such as Nachman Syrkin, Dov Ber Borochov, and Moshe Hess, and later Haim Arlozorov and Berl Katznelson, thought more in terms of a workers' society and less in terms of a state. In this sense, the socialist current is perhaps the best example that illustrates the existing confusion between left and right as perceived in the Israeli discourse. The explanation is simple: Nationalism contradicts the principles of socialism because it divides humanity on an ethnic (and sometimes also religious) basis, but socialism divides human society according to class without ethnic affiliation. As Borochov wrote,

> The Jews in the Diaspora were always considered foreigners, with social, mental, and especially physical characteristics (accent, face, appearance, movements, way of walking). They lacked property and territory, and the attitude towards them was based on the fact that they were Jews. The hatred of Israel was seen as enmity towards the Jew just like that, without any guilt or justification, which arose from the material, and general living conditions of society. Even the intellectual progress of those layers of society imbued with hatred of Israel did not weaken the hatred, but on the contrary increased it. As progress improved the condition of the population, it gave the residents the right to vote, courts of judges and juries, and as the differences between the upper and lower layers of society weakened, so the hatred of Israel from above merged with the hatred of Israel from below and from the sides, highlighting the Jews as a crowd of foreigners.[15]

Here is another paradox. If Borochov supported the establishment of a just and egalitarian society only in the Land of Israel—that is, he was a Zionist (return to the land of the ancestors) and a socialist (a just society)—is he a man of the right or the left?

Borochov is not alone in this sense. Moshe Hess wrote as early as 1862 about returning to the land of the ancestors, creating a working life, and establishing a society in which the means of production and the treasures of nature would belong to the whole and in which there would be equality in the spirit of the prophets of Israel. In 1897, the Bond movement arose in Russia, whose founders believed that the immigration of masses of Jews to the Land of Israel was not realistic and would not solve the Jewish problem. Instead, it supported granting national cultural rights within the framework of autonomy to Jews as a minority living in Russia. Where, therefore, do we place Hess on the continuum from right to left? If he dreamed of a society in the spirit of the vision of the prophets of Israel, is he a religious Zionist? If he favored an egalitarian society where the means of production belong to everyone, is he located on the left side of the continuum, being a socialist whose economic views are identified with the left? Hess was not talking about the borders of the Land of Israel in 1862, but if he was referring to its borders during the time of the prophets, then he is a man of the Land of Israel. That is, in today's terms, is he a "complete rightist" based on the primordial approach? According to this attitude, God had promised land to the Sons of Israel in the Bible on four different occasions, though its size varies from promise to promise.

Socialist Zionism led, at the beginning of the twentieth century, to the establishment of the Zion Youth Movement, which established Hapoel Hatzair (The Young Worker) as a national labor movement in 1905. Its leader, Aharon David Gordon, devoutly called for the redemption of the Jews—as individuals and as a nation—through manual labor in the Land of Israel. In modern terms, this is a form of nationalism that combines primordial elements and territory, in which religious Zionists also believe. Gordon grew up in a religious home and was later nicknamed the "secular *tzaddik*" (righteous). Even after he was stabbed and shot by Arabs in Jaffa in 1908, he continued to believe that the moral right of the Jews to the Land of Israel was bought through labor and production, not by force of arms. After the Battle of Tel Hai in March 1920, he said that it would be desirable for the Jews to have peaceful and friendly relations with the Arabs, but this was not the time, nor was violence the way.

Gordon also believed in the secularity of religion; that is, he rejected the assumption that religion was given by divine revelation. At the same time, he did not deny his Jewish roots as someone who grew up in a religious home. In his view, the individual does not stand alone in the world but is dependent on and identifies with the group. Therefore, Gordon's view was that religion (like nationalism) is a creation of human beings. Hence, Gordon believed that everyone takes a subjective position in relation to the laws and *mitzvot* of religion.[16] An attempt to place Gordon, according to the lines of his life's trajectory and views, between the poles of right and left is a real intellectual challenge because his personality, sociopolitical beliefs, and actions combine the two poles as they are interpreted in the Israeli discourse today. Gordon, Sirkin, and Borochov, three of the spiritual fathers of Poale Zion (Workers of Zion), also influenced prominent political figures in the early twentieth century, including David Ben-Gurion and Ze'ev Jabotinsky (see "The Revisionist Current").

There is another angle that must be considered in this analysis of socialist Zionism before it can be identified as left or right in the Jewish-Israeli context. The difficulty in doing so stems from, among other things, the position of the leaders of Mapai (Workers' Party of the Land of Israel, founded in January 1930) regarding the treatment of Arabs. Discussions on this question have been a regular part of the discourse of the Jewish community since the beginning of the twentieth century, and it became clear that quite a few of the party's leaders supported the idea of a transfer—that is, the removal of the non-Jewish population from the borders of the Jewish state they sought to establish. During the Zionist Congress convened in the summer of 1937 in Zurich, Switzerland, it became clear that there were two camps within the socialist current. One supported the removal of Arabs from the country, based on precedents of population exchange, to create distance between rival groups (on an ethnic or other basis). Supporters of the transfer in the ranks of Mapai justified their position by mentioning that the Norwegian explorer Fridtjof Nansen had received the Nobel Peace Prize in 1922 for repatriating populations to resolve conflicts. The other camp, which included figures such as Golda Meir, Yitzhak Tabenkin, and Ya'akov Hazan, opposed the transfer, mainly due to their assessment that the chances of realizing it were low.[17]

It is worth considering the spirit of the things that dominated the references of Mapai members, who were socialists in the socioeconomic sense but not reformers in the national-political sense, certainly not when it came to relinquishing land or the removal of Arabs from the territory intended for the Jewish State of Israel. David Ben-Gurion wrote the following to his son Amos on October 5, 1937:

> My assumption is—and that is why I am an enthusiastic supporter of the state, even if it involves division at this point—that a partial Jewish state is not an end but a beginning. When we purchase a thousand or ten thousand *dunams*, we are happy, and the feeling is not hurt that we did not thereby purchase the whole land. Because the purchase is important not only for its own sake—through it, we increase our power. And every reinforcement helps to acquire the whole country. The establishment of the state—even partially—is a maximum reinforcement of power during this period. And it will serve as a powerful lever in our historic efforts to redeem the country in its entirety.[18]

In other words, Ben-Gurion saw his acceptance of the Peel Commission's proposal as a tactical move that would allow him to increase Jewish power (the Jews would have territory), and then they would continue to work for the liberation of the entire Land of Israel. This position allows us to conclude that Ben-Gurion does not meet the parameters of left or right if these terms are examined according to the four elements proposed above: economy, land, position toward non-Jews (who will be a minority in the future), and religion within the official establishment of the state.

How did it happen, then, that Ben-Gurion is labeled in the Israeli discourse as a "leftist"? While he agreed to the proposal of the Peel Commission in 1937, he did not give up 80 percent of the land in Israel since the Jewish settlement did not have sovereignty over the entire area at that time. The answer we offer is simple: He was conceptualized as being on the left side of the spectrum compared to the positions of Ze'ev Jabotinsky, who proposed an uncompromising approach toward the Arabs.

Arthur Rupin, a senior member of Mapai, expressed a similar position regarding the transfer of the Arab population:

> First, suitable land must be prepared in the Arab country for the farmers, and only then should one try to bring them there, as much as possible out of a desire and only if no other way is found—through expropriation [i.e., forcefully]. Without the relocation of the Arabs, the new Jewish state will have enormous difficulties with them from the point of view of internal politics

(the protection of minorities), from the point of view of external politics (the relations of the Arabs in the Land of Israel with Arab countries), and from the economic point of view (since we will then be forced to give them equal rights).[19]

In other words, Rupin never thought of giving rights to minorities since he conceptualized a country where the Jews are the owners of the house and are entitled to special rights. How, for example, is this different from the platform of the right-wing parties that ran in the elections for the twenty-fifth Knesset in November 2022? On a conceptual level, there is no difference between the discussions held in 1938 and 2022 regarding the Arab transfer. Even if the possibility of such a transfer in 1938 was weak to non-existent due to the British control of the Land of Israel, such discussions nevertheless took place, and perhaps the fact that they had no possibility of succeeding strengthens the claim. Ideologically, this reflects the same wishful thinking of Mapai and right-wing parties in the twenty-first century.

In 1937–1938, these discussions led to the establishment of a committee within the Jewish Agency for Israel, whose role was to discuss the technical aspects of moving the Arab population outside the borders of the Jewish state, as recommended by the Peel Commission. Theoretically, it can be argued that Jewish support for the idea of transfer originates from an attempt to match Britain's position, since the Peel Commission recommended population exchange, but this is a one-point argument that does not reflect the full picture. The discussions on the transfer of the Arabs of the Land of Israel continued for about a decade after the publication of the Peel Commission's conclusions, illustrating the Jewish leadership's interest in this idea. Moreover, an attempt was made to move Bedouins in the Ghazuya tribe from the Beit Shan valley to the eastern side of the Jordan. This began in 1938 and ended in 1947, indicating the difficulty of realizing the transfer—forced or voluntary—of Arabs in the country.[20] These positions of senior Mapai members illustrate the vitality of the idea within the party. It also puts a significant question mark on the statement that Mapai is a left-wing party. At most, the socialist Zionist current until 1948 can only be called "left" in a socioeconomic context due to its pursuit of equality for all, in contrast to the divergent right-wing position that arose when a disagreement emerged between those who sided with the continuation of the old social order and those who sought a revolution.

These positions received a practical expression after the establishment of the State of Israel when Mapai became the ruling party. One of the first decisions made by the interim government was that refugees who left the country were not allowed to return to it. This policy was never changed, and in fact, changing it has never been considered. In September 1948, a military government was imposed on the Arabs of Israel, who became the minority community. Ben-Gurion refused to end military rule, despite pressure from the left and the right in the 1950s, until the end of his term in 1963. On November 8, 1966, his successor, Levi Eshkol, notified the Knesset of his intention to abolish the military government, but this was done only in January 1968 because of the fear that Israeli Arabs would become a fifth column if war broke out, as indeed happened in June 1967.[21]

Israel's decisive victory in the June 1967 war incentivized Mapai's leadership to present its security positions concerning landholding, which is one of the variables through which I argue for an artificial mix between left and right. At a meeting of the Israeli government on August 20, 1967, the discussion was aimed at determining the government's policy regarding the future of the West Bank, which had been occupied during the war. The minister of the interior, Haim-Moshe Shapira, a religious Zionist, said, "I accept the proposal of Defense Minister Moshe Dayan that in some places, it is necessary from a security point of view for us to resettle our army. We will set up an army, but not for settlement." Levi Eshkol, the prime minister, noted that "even Mr. Begin does not want a million and a half Arabs among us, and if it were up to us, we would take all the Arabs to Brazil."[22] Subsequently, Eshkol shared with his ministers his view of the land located in the West Bank: "We received information that if we cross the border of Jordan, on the border there is an area of 150,000 state *dunams*, and it is said that there is also land in the Dotan Valley, which, although it is private, it is possible to concentrate 250,000 to 300,000 *dunams* of land there. If it is possible to lease this land, it will be possible to settle Jews there. The question is who we will settle in these areas."[23] The minister of police, Eliyahu Sasson, a member of Labor (an offshoot of Mapai), warned against the formation of a binational state and the security threat posed to the State of Israel based on the following demographic calculation: "There are 2.3 million Jews in Israel and about 1.5 million Arabs if you add the number of Israeli Arabs, the Arabs of Gaza, the Arabs of the West Bank, and those living in East Jerusalem. In such a situation, all Jews will have to mobilize to defend the Jewish state." Ze'ev Sharf, the minister of commerce and industry and also a member of Labor, was troubled by the internal Arab threat within the borders of the State of Israel when he estimated that the country would be constituted of about 30 percent Arabs, potentially translating to thirty-six Knesset members.

We conclude from these statements that Eshkol, the man at the head of the political system, thought aloud about the settlement of civilians in Judea and Samaria shortly after these areas came under Israeli control. The ministers were not in a hurry to propose a territorial compromise, and the impression is that there was consensus that the homeland had returned to its historical owners. The concern was about the Arabs living in the territories now controlled by Israel. The conclusion, therefore, is that the land variable places Mapai (and then Labor) far from the position of the left as is understood in the modern public discourse of Israeli society.

These attitudes soon translated into demographic changes in Judea and Samaria. With the encouragement of Labor, Jewish settlement in these territories began as early as 1968. In 1971, work began on the construction of Kiryat Arba/Hebron district, and later, Jews entered Beit Hadassah in the city of Hebron. In 1975, the first nucleus of the Elon Moreh settlement was founded in Samaria. The settlement's official website states, "They aspired to settle around the city of Nablus, the place of the beginning of the settlement in Israel by Avraham Avinu. . . . Supporters of the struggle came from members of the labor movement [the Labor Party], members of *kibbutzim* and *moshavim* (Ein Harod, Ein Vered, Ram On, Hanita, and more), members of the Knesset, writers and professors from all universities, students and members of youth movements."[24] This is a clear expression of the labor movement's attitude to the land aspect and expresses a continuous line of thought that began with Mapai, continued in the Labor Party, and then continued in Likud regarding the need for Jewish settlement in Samaria. In the same context, it is worth mentioning the statement of Moshe Dayan, a member of Mapai, in 1956, according to which "Sharm al-Sheikh without peace is better than peace without Sharm al-Sheikh," expressing the attitude to national territory on a primordial and historical basis.[25] Consequently, from any point of view, this party cannot be classified as a leftist party according to the territorial component of our model.

We can also point to a trend in the opposite direction. Ariel Sharon, the prime minister from 2001 to 2006, led the process of disengagement from the Gaza Strip (August 2005), which, by any measure of the Labor Party, was one of the places that must be settled by Jews. Sharon was the leader of Likud, a right-wing party (according to Israeli public discourse). Nevertheless, his position regarding disengagement and its implementation, at least regarding the settlement of all the homeland's territories, does not reflect a right-wing view.

Since the 1980s, it has become increasingly difficult to identify socialist Zionists as a camp of the left and liberal Zionists as a camp of the right regarding economic concepts. Asher Arian and Michal Shamir argued as early as 1983 that there is no distinction between "left" and "right" government in Israel because the left does not represent a workers' party (according to a sociological key) and the right does not necessarily represent a free economic class. They also claimed that most of the public in Israel believes that there is no place for such a diagnosis.[26] In a later essay, Arian claimed that the difference between the right and the left blurred not only in social and economic matters but also in security matters, and this trend continued in the election campaigns for the thirteenth and fourteenth parliaments in 1992 and 1996. Moreover, Benny Neuberger claimed that in the 1990s, Likud recognized the Histadrut (the General Organization of Workers) and supported a welfare state.[27] The coronavirus crisis (2020–2021) somewhat strengthened his claim when the "right-wing" government, led by Benjamin Netanyahu, intervened significantly to deal with the economic crisis created in the Israeli economy, as is customary in regimes of a socialist nature.

The Religious Current

Religious Zionism supports the idea that Judaism combines religion and nationality, and that the establishment of the State of Israel as a home for the Jewish people, in the sense of a community seeking sovereignty, is in fact an obligation arising from the Torah, the holy book of the Jewish religion and the people of Israel.[28] The roots of this movement lie in the thought of Rabbi Zvi Hirsch Kalischer (1795–1874), who, in his book *Derishat Zion* (*Making of Zion*), wrote that the beginning of redemption—that is, a return to the land of the ancestors—depends on the initiative of human beings. His book was a milestone in the history of Zionism because he suggested moving from waiting for the coming of the Messiah to taking responsibility and making moves that would advance redemption.

Kalischer was not alone in this sense. Rabbi Eliyahu Guttmacher called for agricultural settlement in the Land of Israel, and Rabbi Yehuda ben Shlomo Chai Alkalai, who lived in Serbia, dedicated his life to settlement in the Land of Israel and even composed a political plan for the immigration of Jews to Israel and the establishment of a Jewish home in the mid-nineteenth century. These three rabbis and their students combined three components in their thinking that they considered inseparable: the Land of Israel, the people of Israel, and the Torah of Israel. Ruth Winkler has described how Alkalai met Bivas and was influenced by his perception that Jews should be brought to Israel. She also pointed out that Alkalai drew from the teachings of Eliezer Papo, who wrote in *Pele Yoetz* (*Wonder of Counsel*), "Her virtue is known because it is great . . . and it is necessary for every person to have his eyes and heart there all the days. . . . Well, let him try with all his might to establish his residence in the Land of Israel."[29]

An important note is required here that contributes to the discussion on the development of right and left in the Jewish/Israeli context. The writings of those philosophers and intellectuals who belong to religious Zionism, as well as those who studied their opinions regarding the Land of Israel, do not express the concepts of "right" and "left" in relation to politics or security. Strange as it may sound, the terms "left" and "right" are not mentioned by the generation that came after Kalischer and Guttmacher either. We can assume that when they thought of proactive action to bring Jews to the land of their ancestors, the territory they were thinking of was the Land of Israel within its biblical borders. Even so, there is no mention of borders in their writings because religious Zionism dealt with the return to Zion without referring to the territory's integrity or the possibility of conceding part of it. At this point, it is worth asking the following question: If it is agreed that all currents of Zionism supported the immigration of Jews to the Land of Israel, then can the land variable distinguish between the left and right in the early Zionist movement?

A reinforcement for the argument that all Zionist currents had the same vision can be seen in the Mizrachi movement in 1902, which was founded in an era when political Zionism was already visible and had been discussed continuously since the First Zionist Congress in Basel in 1897. This chronological closeness is not accidental: While Herzl and his school strove for a secular political Zionism, the Mizrachi movement sought to preserve the affinity to religion. The idea of giving Zionism religious support came in 1893 from Shmuel Mohliever. The demand raised at the Fifth Zionist Congress (Basel, December 1901) to allocate resources to secular education hastened the decision among the Orthodox to establish a movement that would preserve the principles of the Jewish religion.[30] The debate about Jewish settlement in Uganda and the cooperation between Herzl and the Mizrachi movement did not address economic, social, political, or security issues in terms of right and left but only in terms of bringing Jews to Israel and the temporary alternative of Uganda as an autonomous territory but not a national home.

The turning point of religious Zionism, which transformed it into a political framework with a right-wing ideology in the territorial context (the complete Land of Israel), came a few weeks before the outbreak of the June 1967 war: an effort to construct and practice a new reality (constructivism) in one of the major religious schools in Jerusalem (Mercaz HaRav yeshiva), founded by Avraham Yitzchak HaCohen Kook. A main point of constructivism is that Israeli control over the territories that belonged to the biblical Land of Israel is a necessary condition for the process of redemption that Israel will go through. At the end of that process, the people of Israel, the Jewish people, will live safely in their land and borders. This would also be a political-security reality that would realize the coming of the Messiah. In a speech called "Psalm 19 of the State of Israel," given on the eve of Independence Day in 1967, Rabbi Zvi Yehuda Kook, the son of the yeshiva's founder, said, "Where is our Hebron—we forget it?! And where is our Nablus—we forget it?! And where is our Jericho—we forget that?! And where is our Transjordan?! Where is every piece of land? Every part of the four corners of the Land of God?! Did we manage to give up a millimeter of them? God forbid, have mercy and peace!"[31] Quite a few of Rabbi Kook's students see these words as a prophetic revelation that led to an awakening and a feeling that the Messiah's coming would be soon. However, it is important to remember that constructivism, which sees the territories of the biblical Land of Israel as the surface of the State of Israel in modern times, refers only to the territorial aspect and connects it with the religious component. There is no reference to minorities or economic aspects, which are used to separate the right from the left.

About a decade after the words of Rabbi Kook, Rabbi Shlomo Goren, who served as chief military rabbi from 1948 to 1971 and chief rabbi of Israel from 1972 to 1983, wrote an article entitled "Problems of Religion and State." In this article, Goren presents a clear position, according to which there is no alternative to a Jewish state based on the principles of the Torah of Israel, and states that "the democratic principle does not apply to the fundamental laws of the Torah." Regarding nationalism, he states that it complements the Jewish religion and creates the uniqueness of the people of Israel, the Jewish people, in contrast to other nations, who built their nationalism on the basis of "race, origin, language, and character."[32]

Researchers of nationalism would associate Rabbi Goren with the primordial approach because of the importance of religion (Judaism) and its basic principles as a factor that produces collective identity. However, Goren proposes other primordial elements (race, language, origin, and character), which are all part of primordialism, for the formation of other nationalities.

Contrary to the Jewish case, he does not add the aspect of land (territory) for those nationalities. Is Goren's position that of the left or the right?

Shifra Mishlov has sought to trace the Zionist views of Rabbi Goren. She believes that although he grew up in ultra-Orthodox educational institutions in Hebron and Jerusalem, Goren was a Zionist. Analyzing his book *The Theory of Philosophy*, Mishlov points out that he stated that one of the steps to redemption is the conquest of the land, and at the same time, "the Jewish political idea is based on the freedom of man in any form and full equality of rights for people in all areas of life and property." Goren does not talk about the extent of the territory to be conquered (exactly like Gordon's socialist philosophy early in the twentieth century), and he has a liberal view when it comes to equal rights (like Jabotinsky). Goren does not see a possibility for the State of Israel unless it exists as a Jewish state according to the principles of *halacha* (the Jewish way of life). Only after the June 1967 war did Goren concretely refer to the territorial aspect when he pointed to the liberation of areas such as the Golan Heights or Sinai. In 1993, Rabbi Goren opposed the Oslo Accords, not because he declared himself a right-wing person but because he thought that biblical homelands should not be handed over to the sovereignty of non-Jews.

It can therefore be stated that Rabbi Goren had a right-wing view regarding Israeli control over territories that were in the Jews' possession during the biblical period, but this was only part of his thought, not the framework of a systematic philosophical vision to which to aspire. If he thought it was, he did not express it.[33] It can also be concluded that there is no real opportunity to define Goren as a leftist or a rightist based on an analysis of the economic variable or his attitude toward non-Jewish minorities.

The Revisionist Current

I have chosen to include a subsection on revisionism not because it offers a different direction from that of practical Zionism but because its philosophical thought can make a real contribution to the discussion of right and left according to the model we propose. The current began in the 1920s, when its founder, Ze'ev Jabotinsky, sought a change in the activity patterns of the World Zionist Organization. When his proposals were not accepted, Jabotinsky resigned from the Histadrut in 1923, mainly because he believed that the conciliatory and moderate path of Chaim Weizmann, the chairman of the Histadrut, was wrong. Jabotinsky founded the Revisionist

Zionist Union in 1925 and poured into this framework an activist subgroup whose principles concerning religion, land, and economics were as follows.

The political-territorial field: A combined political and military struggle until the establishment of a Hebrew state in the Land of Israel on both banks of the Jordan River. Regarding the territorial aspect of the Land of Israel, it seems that the distinction between right and left sharpened for the first time in the late 1920s. Jabotinsky wrote his poem "The East of the Jordan" in 1929 as a protest to criticize the British decision to divide the territory and establish the Hashemite Kingdom on the east bank of the Jordan River. In the first stanza of his poem, Jabotinsky writes,

> As a bridge is held up by a pillar,
> as a man is kept erect by his spine,
> so Jordan, the Holy Jordan,
> is the backbone of my Israel.

The poem's lyrics give a dimension of sanctity to the river, which extends for the full length of the territory, as its second stanza makes clear. If the poem had ended here, it could be concluded that the revisionist current, which viewed all the territory subject to British rule as Israel's future sovereign territory, is on the political right. But the argument here is that it is an arbitrary association for two reasons: First, right and left were not originally divided according to one's attitude toward the land; and second, as we have already seen, the socialist current also supported and promoted Jewish settlement in all parts of the country.

However, in the third stanza, the author suggests that the heavenly waters of the holy river (the Jordan) will also be used by "the Arab, the Christian, and the Jew, for our flag is a pure and just one." In other words, Jabotinsky advocates an egalitarian (socialist) view of the distribution of natural resources. The paradox here is simple: Socialism as a socioeconomic concept belongs to the revolutionaries, such as those who sat on the left side of the hall where the National Assembly was held in France in 1789.[34] No less surprising is the fact that some of the members of Ahdut HaAvoda (Unity of Labor), which was not a revisionist movement, supported annexing the eastern part of the Jordan to the territory of the future Jewish state. These members were not seen as right-wing because their socioeconomic view was socialist.

The territorial aspect of holding both banks of the Jordan was not Jabotinsky's sole consideration. Granting rights to minorities (meaning the

Arabs of Israel, the Arabs of East Jerusalem, the Palestinians in Judea and Samaria, and the Palestinians in the Gaza Strip), which is a significant issue concerning the division of right and left in Israeli society today, is another real difficulty when presenting Jabotinsky as right-wing. In the constitutional outline he proposed, section 4 stipulates: "There will be no objection to the appointment of an Arab as the head of state, and there will be no objection to him bearing the title of 'Emir' if a Jewish prime minister with powers is appointed."[35] In response to Itamar Ben-Avi, who suggested dividing the country into cantons, Jabotinsky wrote: "If we were a majority in the country, we would first of all create a situation of complete equality of rights here. Jew or Arab or Armenian or German, there is no difference before the law—all roads are open to him, he could even become prime minister." He also suggested that "we would offer each and every nation an autonomous organization, with its own 'national council,' with the right to collect taxes, with the right to arrange all its internal affairs as is good in the eyes of its members, with the right to create schools from kindergarten to university. This will be an example to the whole world of how a multinational state should be run."[36]

Total equality of rights and a multinational state are not part of the agenda, as the view has developed since eighteenth-century France. In Israel in late 2022 and early 2023, such a position that supports complete equality of rights and a multinational state cannot be associated with ideological and political factors within the right. How, therefore, is Jabotinsky placed between right and left? The answer we offer is that he expressed positions of the political right and the social left because he combined Jewish nationalism with universal liberalism. Colin Shindler claims that the Third International Betar Conference in 1938 was the turning point where nationalism prevailed over liberalism, mainly because the national bloc within the revisionist current, with members like Menachem Begin, Uri Zvi Greenberg, and Avraham (Yair) Stern, became dominant.[37]

REVISIONISM AND THE ECONOMY

At first glance, it seems that the economic outlook of the revisionist current, founded by Jabotinsky, supports a free and liberal economy. In fact, the picture is much more complex, and it is difficult to categorize this view as being on the right of the socioeconomic (and political) spectrum. Jabotinsky admitted to various influences that shaped his own position, which ranged between socialism, communism, and liberalism. For example, in an article from 1910 titled "I Don't Believe," he wrote that "the nationalization of the means of production is a necessary and desirable result of the social process, and I admit that the subject of the revolution is the working class."[38] Jabotinsky continued to adhere to this line even in the 1920s. In 1925, he published an article called "Left," in which he praised the working class' contribution to the building of the country and defined their work as "great activity and dedication."[39] The explanation for this is simple: He saw the endless effort of the workers as a contribution to the national struggle for the Land of Israel; that is, he connected socialism with nationalism. Even when he went to study law in Rome with Enrico Peri and Antonio Labriola, he continued to adhere to socialist thinking and even wrote that his teachers influenced him in this regard.

The Religious Aspect

What was the attitude of the founder of the revisionist movement toward the role of the Jewish religion in the life of the state? Here, too, those seeking to understand his position will find it difficult to do so, as Jabotinsky's view of the status of religion changed over the years. Eliezer Don-Yehiya has proposed dividing Jabotinsky's views into three different periods. The first lasted about twenty years (1905–1925) and was characterized by criticism and reservations about religion. These were the years when Jabotinsky began to stand out in his public activity. The second period lasted for about a decade (1925–1935), during which there was a certain moderation in his attitude toward religion. The third period (1935–1940), which ended with his death in 1940, was one of a positive attitude toward religion. Nevertheless, Don-Yehiya states that in no way can Jabotinsky be defined as a religious or God-fearing person.[40]

Summary

This chapter took a historical point of view to examine the development of the terms "right" and "left" from the time they were coined in France in the late eighteenth century until they took root in Israeli sociopolitical discourse. The direct interface between Jews and those who coined the terms (in France and later throughout Europe) made them accessibleand allowed some to believe and hope that in the division into right (conservatives) and left (reformers-revolutionaries), Jews would have an opportunity to change their inferior situation compared to Christians across the continent. In practice, a long line of thinkers arose among the Jewish people, all of them Zionists, who proposed different ways of using the revolutionary idea of redistributing human society.

Over the years, there emerged five currents of Zionism, the practical meaning of which is to bring Jews to the Land of Israel and establish a state for them. Each current offered its own course for a long list of topics. Of these, this chapter has focused on four significant ones that relate to attitudes toward land, the place of religion in the life of the state, attitudes toward a free economy, and attitudes toward non-Jewish minorities. Our main conclusion is that basing the division of right and left on an economic worldview in the Jewish society of the Land of Israel from the end of the nineteenth century until the establishment of the state is only partial and does not present the complexity of the issue. For example, the socialist movement, which supported an egalitarian society and economy (see, e.g., the idea of the *kibbutz* as a social structure), did not support Arabs remaining in the future Jewish land. Some, including senior officials, spoke openly about the transfer of Arabs as a necessary solution. In the opposite direction, the revisionist Zionists, who were standard-bearers for a complete Land of Israel, were ready to grant equal rights to the non-Jewish minorities who would live in the State of Israel. Moreover, Jabotinsky and his student, Menachem Begin, did not propose a transfer as a solution to the Arab question. After 1948, Begin also struggled to remove the military administration imposed on the Arabs.

This conclusion is also valid for ultra-Orthodox Zionist parties, such as Shas, which was established in 1984 and did not express its objection to Zionism. Shas cannot be placed between right and left. The reason for this is simple. On the one hand, Shas supports a socialist economy—the state distributing budgets at increased rates to the ultra-Orthodox student society, instead of encouraging them to work and be part of the productive economy. According to this parameter, Shas belongs to the left according to the values of the French Revolution (equality for all). In universal terms, this is a position of the economic left. In Israeli terms, this is differential socialism, which distinguishes between Torah students and the secular society of students.

On the other hand, Shas has changed in its attitude toward land: Its spiritual leader, Rabbi Ovadia Yosef (1920–2013), supported a territorial compromise, but his successors, led by Aryeh Deri, oppose it. The political (but not ideological) paradox is this: Though economically a left-wing party,

Shas allies with Likud, headed by Benjamin Netanyahu, which is seen in Israel as a right-wing party. Likud uses the instruments of an egalitarian (socialist) economy to maintain its political power thanks to this alliance with an ultra-Orthodox party. Likud also channels high sums of money to ultra-Orthodox studies in yeshivas instead of leading a liberal economy, as would be expected of a party that presents itself as right-wing.

Our conclusion is that the terms "left" and "right" are not relevant to the mapping of political forces in Israel either ideologically or sociologically (socially). In the Israeli discourse, the terms distinguish between two camps, classified as such by leaders of public opinion (who call themselves right-wingers). The first is a national camp, which supports a complete Land of Israel (although, as we have seen, this is also a correct definition for an economically and socially leftist party such as Mapai). At the same time, this camp supports a harsh and uncompromising policy against Arabs, without distinguishing between Palestinians and Arabs who are citizens of Israel. This camp also tends to attribute a closer connection between land and religiously based primordial foundations and justifications, but this does not distinguish the two camps much either because Labor began the return to Hebron, the city of the ancestors, immediately after the June 1967 war. The second camp, standing against the national camp, according to this division, includes the leftists, a term that refers to anyone who is supposedly ready for a territorial compromise, for peace with the Arabs at any cost, and for the separation of religion and state.

The explanation I offer for this paradox is that the camp that defines itself as right (national-religious) attributes itself to a holy territory, the land promised by the Holy One. In this way, two camps were indeed created in Israel, but these are not left and right but split according to the division between state and religion. This rift is the subject of the next chapter.

Chapter 3

Statehood and Religion

Background and Definitions

Sometime after the results of the elections for the fourteenth Knesset in 1996 became widely known, when Benjamin Netanyahu marginally defeated Shimon Peres by a few tenths of a percent, the loser declared, "The Jews defeated the Israelis."[1] Usually, candidates who lose in elections, especially when the results are so close, express themselves differently, ranging from recognizing the loss to defying the result or blaming a culprit. Peres's statement reflected a new reality for the Jewish citizens of the State of Israel—a reality in which a citizen, who until then considered their identities as a Jew and an Israeli in the same context, found themselves, voluntarily or involuntarily, defined not as a balance of the two terms but as a person for whom one of these components is dominant while the other is secondary. In other words, the citizen is first a Jew and then an Israeli or vice versa.

Although Peres was the first to use the phrase "the Jews defeated the Israelis," the fault lines between "Judaism" and "Israelism" began to emerge long before that. Over the years, particularly against the background of the five election cycles from 2019 to 2022, these terms have become more dichotomous concepts that threaten to create a kind of zero-sum game. In other words, every Israeli-Jewish citizen will ultimately be forced to choose between two poles. On one side is the state of *halacha*, which concerns religion/faith, and the form of the regime is either a theocratic dictatorship or an illiberal democracy. On the other side is a Jewish state that maintains a regime in the format of a representative and liberal democracy.

The deepening rift between the Jewish identity and the Israeli identity further blurs the (artificial) differences between the right and left in Israeli society and makes (perhaps contrived) connections between the "left" and the "state bloc" and between the right and the "religious bloc." The reason I reject this artificial connection is quite simple: In the state camp, one can find religious figures, and in the religious camp, there are people inclined toward the state.

This chapter will begin by defining the basic concepts of "state" and "faith" in the conceptual and political context of Israeli society. From a historical point of view, since religions came into the world long before the idea of the modern state and certainly long before the establishment of the State of Israel, the mutual relations between "state" and "faith" can only be discussed from the beginning of Zionism, since Zionism is what introduced the idea of the state into the Jewish discourse. Subsequently, the discussion will extend to the question of democracy in the State of Israel and examine whether the state-faith relationship overlaps completely or only to the extent of the relationship between democracy and "non-democracy." This discussion will require us to deal with a relatively new concept that has appeared in the field of political science—"illiberal democracy" or, as it is sometimes called, the "democrature," which is formally a democracy but de facto a dictatorship.

When we define the term "of the state" in Hebrew, we encounter a certain difficulty because the simple definition is "of the kingdom" or "belonging to the kingdom." However, the leading Israeli dictionaries, such as the *Even-Shoshan Dictionary*, define it as meaning "belongs to the state." Israel is not a monarchy but a republic, and therefore we will interpret "state" as meaning "belonging to the state." The word "faith" also requires a precise definition suitable for use in the Israeli sociopolitical context. "Faith," whether in a person or an idea, refers in the Israeli context to the Jewish religion. As such, a "believer" in the Israeli sociopolitical context will be defined for the purposes of this discussion as a "religious Jew" or a "traditional Jew."

The definitions of these two concepts are still not sufficient to understand the development of the system of interrelationships and, moreover, the fault line between the "state" and "faith." To gain a better understanding, one must analyze another concept—statehood, or the "strength of a state"—and note two main approaches. The first is that of Max Weber, one of the fathers of sociology, who claimed that the strength of a state is evident in its ability to enforce and control its subjects in a defined territory. In other words, a strong state is a state in which the monopoly on the exercise of force is in the hands of the state authorities, and it expects the citizens to obey its laws.[2] The second is that of John P. Nettl, who wrote that every country experiences ups and downs in its level of "statehood" and that, at any given moment, the level of statehood can be examined using three parameters: centralization, which refers to the state mechanisms' control over what is done and its ability to satisfy the needs of the citizens and enforce the laws; cohesion, which is measured by the strength of the country's citizens' sense of belonging to it; and territoriality, which refers to the existence of clear and recognized borders.[3]

State and Faith from the Forerunners of Zionism to the Founding of the State of Israel

The interrelationship between "faith" and "state" among Jews began to appear in the second half of the nineteenth century in the words, thoughts, and actions of a number of individuals who were nicknamed the "harbingers of Zionism." What they all had in common was that they believed that the redemption of the Jewish people would come naturally, not experimentally. As such, the Jews needed to act to return to their land and develop a life of agriculture, commerce, and economy in it. Not all of them spoke about a Jewish state, but there were those among them, such as Rabbi Bivas, who argued that the Jews should even take up arms in order to establish their own state in the Land of Israel.[4]

The Zionist movement, established in 1881 with the foundation of the first Hovevei Zion (Lovers of Zion) organizations, aspired to establish an independent political entity, a Jewish state, in the Land of Israel. There were several currents of Zionism (see chapter 2), and all of them strove for an organization with such a color. As the the Jewish state turned from a theoretical interest to something practical, it became clear that there was a rich range of options for how to define that future state, though each entailed a different mix of religious and state components. The founder of political Zionism, Benjamin Ze'ev Herzl, wrote in his book *The Jewish State*,

> Well, shall we finally have a theocracy? No! . . . The theocratic impulses of our clergy cannot be allowed to rear their heads. We will know how to keep them in their synagogues, just as we keep our standing army in barracks. Army and clergy will be highly respected, as necessary, and appropriate for their beautiful

positions. In the affairs of the state, with all respect for them, they should not interfere, lest they bring difficulties to it from home and abroad.[5]

Chaim Weizmann, the first president of the State of Israel, addressed this issue decades later, upon the establishment of the state, and said, "It is our duty to make it clear from the outset that although the state will treat the religious feelings of the community with full respect, it will not be able to turn back the clock to make religion the main principle in the state's leadership. Religion will be reduced to synagogues and the homes of families who want it; it will occupy a special place in schools but will not supervise government offices."[6] At the opposite pole, the thinkers of religious Zionism bound the future Jewish state to the fulfillment of the religious commandments and, in fact, supported the establishment of a halacha state. Rabbi Avraham Yitzhak HaCohen Kook, who is considered the central thinker of the religious Zionist current, saw the Jewish state that was about to be established as "the foundation of God's throne in the world" and as one whose role would be to demand and reveal the kingdom of God.[7] Rabbi Ben-Zion Meir Hai Uziel believed that "the Torah and the state were and will be in Israel one and united body in which there is no division, because each of them is conditioned by the existence of its fellow."[8]

The revisionist current within the Zionist movement, from which the Freedom Movement and Likud later sprang, was ambiguous regarding the relationship between religion and state, which is clearly evident in the change of positions expressed by its leader, Ze'ev Jabotinsky. At the beginning of his public activity in the first decade of the twentieth century, he stressed the universal and civil aspects of the Zionist movement, emphasizing the granting of full equal rights to women, but as the years passed, he changed his position slightly. In 1935, he wrote to his son Ari that he supported the state being established "in the spirit of the Torah of Israel," although he emphasized that this spirit did not mean religious coercion but that its concern was universal justice and morality and that he continued to support freedom of opinion. Jabotinsky advocated freedom of religion for all sects in Judaism and even asked the state not to harm the holy places of other religions.[9]

The initial official definitions regarding the State of Israel's purpose and its nature are given in the Declaration of Independence. The first hint of the purpose, character, and identity of the Jewish state is given in the fifth paragraph, in the middle of the historical review, which states, "The catastrophe which recently befell the Jewish people—the massacre of millions of Jews in Europe—was another clear demonstration of the urgency of solving the problem of its homelessness by reestablishing in Eretz-Israel the Jewish State, which would open the gates of the homeland wide to every Jew and confer upon the Jewish people the status of a fully privileged member of the comity of nations."[10] This reflects a contemporary attitude according to which the Jewish state served first and foremost as a state of refuge for every Jew. In it, the first seeds were already being planted for the growth of the state as a sovereign political entity where Jews would have superiority over non-Jews, which was reflected legislatively quite quickly. The enactment of the Law of Return in 1950 made the State of Israel the only country in the world that automatically granted citizenship based on religious affiliation. Moreover, this became Israeli policy despite being a multicultural and multi-religious country in which an ethnic-national-religious minority exists. This determination thus strengthened the element of religious in the dynamic between religion and state.

Israel was founded as a state without a constitution. Constitutions not only define the nature of a country, but in countries with a constitution, it is often also very difficult to cancel or change it. In my understanding, this lack explains the schism between the state and religion and to reflect their flexible relationship. The members of the first Knesset disagreed regarding the drafting of a constitution, mainly because religious circles opposed it. The compromise adopted was the enactment of Basic Laws, which were defined as "laws with constitutional status."

However, reality has shown, particularly during the repeated election cycles in 2019–2022, that there is no real difficulty in changing or even repealing Basic Laws with a minimum majority of sixty-one members of the Knesset. In the absence of a constitution and given that the Basic Laws are not firm, no rules have been set regarding two main issues that have affected the relationship between faith and state over the years: the definition of an Israeli citizen and the definition of the state's borders.

The following paragraphs in the Declaration of Independence are particularly interesting:

> The State of Israel will be open for Jewish immigration and for the Ingathering of the Exiles; it will foster the development of the country for the benefit of all its inhabitants; it will be based on freedom, justice and peace as envisaged by the prophets of Israel; it will ensure complete equality of social and political rights

> to all its inhabitants irrespective of religion, race or sex; it will guarantee freedom of religion, conscience, language, education and culture; it will safeguard the Holy Places of all religions; and it will be faithful to the principles of the Charter of the United Nations. The State of Israel is prepared to cooperate with the agencies and representatives of the United Nations in implementing the resolution of the General Assembly of the 29th November, 1947, and will take steps to bring about the economic union of the whole of Eretz-Israel.[11]

According to this section, the state will maintain complete social and political equality of rights for all its citizens without distinction of religion, race, or gender and will guarantee freedom of religion, conscience, language, education, and culture, although there is no explicit mention of the word "democracy." Even so, it refers to all the elements of a liberal democracy. In other words, this self-image of the state allows the citizens of the State of Israel to be "Israelis" even if they are not Jewish and also allows for the concept of a "Jewish and democratic state." However, we believe this is no longer a concept whose elements can be merged since the religion-state divide has deepened.

Israel was founded following a civil war that, in the Israeli-Jewish ethos, has been labeled "the war of liberation," or "the war of independence." The young country fought for its life from the first moment of its declaration in a bloody war that claimed the lives of over six thousand citizens and soldiers. However, even during the chaos of the war, when it seemed that the entire Jewish community was united around a common goal (victory in the war and the establishment of the State of Israel), there was no agreement regarding the roles of religion and state. The ultra-Orthodox in the Jewish community, particularly in Jerusalem, which was under siege, divided into two main currents. The moderate current, led by Agudat Yisrael, was not Zionist. However, from the 1930s on, it conducted a continuous and constructive dialogue with the leaders of Zionism while adopting a strategy of negotiations and, at times, cooperation with the Zionist movement and its institutions, knowing that this was the only way to achieve ultra-Orthodox aims and influence, even partially, the character of the Jewish community in Israel. This current even agreed that a small amount of ultra-Orthodox youth would be mobilized and actively participate in the war. In contrast, there was an extreme current, albeit a much smaller one, that denied any connection between Jerusalem (in the ultra-theological sense of Jewish settlement in the Land of Israel) and the Jewish *Yishuv* (the new settlements from 1878 inward) and saw the establishment of the State of Israel as an act of treason and heresy.[12]

State Versus Religion Until the June 1967 War

After the 1948 war ended and the Rhodes Agreements were signed in 1949, the sovereignty of the State of Israel was applied to a larger area than that allocated to it in the UN Partition Plan—about 78 percent of the territory of Western Israel compared to the 56 percent stipulated by the UN. However, this area still did not include places now seen by the religious camp as holy places, including the Jewish Quarter in Jerusalem, the Cave of the Patriarchs in Hebron, Joseph's Tomb in Nablus, and the Tomb of Joshua in the village of Kifl Harith (south of Nablus). The boundaries of the Rhodes Agreements were also far from the expansive interpretation of the "borders of the promised land" mentioned in the Bible: the East Nile estuary to the southwest, the Syria-Anatolia border to the north, and the Arabian Desert to the east.[13]

The armistice lines of 1949 demarcated a small country in terms of its territory that did not control what are known as the "holy places of the nation." Therefore, we suggest seeing the Jewish state in the period between the end of the 1948 war and the outbreak of the 1967 war as a "sanctuary state"—a dominant concept in Herzl's teachings—for all members of the Jewish people. The Law of Return in 1950 granted any Jew who expressed their desire to settle in Israel the right to immigrate to Israel (*aliyah*) and receive an "immigrant certificate," which entitled the holder to receive Israeli citizenship immediately.[14] However, there are problems and complexities even with the perception of the state as a place for refugees, both in the definition of "who is a Jew" (do second and/or third generations count?), which is becoming more and more confused as various parties try to expand or narrow it, and because such a state can serve as a refuge for Jews only as long as they constitute a solid majority of citizens. Demographic permutations such as birth rate, mortality rate, assimilation, conversion, and immigration mean that at some stage, Jews might no longer form a solid majority in Israel and may even become a minority.

From 1949 to 1967, the Israeli government was led by Mifleget Poalei Eretz Yisrael (Mapai, the Workers' Party of the Land of Israel), which later became the Labor Party. In these governments, there were religious partners, such as the Mafdal (National Religious Party). Emphasis was placed on instilling "Israeli" content in the young country while highlighting the values of work, military service, economic development, cooperation, and policies based on socialist Zionism. However, even then, there was no separation between religion and state, which was reflected in the statements of the first prime minister of the State of Israel, David Ben-Gurion, according to whom the two should not be separated. Ben-Gurion justified his position by saying that "there is a shared destiny between the State of Israel and the Jewish people." He also said that it is better for the State of Israel to maintain some level of control over religion and not allow a situation where religion becomes an independent factor with which the political government would have to deal.[15]

From its first day, the State of Israel was a country where the government's symbols were primarily Jewish religious symbols. The state flag was designed to be very similar to the prayer shawl (*tallit*), and the state symbol was determined to be the seven-branched candelabrum (*menorah*) from ancient times when the Jews had their Mishkan and the Temple in Jerusalem. The official day of rest was determined to be Saturday (*Shabbat*), Jewish holidays were determined to be vacation and sabbath days, food in government offices and its security arms was kosher, and there was no public transportation on Saturdays, except in places such as "Red Haifa." In the education system, the picture was more complex, perhaps reflecting more than anything the range of possibilities on the state-religious spectrum. Since unanimity was not reached regarding the nature of the education system, it was determined that there would be three separate systems: state education, which was formed from the agreements reached between Mapai and the General Zionists party; state-religious education, which reflected the worldview of the Mizrahi (established in 1902 in Eastern Europe), meaning religious Zionism; and independent education among the ultra-Orthodox community.[16]

The existence of three separate education systems in the same country eroded the principle of statehood because each system could determine syllabus contents according to its own view. Mainly secular students studied in the state education system and were also exposed to religious educational content, including Torah lessons and oral Bible studies (Toshba'a). In contrast, the religious education system contained almost no state subjects or content, such as citizenship and history lessons. Mathematics and English (now known as "core studies") were studied at a superficial level or not at all. In the state-religious education system, there was a more significant balance between secular studies and religious studies in a way that allowed students not only to enjoy both worlds but also to integrate into the various state systems and, much later, even become an influential force in the labor market, the army, or the public administration.[17]

One of the main issues in the long-standing dispute between the two camps (at least between the secular and ultra-Orthodox groups) that produces an almost abyssal rift is the issue of enlisting with the Israel Defense Forces (IDF). Even before the state's establishment, in March 1948, Yisrael Galili, chief of staff of the Haganah, instructed all divisions of the paramilitary group to exempt established yeshiva members (according to approved lists) from military service. In October 1948, Prime Minister Ben-Gurion announced in the State Council's Security Committee that four hundred yeshiva students would be released from military service, and the following year, he decided to grant recruitment rejection of yeshiva students in an orderly manner.

Although the number of religious students who received an exemption from service was negligible in the early days of the State of Israel, the principle of equality before the law regarding citizens of the state was violated even then, a phenomenon that gradually spread to other areas over the years. This is a tangible example of how the state-faith divide was expressed in a political decision in the state's early days. We do not propose to see this as affirmative action in favor of the ultra-Orthodox minority but rather to point out the inequality in the state burden—in this case, serving in the army of an embryonic state that was (and partially remains) surrounded by enemies. The Israeli legislator created inequality in the security service law and thus, in fact, set a precedent for apartheid based on faith and deepened the rift between the religious camp and the state.[18]

At this point, it is worth considering Rabbi Kook's address in May 1967 because, historically, it is a significant point that clarifies the religious-state rift. In his address, Kook mentioned that there were few regions outside the state's rule. Additionally, Kook commented on his feelings on the night of the vote on the establishment of the State of Israel at the UN on November 29, 1947:

> Nineteen years ago, on that famous night, when the positive decision of the governors of the nations of the world for the establishment of the State of Israel arrived in Israel, when all the people poured into the streets to express their feelings of joy, I could not go out and join in the joy. I sat alone because it was

a burden on me. To come to terms with what is happening, with the same terrible news, because word of the prophecy in Teri-Esher will indeed be fulfilled—"And they divided my land!"[19]

Referring to the State of Israel, Rabbi Kook likened it to his *mitzvot* and described it as the fulfillment of the vision of the prophets:

> And compared to what was said: "Is this the country that our prophets foresaw?" I say: This is the country that the prophets foresaw. Of course, the state is not completely perfect, but our prophets and our elders, their successors, said that the state would be like this: the seed of Abraham, Isaac, and Jacob would return and establish a local revival and an independent political government in it. . . . We were privileged, and we are privileged even now, to fulfill this word of God by the glory of the valor of our army. In other words: the State of Israel and its army, together with being considered the "end of exile," was an explicit and important mitzvah, an all-Israeli mitzvah.[20]

Rabbi Kook's words expressed the concept that the State of Israel is supposed to be a state of halacha in the spirit of the prophets of Israel, ruling over the entire territory of the Land of Israel and bringing about the fulfillment of a divine mitzvah of conquering the land for the sake of heaven. The IDF, in his view, was closer to the definition of the "Army of God" before it became the Defense Forces of the State of Israel. Over the years, this concept has become the ideological basis of personalities in the religious Zionist movement, such as Rabbi Haim Druckman and Rabbi Dov Lior, or elected officials, such as Hanan Porat, Nissan Slomiansky, Shaul Yahalom, and, in the twenty-fifth Knesset (which began to serve in January 2023), Bezalel Smotrich and Itamar Ben-Gvir. There is a clear difference from the statesmanlike ethos of both Ben-Gurion and Jabotinsky, according to which the development of institutions and society in the State of Israel comes before promoting religious matters.

These concepts have become more than merely abstract ideas. In March 2023, during a constitutional crisis in Israel concerning a reform of the judicial system, the reform's supporters protested with signs that read "This is the time to do for God" and "Join God's army, they [the statehood camp] will not steal the Torah and the Holy Land from us." The reform's opponents, who sought to maintain a state/kingdom with a complete separation of powers, as is expected in a democracy, were called anarchists in the same posters.

From the Six Days War to Oslo: The Religious Element Between Disobedience and Political Constraints

The June 1967 war brought a major change not only in the balance of power between Israel and its neighbors but also, and perhaps above all, in the perceptions within Israeli society and politics regarding the territories—Judea, Samaria, the Gaza Strip, East Jerusalem, the Sinai Peninsula, and the Golan Heights—that came under Israeli control after the war. These perceptions had and still have a direct impact on the state-religion divide in the Israeli context. The regional security changes had a significant effect on the perception of the identity of the Jewish citizens of the State of Israel and the ways in which different groups saw the future and character of the state.

After the war, Israel controlled areas that, according to international law, are considered "occupied territories" where military rule applies. In June 1967, the State of Israel asserted its sovereignty over East Jerusalem, although its residents were only granted permanent residency, not citizenship, and in December 1981, Israel fully asserted its sovereignty over the Golan Heights.[21]

A series of significant events that have taken place in the internal and external arenas since the war in 1967 allows us to draw the lines of the state-faith divide on a timeline and to discover that the identity crisis that we placed at the center of our research has never been close to a solution. A series of political agreements that enabled the continuous functioning of governments did not erase the existence of two camps—state and faith—that still stand opposite each other at the beginning of the third decade of the twenty-first century. An ideological chasm has now opened between them: One camp holds the Jewish religion as the basis for a correct human society, while the other holds the religion of liberal democracy as the cornerstone of such a society.

The significant events that befell Israel also included territorial changes. In 1982, Israel completed its withdrawal from the Sinai Peninsula following the signing of a peace agreement with Egypt that granted Israel the Gaza Strip, which the Egyptians did not want to accept. Egypt also insisted that the peace agreement include clauses granting autonomy to the Palestinians in the West Bank and the Gaza Strip. In 1994, Israel withdrew from most of the Gaza Strip and the city of Jericho in the West Bank as part of the first phase of the Oslo Accords. The second phase, which was completed in 1995, transferred full civil and security control of all the large cities of the West Bank (Area A) and civil control of most of its rural areas (Area B) to the Palestinian Authority. The uninhabited areas of the West Bank (Area C) remained under full Israeli civil and security control. Yitzhak Rabin's assassination on November 4, 1995, and the 1996 election interrupted the progress toward a permanent settlement. However, Israel handed over territories to the Palestinians even after that—in the West Bank as part of the Hebron Agreement (1997) and the Wye River Memorandum (1998), followed by the unilateral disengagement from the Gaza Strip and the evacuation of four settlements in northern Samaria (2005).

It is worth noting that in all these cases, it is possible to identify a gap between the statehood camp and the faith-religious camp that does not correspond to the traditional rift between "right" and "left." The withdrawal from Sinai was carried out by the right-wing government headed by Menachem Begin, the Israeli withdrawal from parts of Samaria in 1997 and 1998 occurred under Benjamin Netanyahu's government, and Israel disengaged from the Gaza Strip during the government of Ariel Sharon. The Oslo Accords were signed by the government of Yitzhak Rabin, who, in 1977, had approved the citizenship of the settlement of Netzer Hazani in the Gaza Strip. The immediate conclusion that emerges from this sequence of historical facts is simple: Using "right" and "left" labels in relation to the land variable in the Israeli case is, at best, a half-truth. It is an artificial labeling because public figures separated into right and left held similar, even identical, views regarding the importance of leaving the land under Israeli/Jewish control. The justification—religious or security—is what separates the two camps.

One of the outcomes of the 1967 war was a large Palestinian population living under Israeli rule in the West Bank, East Jerusalem, and the Gaza Strip. The war also brought international pressure to withdraw from the occupied territories in exchange for peace agreements that would guarantee Israel an existence within recognized and safe borders (Security Council Resolution 242). The new geopolitical and demographic situation led to internal Israeli discourse concerning what should be done in the occupied territories. At a government meeting in August 1967, there was a broad consensus that the new territories would not be returned to Jordan or handed over to any other political entity.

The political upheaval that took place in Israel in May 1977 brought Likud to power, a party that was unjustly perceived as right-wing due to its position on economic and territorial issues (see chapter 2). Throughout their years of public service, senior members of Likud, such as Menachem Begin, Yitzhak Shamir, and Ariel Sharon, who all reached the status of prime minister, demonstrated statesmanship and non-religious positions, just as Labor's leaders did. It is the ultra-Orthodox parties (Agudat Yisrael and, from 1984, Shas) that illustrate the gap between the statehood camp and the religious camp. Religious (non-ultra-Orthodox) political power was divided between these two camps from 1948, even more so after 1967. This rift not only manifested in customs and forms of clothing but also in attempts to erode the status quo between secular (state) and religious/Orthodox, including Israel's national airline (El-Al) operating flights on Shabbat, the operation of movie theaters on Shabbat evenings in mixed communities (Jerusalem, Petah Tikva), closing streets for vehicles to pass on Shabbat and holidays (e.g., Bar-Ilan Street in Jerusalem), and, since 2017, carrying out infrastructure works on the Tel Aviv Light Rail system in the city's ultra-Orthodox suburbs on Shabbat evenings.

The elections of 1984 and 1988 ended in a stalemate. In 1984, the formation of a National Unity government was necessitated, as well as a rotation of the position of prime minister from Yitzhak Shamir of Likud to Shimon Peres of Labor. The 1988 general election resulted in the formation of a government led by Shamir. In both cases, there was no real cleavage within the ruling coalition because these two governments relied on a substantial parliamentary majority of about ninety members of the Knesset, the vast majority of whom belonged to the statehood camp. Therefore, the religious-faith side had no real influence on the character of the state in those years. There was no move toward the separation of religion and state or the mass recruitment of ultra-Orthodox yeshiva students to the army, and most secular citizens did not feel that they were in danger of disproportionate religious coercion.

Domestically, Israel faced a great challenge in the 1980s that highlighted the dominance of the state element in the political system. The sharp increase in military expenditure, the failure of the monetary reforms, the devaluation of the local currency against the dollar, and the regulation of bank shares led to a severe economic crisis that reached its peak in 1984 with inflation of 445 percent.[22] The unity government of 1984 succeeded, despite the bitter ideological rivalry between the political camps, in launching an economic stabilization plan in which each side made significant and real concessions for the sake of the national economy. The statehood camp, which included parties with a socialist tone (which is why they were called leftist) and parties with an economically liberal tone (which is why they were called rightist), agreed to dismiss civil servants, freeze the wages of public sector workers, cut government subsidies, impose additional taxes on companies and the self-employed, and impose controls on the prices of many products. This program succeeded beyond expectations. At the end of the 1980s, inflation in Israel dropped to single digits, and the Israeli economy was ready to successfully absorb about a million immigrants from the Soviet Union and prepare itself for the era of technological breakthroughs of the 1990s.[23]

It is not possible to fully understand the transfer of the artificial fault line in Israeli society between left and right to the real and more significant divide between religion and state (or between a statehood camp and a religious camp) without analyzing the contributions of religious Zionism. Until the 1967 war, the messianic elements in this movement, educated on the teachings of Rabbi Kook, constituted a marginal minority. The overwhelming majority consisted of bourgeois Zionists who were also members of Labor governments. After the war, there was a fundamental change in religious Zionism because the dream or vision of a complete Land of Israel under Jewish control became more tangible due to the takeover of the territories of Judea, Samaria, the Gaza Strip, the Sinai Peninsula, and the Golan Heights. This takeover gave Israel actual control over the holy places of Judaism—the Temple Mount and the Western Wall in Jerusalem, Joseph's Tomb in Nablus, the Cave of the Patriarchs in Hebron, and Mount Sinai.

Historically, the claim that the two camps both opposed a territorial compromise is true. However, the explanation for their opposition exposes the depth of the gap between them: While the statehood camp rejected the compromise proposals for political and security considerations, the religious camp did so for primarily theological reasons—holding the territories and settling in them as an instrument for redemption. Within the religious camp, some pragmatic members were national Zionists and emphasized the military-strategic narrative, according to which these are strategic territories necessary for the defense of the State of Israel.[24]

One of the main issues that deepened the gap between the two camps was compliance with the law in the Jewish/Israeli settlement enterprise in the territories captured in the June 1967 war. Chapter 2 already proved that the argument about right and left in this context is irrelevant because Labor sent the first settlers to build their homes in the territories of the homeland east of the Green Line. The question of whether to respect the laws of the state (or the kingdom) became contentious because the parties differed on the scope and pace of construction for Jews in the occupied territories.

The members of the extreme current in religious Zionism believed that if there was a conflict between them and the state on the question of settlement, then the institutions of the state should not be obeyed because settlement in all parts of the Holy Land stands above Israeli law and because "there is nothing more important than God's decree." The people of the moderate current thought it would be beneficial to reach an understanding with the state, but if such an understanding were not reached, then disobeying the provisions of the law would not be a failure to recognize the will of the State of Israel and, at most, reflected Israeli society's culture of disobedience. Certain circles even compared the illegal settlement enterprise as parallel to the illegal Zionist settlement enterprise during the British Mandate period.[25]

The radicalization within religious Zionism in the late 1970s and early 1980s led to the establishment of the "Jewish underground," which sought to carry out terrorist attacks as revenge for the damage done by Palestinians to Jewish settlers in Judea and Samaria. The underground cells, isolated from each other, mainly included activists on the extreme fringes of the religious Zionist current. They carried out a series of actions against Palestinian institutions and mayors and even planned to blow up the Dome of the Rock located on the Temple Mount in Jerusalem to provoke a war that would ultimately lead, according to their belief, to the redemption of the people of Israel.

The activity of the underground was brought to an end in 1984 by the Israeli Security Agency (Shabak). The Jewish underground did not receive support from the rabbis of religious Zionism at the time. Apparently, it was considered a marginal issue, but its activity illustrated that there were extremist elements among the religious public in the State of Israel, ready to commit acts that would endanger the security of the state and its citizens and take the law into their own hands while relying on the justification of their growing beliefs about the state's laws and institutions.

"Left-Right" Becomes "State versus Beliefs"—1992 to 2009

Early in the 1990s, two fundamental processes took place in Israel that had a significant role in transforming the sociopolitical discourse in Israel from a discourse of "left versus right" to one of "state versus faith": the constitutional revolution and secret negotiations between Israel and the Palestinian Liberation Organization (PLO), which culminated in the signing of the Oslo Accords in September 1993. These two processes were accompanied by another, which is still in the making—a demographic change to majority and minority relations within the Jewish majority group in Israel in favor of the religious camp. It is important to remember that the arrival of approximately one million immigrants from the former USSR, the vast majority of whom were secular, delayed the shift of the demographic balance to the religious side by twenty to thirty years.[26]

The constitutional revolution is a term for the process of expanding judicial reviews of Knesset laws, based on the increasing dominance of the school of "judicial activism" led by justice (and later president) of the Supreme Court, Aharon Barak. According to this approach, "everything can be judged." This interpretation is in line with the Declaration of Independence's principles, and it found its expression in two Basic Laws—Basic Law: Human Dignity and Freedom, enacted in March 1992, and Basic Law: Freedom of Occupation, enacted in 1993. These laws were of great significance: They tilted the "balance of democracy" toward a liberal democracy, similar to that practiced in most Western countries—that is, a democracy in which, in addition to the basic element of holding elections and majority decision, there are significant layers of human and civil rights, protections for minorities, and strong elements of freedom of expression and freedom of association. In addition, the enactment of these laws, especially the Basic Law: Human Dignity and Freedom, was seen by many as giving the courts a new role: to examine the Knesset's legislation and determine that a law that unlawfully violates human rights is not valid. Referring to these laws, Justice Barak said,

> With their enactment, there was a fundamental change in the status of human rights in Israel. They became constitutional rights. They were given a supra-legal constitutional status. A "normal" law of the Knesset cannot change them. Ordinary legislation cannot harm a protected human right unless the requirements stipulated in the Basic Laws are met. Failure to meet the constitutional requirements turns the ordinary law into an unconstitutional law. This is a constitutionally flawed law. The court may declare it null and void. Israel is a constitutional democracy. We have now joined the community of democratic countries (including the United States, Canada, Germany, Italy, South Africa) that have

a constitutional Bill of Rights. We became part of the human rights revolution, which characterizes the second half of the 20th century. Indeed, the lessons of World War II, centered on the Holocaust of the Jewish people, as well as the suppression of human rights in totalitarian countries, put human rights at the top of the world agenda. International documents on human rights were struck down. Israel joined them. International human rights tribunals were established. The new constitutions include extensive chapters—usually at the top of the constitution and within a unique armor of some rights—regarding human rights. The judicial review of the constitutionality of laws that violate human rights has become the domain of the majority of countries. This revolution did not escape us either. We joined it in March 1992.[27]

Opponents of the "constitutional revolution" claim that although the Basic Law: Human Dignity and Freedom, which is at the core of the matter, was enacted by the Knesset, it was, in fact, the handiwork of the Supreme Court, which assumed, without any authority, the role of establishing the constitution in Israel. According to the opponents' understanding, the Supreme Court harms the status of the Knesset, which, as the House of Representatives, represents the sovereignty of the people, thus marking a violation of democracy. Although a significant portion of the opponents of the constitutional revolution came from the statehood camp, including some associated with the liberal right, the feeling of alienation from the Supreme Court among the ultra-Orthodox and religious public grew stronger over the years. This happened because, according to their perceptions and beliefs, the judicial authority harmed their religious worldview and way of life.

A prominent incident that illustrated this position occurred on February 14, 1999. It turned out, in hindsight, to be a crucial event. The religious camp, which included Zionist and ultra-Orthodox figures, organized a large-scale demonstration (according to police reports, about 250,000 people) to protest over High Supreme Court verdicts that violated the status quo in matters of religion and state. For example, the Supreme Court had ruled that in a divorce suit, the rabbinic courts must discuss matters of property division according to the laws of the Knesset and not the laws of halacha.[28]

The ruling of the High Court of Justice on the personal status of the person (citizen) embodies the state-religious divide regarding individual freedom and the right to personal property. This is a fault line that cannot be reconciled at the conceptual level because the religious camp will always prefer the laws of the Jewish halacha over the laws of the state. On this issue, the Supreme Court is perceived, in the eyes of the ultra-Orthodox public and among elements of religious Zionists, as a liberal democrat and not as a Jew. Conversely, the massive demonstration of February 1999 was a warning sign for the statehood camp, which saw the event as a tangible expression of a view that was a danger to democracy.

In the 1990s, the state-religious fault line was obscured by the guise of a fault line separating left and right. The real dispute was over the definition of democracy in the State of Israel. If, until the constitutional revolution, the State of Israel was considered only a representative parliamentary democracy, then following the constitutional revolution, many in Israel and in the world also saw it as a liberal democracy, where one of the functions of the judicial system is to make sure that the elements of liberalism are respected and that the legislative and/or executive authority does not infringe on the rights of the citizens. The opponents of the constitutional revolution, among whom the religious element was growing, had aspired since the 1990s to establish a democratic regime in Israel that was less liberal and more conservative in nature. There were prominent public figures within the religious camp, such as Rabbi Moshe Levinger, who stated that while Israel would continue to be a democratic state, democracy is ultimately secondary and must be subordinated to the needs of the people of Israel, which include religious values.[29]

At the same time as the constitutional revolution, Israel strove to end the conflict with the Palestinians and conducted negotiations that culminated in the signing of the Oslo Accords. This political development deepened the state-religious divide and separated the two camps, though not necessarily in terms of right and left. A study of Yitzhak Rabin's speeches in the Knesset (and outside of it) shows that a complete Land of Israel was part of his worldview. Conversely, Benjamin Netanyahu, who won the Knesset elections in 1996, continued the outline of the Oslo Accords, which were signed by a government mistakenly identified as left-wing. Both Rabin and Netanyahu belong to the statehood camp, so the rift is between this camp and the religious camp.

The Oslo Accords were signed after a long process that started with the outbreak of the First Intifada (1987); the decision of King Hussein of Jordan to secede from the West Bank (1988); the first Gulf War, which damaged the PLO's revenues; and the convening of the Madrid Conference (1991). In the internal Palestinian arena, the establishment of Hamas led to the strengthening of the religious current in the territories and raised the level of concern in the ranks of the PLO about the loss of its hegemony in Palestinian society. This sequence of events increased Israel's need to find a solution for the future of Judea, Samaria, and the Gaza Strip. Although the Israeli public did not provide a solution in the 1988 elections, public discourse did focus on the demographic changes taking place in the State of Israel. It should be noted here that a scientific study published by the demographer Sergio Della Pergola in 2016 suggests that the Jews are already a minority in the Land of Israel in the area from the sea to the Jordan River.[30]

The Oslo Accords were a watershed in all that has been said regarding the array of political forces in Israel and accelerated the shift of the Israeli fault line from a right-left axis to a religious-state axis. For the first time, a strong connection formed between the state's liberal right-wing and religious elements against the background of their fierce opposition to the agreements. Each element of this new composition had different reasons for opposing the agreements: The liberal right-wing objected mainly for security and national reasons, while the religious element opposed them due to religious-theological considerations and saw the relinquishment of territories in the Holy Land as an inviolable commandment.

It was clear to the two sides of this new political bloc, which would later create the "faith camp," that if the Oslo process moved in the direction of a permanent settlement between Israelis and Palestinians, this would affect their ideological cornerstones: the holy places in Judea, Samaria, and Jerusalem; the settlement project in the West Bank and the Gaza Strip; and, of course, the state's permanent borders.

The most significant clash at that time between the religious narrative and the state narrative occurred on November 4, 1995, when Yigal Amir, a law student at Bar-Ilan University, shot dead the prime minister of Israel, Yitzhak Rabin, while wearing a *kippah*. In his interrogation after the murder, Amir said, "Everything I did, I would not have done other than out of my religious duty to protect the people of Israel from the 'moral' side of the law to which Rabin belonged, as was said by many rabbis."[31] This was the first time the general Israeli public was exposed to halachic-theological concepts such as the Law of the Pursuer and *din moser*. The "persecutor," according to halacha law, is a person who commits an act that, due to its seriousness and consequences, allows another person to prevent them from committing the act, even at the cost of killing them.[32]

The comprehensive investigations that followed Rabin's murder ultimately did not lead to the prosecution of rabbis for incitement. However, many testimonies show that quite a few rabbis became concerned with the question "Is the Law of the Pursuer relevant for Rabin as the main politician who decided to withdraw from the Jewish territories set out in the Bible?" This discussion was an incentive for Amir's decision to assassinate Rabin. Law enforcement officials even investigated a series of letters that Eliezer Melamed, the rabbi of the Har-Bracha settlement and a religious Zionist, sent to various rabbis in February 1995, in which he pointed out a series of situations in which individuals would take the law into their own hands. Moreover, he even asked whether there is any place for public figures to warn the prime minister and government ministers that if they continue to hand over territories to murderers, according to halacha law, it will be necessary to bring them to a public trial and punish them.[33]

Rabin's murder was the most severe clash between religious and statehood values in Israel since 1948. Arie Nadler described the incident in his book *Incitement and Political Murder* in which he claimed that Amir was the emissary of a group that developed an alternative justice system and that, in its view, was threatened by the policies of the Rabin government. The murderer translated into action the negation of the leader's legitimacy, the denial of his humanity, and the verbal accusations hurled at Rabin. The killer felt that he enjoyed support for his murderous act. He is the one who carries out what others have asked. From his point of view, he is a self-chosen hero, and he realizes the ideals of his group.[34]

Most of the religious camp condemned Rabin's murder, but these condemnations were not enough to stop the deepening of the state-religious rift. One of the explicit expressions of this was a feeling—not necessarily true—that arose in the statehood camp, especially among the secularists, that everyone who wears a kippah belonging to the so-called religious camp supports political murder for the realization of national-religious goals. In a television program that interviewed religious and secular young people, Yigal Klein, a right-wing activist, said,

> The kippah was enough, the shape of the kippah, the style of the kippah. If you belonged to the kippah, you would be labeled guilty, even indirectly, of murder. At the time of the murder, I was on my regular protest shift, a high school student handing out stickers against the Oslo Accords. When the murder happened, people stopped, got out of their jeeps, and started beating us because we were the "guilty" ones. And for me, that was start of what awaited us.[35]

Shortly after Rabin's murder, Israel had to deal with two additional campaigns: security and political. The first half of 1996 was marked by a wave of lethal terror attacks by Hamas and the Palestinian Islamic Jihad (PIJ). Many people in both camps—religion and state—called for a reexamination of the Oslo Accords.

In May 1996, the elections for the fourteenth Knesset were held. In this election campaign, Netanyahu was assisted by Arthur J. Finkelstein, an American political consultant who later earned the nickname "the consultant who divided Israel." This nickname was puzzling because Israeli society had been polarized between right and left (an artificial classification) for many years, as evidenced by the close election campaigns and even the violence in the 1970s and 1980s. In 1996, Finkelstein led the Likud party's campaign and did not present the option of choosing between "right" and "left" to the Israeli public but the choice of "Jews" or "Israelis." Two slogans that highlighted the new fault line are remembered from this campaign: "Netanyahu is good for the Jews" and "Peres will divide Jerusalem." These two slogans were intended to express the religious-nationalist feelings of the voters, as well as to create a common denominator for the entire religious public in the State of Israel and bring them entirely to Netanyahu's side.[36]

The 1996 elections were the first in which the division between "Jew" and "Israeli" was visible above the surface, and following the results, the foundations were laid for the future connection between the liberal right and the entire religious camp. Netanyahu's first government did not cancel the Oslo Accords but in fact made progress in implementing its additional stages, including handing over territories to the Palestinians, despite a fragile security reality that included attacks against Jews. In January 1997, Israel handed over the Arab territory of the city of Hebron as part of the Hebron Agreement and, in 1998, significant parts of Judea and Samaria (13 percent of Area C and another 14.2 percent of Area B) as part of the Wye River Memorandum, which was frowned upon by many in Netanyahu's camp—both the liberal right and the religious bloc. This was the second time a right-wing party had handed over Jewish territories—according to the Bible—to non-Jewish sovereignty. This development, as well as the disintegration of parts of Netanyahu's coalition for various reasons, led to the dissolution of the government and more elections in 1999. In these elections, Ehud Barak defeated Netanyahu, and his coalition, One Israel, which included David Levy's Gesher (Bridge) and the moderate right-wing party Meimad (Dimension), was the largest faction.

The Barak government lasted for less than two years due to a variety of factors, including the economic crisis that resulted from the bursting of the "high-tech bubble," disagreements with the religious parties on issues of religion and state, and the failure of the Camp David talks with the Palestinian Authority (July 2000) and the outbreak of the Al-Aqsa Intifada (September 2000). In the prime ministerial elections held in 2001, Ariel Sharon defeated Barak by a considerable margin of about 25 percent, but since there were no Knesset elections that year, a unity government was formed comprising Likud, Israel One, Shas, Yahadut HaTorah, Yisrael Beiteinu (led by Avigdor Lieberman), the National Religious Party, and some Center Party members. This coalition brought together the liberal-economic right and religious elements.

The first Sharon government served for about two years until the 2003 elections and did not deal with matters of religion and state at all due to serious security problems, culminating with Operation Defensive Shield (April 2002). This operation aimed to disrupt the infrastructure of Palestinian terrorists in northern Samaria, mainly in the Jenin refugee camp. Economically, this government faced a high-tech industry crisis, so it launched Operation Economic Defensive Shield, designed to rescue the State of Israel from an economic crisis. The plan included wage cuts in the public sector, cuts in many national insurance allowances, and sharp cuts to child allowances. Netanyahu, who served as this government's minister of finance, said at the time,

> Entire populations in the Arab public, and the ultra-Orthodox public in particular, have become accustomed to children's allowances to the point that a person's job is, in fact, the birth of children. He has children, and later he will raise children whose job is to have more children. Because the allowance increases the more children he has, there is an incentive here that will simply bring us to collapse, and the collapse is, by the way, both economic and social. . . . I want people to have children that they can provide for. . . . A person can and should raise a family with as many children as he wants, but he must understand that he has the primary responsibility to provide for them, educate them, and take care of their future. He cannot shirk this responsibility and transfer all or most of it to the state. Most of the responsibility is on his shoulders.[37]

The cut in child allowances obviously hurt the ultra-Orthodox sector, which fully supported Netanyahu in the 1996 and 1999 elections. In carrying out this plan, the Likud government preferred values of the state and its general pubic over the sectoral interests of a significant part of the religious camp, which, after the 1996 elections, gave up its neutral position between "right" and "left" parties and adhered to conservative and religious values, which have been attributed to political frameworks with a right-wing view since the French Revolution. In Israel, at the beginning of the twenty-first century, such right-wing conservative positions were the ideology of parts of the Jewish public who belonged to the religious camp and of the public who defined themselves as the secular right in terms of territory and economy only.

The next landmark in the faith-state fault line was the disengagement plan of the second Sharon government that was accepted at the end of 2004 and implemented in the summer of 2005. In accordance with this plan, Israel unilaterally withdrew from the Gaza Strip and northern Samaria, involving the forced evacuation of nearly nine thousand Jewish settlers. The plan met with strong opposition from the religious-nationalist public, with the strongest opposition coming from the religious Zionist movement. In *The Loss of Innocence: The Effect of Disengagement on Religious Zionism*, Yair Sheleg pointed to the religious Zionist current as the factor most significantly affected by the plan since most of the evacuees were from this current. For these people, it was a triple trauma: a personal loss for the thousands of people evacuated from their homes, the destruction of flourishing communities, and an ideological destruction of faith in the vision of a complete Land of Israel. In the months after the disengagement, voices in religious Zionist circles called for a dramatic change in their relationship with the state: some called for a separatist, ultra-Orthodox approach to the state, at the heart of which is no longer seeing statehood as a value; no more Independence Day celebrations; no longer saying prayers for the peace of the state on Shabbat and holidays; and avoiding conscription for the IDF. Others in this faith camp called for a democratic, nonviolent takeover of the state's leadership.

Sheleg concluded by asserting that although the essential barrier between the majority of religious Zionists and the state had not changed and that they remained Zionists, which means believing in the importance of the state, military service, and contributing to society, the religious Zionism current ultimately began to be less state-like and less romantic in its relationship with the state. It even revealed more signs of cynicism and a willingness to fight the country if its path did not seem worthy. Additionally, there was radicalization among the religious Zionist movement toward domestic political opponents and level of violence toward the Arab public, both in the territory of Judea and Samaria and within the Green Line. Religious Zionism began to have an adversarial, sometimes militant discourse with the country's media, cultural, and intellectual elites and moved from an action pattern of courting these elites to one of "restoring war."[38]

Israel's unilateral disengagement from the Gaza Strip and northern Samaria caused an earthquake on the political map of Israel. In November 2005, Prime Minister Ariel Sharon decided, against the background of this internal political crisis, to withdraw from Likud and form a new party called Kadima (Forward), which was joined by some Likud MKs and several figures from Labor, including the former prime minister, Shimon Peres. This new political group reflected the ability of political personalities with a statehood vision to coalesce under one roof, if only temporarily. The split in Likud and the establishment of Kadima created a situation in which the ruling party, which claimed to represent the liberal right in Israel, was, in fact, a statehood bloc that stood against an opposing bloc whose ideology was dominated by its religious component. This rift influenced Likud, which originally had a liberal-right ideology. After 2006, it began to distance itself from those liberal values enshrined in its name (the Liberal Freedom Party) and move closer to nationalist-religious values.

In January 2006, two months before the elections for the seventeenth Knesset, Sharon, the prime minister, suffered two strokes, putting him in a state of paralysis. Ehud Olmert took his place as the head of Kadima. The elections in March led to the establishment of a coalition government formed by Kadima, Labor, Shas, and Gil (Generation Who Built the Land), a newly formed party. Likud, which fragmented due to the disengagement process, failed in these elections, receiving only twelve seats. The religious bloc in the Knesset was not yet coherent, but even then, behind the scenes, a connection was formed between the old national-religious party and secular and religious political parties, who found an ideological home in the Homeland party, which was known to propose, among other things, the transfer of Palestinians living in the territories. This was the same position that, decades earlier, had been part of Mapai's discourse, which was mistakenly labeled as a leftist political party.

The Olmert government collapsed when the prime minister resigned in September 2008 following the police's recommendation to prosecute him for a number of crimes, including accepting bribes. His resignation led the country to further elections in March 2009. These elections were held against the background of significant external developments, including the victory of Hamas in the Palestinian Authority elections (2006), the Second Lebanon War (2006), Hamas' takeover of the Gaza Strip (2007), and Operation Cast Lead (December 2008–January 2009).

Between 2009 and 2019, Israel saw three governments led by Netanyahu. It was a decade in which the contours that clearly distinguish the camps among the Jewish majority in Israeli society took shape: a statehood camp versus a religious camp. Until 2015, Netanyahu aspired to form governments that were as broad as possible, though he preferred to incorporate statehood elements into them, such as Labor, Yesh Atid (There Is a Future), and Yisrael Beiteinu. All these, to use anachronistic terminology, embodied currents of the artificial sociopolitical partition between "right" and "left." After the elections in 2013, Netanyahu established a government with statehood parties (Yesh Atid, Hatnua) and Jewish Home, a religious Zionist party that combined statehood and faith. This party was headed by Naftali Bennett and had members whose worldview was traditional, religious, and nationalist, such as Uri Orbach, Uri Ariel, and Moti Yogev. Netanyahu chose to leave the ultra-Orthodox parties out of his coalition. Two years later, in 2015, the government that was established was perceived as right-wing, but in fact it was a government in which the religious component had an increasing dominance, which was reflected in the fact that all the religious parties were members of it.

The tilting of the political discourse in Israel from right-left to religion-state in these years was accompanied by a process of opening up the connection between Judaism and democracy and turning these two concepts into a zero-sum game. This was mainly reflected in the statements of political and social figures in the religious camp who highlighted the superiority of Judaism over democracy. For example, in July 2011, Dov Lior, one of the top rabbis of the religious-nationalist community, said, "The foreign work of our generation is democracy. Once it was marriage and wealth. Today it is democracy. Instead of democracy being a form of government, it has become a value. This is good for people who live a promiscuous life, because they do not want to restrain themselves."[39] In 2012, Benny Katsover, one of the leaders of the settlers in Judea and Samaria, said, "I would say that Israeli democracy has one major job today, and that is to disappear from our life. . . . Israeli democracy has finished its job, and it must disintegrate and bow to Judaism. Today, all events are leading to the recognition that there is no other way than to put the Jewish matter at the center over every other matter, and that is the answer for all situations and threats."[40] In 2014, Sheldon Adelson (1933–2021), former owner of the *Israel Hayom* newspaper and patron of the religious camp, said, "It's not bad if Israel is not a democracy because it isn't written in the Bible."[41]

The question thus arises of whether there is a Gordian connection between "statehood" and "democracy." Many nondemocratic countries are run in a manner entirely compatible with statehood in terms of the functioning of the institutions and the citizens' sense of identity with the state. This is the case, for example, in China and Egypt and, in the past, in the nondemocratic countries of the Eastern Bloc. In Israel, on the other hand, the situation is different. Israel was established as a Jewish and democratic state, and the content of the Declaration of Independence even positioned it as a liberal democracy. Therefore, calls for the Jewish element to prevail over the democratic element are a violation, at least regarding the recognition of the principle of statehood. This was best expressed by the tenth president of the State of Israel, Reuven Rivlin, who defined Israel as a country with four main tribes: the secular, the religious-nationalist, the Arab, and the ultra-Orthodox (and not as a country where there are "rightists" and "leftists"). In his last speech as president in the Knesset, Rivlin referred to the tension between the Jewish state and a democratic state:

> A Jewish state is not a matter of course. A democratic state is not a matter of course. There will be no Israel if it is not democratic and Jewish, Jewish and democratic, in one word. The internal tension that bubbles within us, between the integrity of the people, the integrity of the society, and the integrity of the country, is a dispute that will end up existing only if we do not deny it. We will succeed only if we know how to hold on to complexity—and reject simplification, which is always so tempting. We will succeed only if we know how to hold this tension, to find the balances and compromises within it. Only then will we be able to keep this miracle, which is our home.[42]

In the eight years between the establishment of the fourth Netanyahu government (2015) and the time of writing, the deepening of the religious-state fault line greatly accelerated. My analysis is that this divide has almost completely erased the divide between right and left.

This erasure was accompanied by a secondary process of crushing the principle of statehood in general, which was reflected in the fact that the political forces that created the "religious" camp—Likud, the religious Zionists, and the ultra-Orthodox parties—intensified the tone of their statements against the state institutions, especially against those perceived as the defenders of statehood and democracy: the Israel Police, the State Attorney's Office, the Supreme Court and the judiciary as a whole, the legal advisor to the government, the state comptroller, and, to a certain extent, the chief of staff. Simcha Rothman, one of the leaders of Otzma Yehudit (Jewish Power), expressed this in a March 2023 interview with the *New York Sun*, stating that the judicial reform, to which the response was a large-scale protest, was, in fact, a religious war.[43] My analysis considers it a war between Judaism as a religion and democracy as a civil religion.

This rift is on an escalating trend and threatens to plunge Israel into a constitutional crisis and dismantle the foundation and balance, fragile from the beginning, of Israel as a Jewish and democratic state. Since 2015, a personal-legal aspect has been added to this rift, which also affects the political system in Israel and the characterization of the two camps. In October 2015, *Haaretz* published an article stating that the employees of *Walla* received instructions to give sympathetic coverage to Netanyahu and his wife Sarah during the period when the website was controlled by Shaul Elovitch, a personal friend of the prime minister. In July 2016, the attorney general, Avichai Mandelblit, announced that he was starting an investigation into the matter, and in December, he officially ordered the police to open an investigation. In February 2018, the police recommended that Netanyahu be prosecuted for crimes of bribery, fraud, and two cases of breach of trust, and an additional recommendation was made in December 2018 to prosecute him in a third criminal case.

In November 2019, the attorney general announced that he had decided to prosecute Netanyahu in all three cases, and in January 2020, an indictment was filed against him in the Jerusalem District Court on one count of bribery and two counts of fraud and breach of trust.[44] Throughout this process, Netanyahu rejected calls for him to resign, as his predecessor, Ehud Olmert, had done. Indeed, Olmert announced his resignation as early as when an investigation was opened against him, though not before Netanyahu had called for Olmert to resign.

The enactment of the Basic Law: Israel—Nation State of the Jewish People in 2018 further diminished the element of statehood in the identity of the State of Israel in favor of the religious element. This law established Hebrew as the state language and lowered the status of Arabic, the mother tongue of more than 20 percent of the country's citizens, from an official language to a language with a special status. It also stated that the state would encourage Jewish settlement. This law is seen by many, not only by the non-Jewish citizens of the country, as a discriminatory and undemocratic law. Many believe that it has the potential to curb and even reverse the trends of integration that have begun to emerge among the growing public in the non-Jewish sectors of the country.[45]

At the end of 2018, Israel was caught in a political whirlwind after Avigdor Lieberman, the minister of defense, resigned due to his inability to implement his policy against Hamas' rule in the Gaza Strip. Lieberman requested a decisive military campaign by Israel to defeat Hamas, but Netanyahu opposed this. The political tumult was encapsulated in the five election cycles in the period between April 2019 and November 2022. None of these political campaigns was a confrontation between a right-wing bloc and a left-wing bloc. Instead, it was between a faith bloc, which was sometimes inaccurately called the "right-wing bloc" or the "Netanyahu bloc," and a statehood bloc, which was erroneously called the "center-left bloc" or the "change bloc."

This statehood bloc was a new political framework for old liberal right-wing elements such as Tikva Hadasha (New Hope) led by Gideon Sa'ar, Yisrael Beiteinu (Israel Our Home), and the National Unity party (formerly the Israel Resilience Party and the Blue and White alliance) led by Benny Gantz. It is important to note that quite a few politicians and political parties, mainly within the religious group, are trying, for electoral motives, to influence the public to see the situation not through a religious-state prism but through a right-left prism. For example, politicians with economically or politically right-wing positions who have moved to the statehood bloc are presented by the religious bloc as "people of the left" or "people who joined the left."[46]

The election cycles from 2019 to 2022 revealed another interesting point regarding the definition of the form of Israel's regime. The statehood bloc supports a liberal parliamentary democracy that includes checks and balances on the power of the authorities and maximum respect for individual freedoms. On the other hand, the religious bloc strives for a much more religiously conservative state that does not necessarily emphasize human and civil rights, especially when these rights conflict with religious-Jewish principles.[47]

These elections also strengthen the central argument of this research: The statehood camp, from which hundreds of thousands are participating in the protest against the legal reform, involves both "right" and "left" people. The attempt of the Israeli government at the beginning of 2023 to color the protest against the reform as a division of left versus right consequently ran into difficulties. The protesters adopted the state flag as a protest flag, emphasizing statehood and Zionism. Dozens of men and women shared their life histories from childhood as descendants of right-wing families, expressing support for the protest.

The statehood bloc in Israel believes that the goal of the religious bloc is ultimately to establish a fully halachic state. At the time of writing (spring 2023), this is not the reality in Israel. However, based on the moves in parliament, the emerging trend is that the religious bloc is interested, at least as an intermediate step, in establishing a regime system known as "illiberal democracy." This is a system in which, even though elections are held, citizens cannot bring to the fore mechanisms of supervision and checks and balances vis-à-vis those who actually control the country due to a lack of civil liberties. In an illiberal democracy, rulers tend to ignore or circumvent constitutional limitations on their rule. They also tend to ignore the wishes and rights of ethnic, religious, class, or other minorities. In an illiberal democracy, elections are usually not pure and are used as a tool to create or legitimize the ruler.[48] As a rule, an illiberal democratic regime is not a democratic regime. Instead, it is an electoral authoritarian, competitive authoritarian, or soft authoritarian regime.[49]

The religious camp in Israel did not invent the idea of illiberal democracy. Since the second half of the twentieth century, there have been many instances of illiberal democratic regimes worldwide. Farid Zachariah defined India as "the largest illiberal democracy in the world." Singapore was an illiberal democracy during the reign of Prime Minister Lee Kuan Yew from 1959 to 1990. The most recent case is that of Hungary under Prime Minister Viktor Orbán, who, in a speech he gave after being reelected in 2014, said that he sees the future of Hungary as an illiberal country.[50]

Under the rule of Recep Tayyip Erdoğan, Turkey has also become a classic case of illiberal democracy. It is a country where elections are held but where civil liberties have been denied one by one to the point that, according to various indicators, it has fewer civil liberties than other countries that do not consider themselves electoral democracies.[51] Another example that fits this model is the Philippines under Rodrigo Duterte and, subsequently, Ferdinand Marcos Jr. ("Bong Bong Marcos").[52]

Summary

This chapter analyzed the process of the formation of two camps: a state camp and a religious camp. A sequence of internal events in Israeli society, such as demographic changes, Israeli government decisions, and security escalations with the Arab minority in Israel and the Palestinians in the West Bank and the Gaza Strip (2000, 2008, 2014, 2021), together with external ones in the wider Middle East, sharpened the differences between the two.

During the election campaigns from 2019 to 2022, parts of the Israeli public already felt that some segments of the religious bloc saw themselves above the state laws and as subject only to halachic law and the instructions of their leaders. At the height of the crisis of the coronavirus pandemic, when the Israeli government imposed severe restrictions on the public, including closing educational institutions, many ultra-Orthodox institutions, especially those affiliated with Yahadut HaTorah and those belonging to the extreme current of ultra-Orthodox society ("the Jerusalem faction"), did not obey the government's instructions, claiming that the ruling of their spiritual leader, Rabbi Chaim Kanievsky, was decisive for them.[53] Another example is the disaster at Rabbi Shimon bar Yochai's party on Mount Meron (near the city of Safed) on April 30, 2021. This disaster, in which 45 people lost their lives and 102 were injured, was caused, among other things, by the political echelon yielding to pressure from the leaders of the ultra-Orthodox public and not limiting the number of celebrants at the site.[54]

The victory of the religious camp in the elections held in November 2022 brought the State of Israel closer to a critical watershed regarding the state's identity. At the time of writing, several bills are being discussed in the Knesset that, if approved, will change the state's character. These include the composition of the committee for selecting judges, which aims to weaken or even eliminate the Supreme Court's ability to invalidate laws enacted by the Knesset and even prevent the government from making significant administrative moves that contradict the principles of the Declaration of Independence. One must also remember that huge budgets are transferred to trusted parties in the fields of education, health, and infrastructure. In addition, the intention is to enshrine in law the exemption from military service that has been given de facto to the ultra-Orthodox population until now. These processes would establish a kind of "religious apartheid" in Israel. Making this official through the legislature may create a situation in which the statehood camp, which bears the overwhelming majority of the burden of military service and taxes, will lose many of its human and civil rights and will continue to finance a population whose essence is not productive and whose vision is a country that is not defined as a liberal democracy.

The far-reaching legal reform that threatens to transform Israel from a liberal democracy to a theoretical dictatorship has opened a chasm between the two camps' identities. From the beginning of January 2023 until the time of writing, Israel experienced an increasing wave of mass demonstrations parallel to a rapid—some would say predatory—advancement of the legislative procedures. Its supporters call it "legal reform," but its opponents define it as a "regime coup" or "the end of democracy." Within this conflict, the term "civil war," which until recently was out of the public discourse in Israel, is often used by politicians, officials, journalists, and public opinion makers. There is also a reasonable possibility of a constitutional crisis that will oblige public service personnel, including those wearing uniforms, to choose between obedience to the law and obedience to elected officials inclined to an undemocratic regime, as the minister of justice, Yariv Levin, has admitted. A public opinion poll from April 2023 revealed that 47.5 percent of the Israeli public believe it is more important that Israel be democratic and then Jewish compared to 36 percent who believe the opposite.[55]

This state-faith split threatens the Israeli national resilience more than any other rift. Above all, it threatens to disintegrate the framework that led to the establishment of a Jewish state that enshrined liberal democratic values in its Declaration of Independence, even if only through the explicit mention of the word "democracy" in the text.

Chapter 4

The Jewish-Arab Cleavage

Let us begin this chapter with the paradox reflected in the following two events. The first happened on March 29, 2022, when an Israeli police officer, Senior Sergeant Amir Khoury, an Arab Christian, was shot dead while attempting to stop an Arab Palestinian who had murdered five people. Thousands of people—Jews and members of the non-Jewish minority—attended Khoury's funeral. The municipalities of Bnei Brak, one of the two scenes of the terrorist attack, and Nof HaGalil, where he lived, decided to commemorate Khoury.[1] The second event took place during Yom Kippur later that year (October 2022), when dozens of Jews attacked a group of Bedouins (Israeli Arabs) driving down one of the streets in Bat Yam (southern Tel Aviv). The police came to the scene and rescued five Arabs who were injured after the crowd had overturned the car, claiming that their trip had violated the sanctity of the day.[2]

This paradox has accompanied the State of Israel from the time before its establishment to the present day, and it remains a central characteristic of the rift that exists between the Jewish majority and the Arab minority, who, at the time of writing, constitute about 21 percent of the country's citizens. The Jewish-Arab divide is manifested in national, religious, and civil aspects. This chapter focuses on the characterization and analysis of this rift that affects not only the lives of Jewish Arabs in Israel but also the state's character, from a conservative Jewish state to a liberal Jewish state to a state for all its citizens.

Introduction to the Jewish-Arab Divide in Israel: From the Beginning of Zionism to the UN Partition Plan

The divide between Jews and Arabs began with the birth of Zionism. Admittedly, during the period of the "harbingers of Zionism," there was no reference to the status of the Arabs in the future Jewish state,[3] but there were references to Arabs in among the first leaders of the Zionist movement. Herzl wrote in his book *Altneuland* (*The Old New Land*, 1902) that "all residents of the Jewish state should enjoy full equality of rights, including the right to vote and be elected. In the Jewish state there will be prosperous Arab villages that take a full part in the development of the land."[4] Herzl's ideological opponent, Asher Zvi Ginsberg (better known as Ahad Ha'am), had already pointed out the Jewish-Arab divide as early as 1891 in his article "Truth from the Land of Israel," in which he wrote that it would be a mistake to see the Arabs as "desert savages who do not see and do not understand what is happening around them" and that if the Jewish settlement pushes out the Arabs living in the Land of Israel, they will strongly oppose it.[5]

The Balfour Declaration (1917), the occupation of the Land of Israel by Great Britain (1917–1918), and the establishment of the British Mandate in the Land of Israel (1920) turned the status of Arabs in the future Jewish state into a central issue among the leaders of Zionism whose movements later led the State of Israel—Mapai leader David Ben-Gurion and the leader of revisionist Zionism, Ze'ev Jabotinsky. Their positions enable us to understand the trends in the formation and expansion of the Jewish-Arab divide.

Chapter 2 analyzed the attitude of the various currents in Zionism toward the Arabs, including the possibility of their expulsion from the country. Mentioning the topic in the current chapter is necessary because it traces not only the roots of the rift but also ideas that still exist today concerning the question of the place of the Arabs, who lived in Palestine/the Land of Israel and later under Isrsaeli sovereignty.

There are different perspectives of Ben-Gurion and most of the leaders of the Labor Party (Ahdut HaAvoda) on the subject of the Arabs of Israel. Shabtai Teveth, known as Ben-Gurion's biographer, claimed that researchers who have labeled Ben-Gurion's approach to this issue as "naive" are mistaken. Teveth argued that until at least the late 1920s, Ben-Gurion and most of his colleagues believed that the solution to the Arab problem in Palestine should be a social-class solution, within the framework of which, when the Arab workers and peasants are freed from the burden of their oppressors (the landowners and the priests), they would gladly accept the "brotherhood of workers" cooperating with their Jewish counterparts. According to Teveth, even during the Ottoman period, Ben-Gurion believed that the Arabs in the Land of Israel had a national movement, that they were opposed to Jewish settlement in the Land of Israel, and that, sooner or later, there would be a violent conflict between them.

At that time, and especially after the events of 1929, Ben-Gurion adhered to the establishment of a privatized Jewish-Arab regime in the Land of Israel in which there would be two areas of autonomy (Jewish and Arab). He also believed that the Jewish settlement should strive to create territorial continuity between the areas of Jewish autonomy. Some see this position as support for the establishment of a binational state. However, according to Teveth, Ben-Gurion actually intended to "gain time" to allow the Jewish settlement to grow.

The events of 1936–1939 (the Arab Revolt), the publication of the conclusions of the Peel Commission (1937), and the publication of the White Paper on Palestine by the British (1939) caused Ben-Gurion to support dividing the country into two states—Jewish and Arab—and thus the Jewish community would have a solid Jewish majority in the state.[6] During this period, Ben-Gurion did not rule out the idea of forced transfer. After the publication of the conclusions of the Peel Commission, including the discussion of the possibility of Britain evicting approximately 225,000 Arabs from the territory designated for the Jewish state, he wrote,

> The forced transfer of the Arabs from the proposed valleys to the Jewish state may give us something that we never had, even when we were standing on our own, both in the days of the First Temple and in the days of the Second Temple. . . . There is a possibility that we did not dream of and could not dare to dream of in our wildest imagination. Does England dare to do this? . . . It is certain that she will not do so if we do not wish to do so and if we do not push her to do so with all the power of our pressure and the power of our faith. If, because of our laxity and neglect and carelessness, this is not done, we lose in our hands an attempt that we have never had before, and who knows if it will ever return. . . . We must uproot from our hearts, and uproot from the root, the assumption that this is not possible.[7]

On the other side of the political map of the Jewish community in Israel stood the revisionist movement led by Jabotinsky. In his thinking, two stages can be distinguished. The first is the struggle between Jews and Arabs over the territory of the Land of Israel. At this stage, Jabotinsky proposed the "Iron Wall" solution—which means Jewish steadfastness and the development of advanced military capabilities through which it would be possible to make the Arabs accept that they are a minority in the Jewish state.[8] In the second stage, when a Jewish state is established in the Land of Israel with a Jewish majority and an Arab minority, the Arabs will enjoy national rights, not just personal ones. Jabotinsky completely ruled out the possibility of dispossessing the Arabs of the country or deporting them and wrote,

> Even after the creation of the Hebrew majority, there will always remain a large Arab population in Israel. And if bad days come to this part of the country's inhabitants at one time, then the whole country will bear the burden of suffering. The stable condition of the Arabs in the political, economic, and cultural sense will, therefore, forever remain the main condition for the healthy and stable condition of the entire Land of Israel. Complete equality of rights of both races, of both languages, and of all religions will prevail in the future Hebrew state. The national self-government of each of the races residing in the country, in matters of communities, education, culture, and political power, should be perfected to the widest and fullest extent. We believe that, in this way, the Jewish people will be able to convince the Arabs living inside and outside the Land of Israel that they must come to terms with the idea of a Hebrew Land of Israel.

Jabotinsky believed that in a state with a Jewish majority, there must be an ethnic balance in the political system as well. In other words, there should be relative representation of the ethnic communities in the government and its mechanisms, starting from the top of the pyramid—that is, it should be possible for an Arab to be prime minister and his deputy to be Jewish—down to the lower levels, in a way that will ensure the proportional participation of Jews and Arabs in both the duties and the benefits of the state, including parliamentary elections, the civil and military service, state budgets, and mixed municipal authorities. However, the equality between Jews and non-Jews, according to Jabotinsky's method, would only apply to those who are already in the country. As for new immigrants, the country's constitution would ensure that only Jews could receive automatic citizenship upon their arrival.[9]

The Jewish-Arab Rift, 1948–1967: Nationalism, Religion, and Civil Affairs

The 1948 war upset the balance of power between Jews and Arabs in the Land of Israel. The armistice lines between the State of Israel and its neighbors and the territory exchange agreements that were signed created a situation where the State of Israel controlled about 78 percent of the territory of Western Israel, but the rest was not established as an independent Arab state. Instead, military or civilian rule was imposed by Jordan (in the West Bank, including East Jerusalem) and Egypt (in the Gaza Strip). From a demographic point of view, there were about 156,000 Arabs in the State of Israel at the end of 1949, constituting about 15 percent of the total population.[10]

Shortly after the start of the war in May 1948, Israel determined its policy toward the Arab population who remained under Jewish sovereignty. It consisted of three principles: military rule over the Arab minority, a refusal to allow refugees to return from exile, and taking control over Arabs' land and property, mainly to house Jews making *aliyah* (immigrating) to Israel. It was a discriminatory policy against Arabs adopted after the evaluation that these Arabs may endanger Israel's survival in the event of another war with Arab countries. The sequence of events that resulted in hundreds of thousands of refugees leaving the territory of the Jewish state during the 1948 war, which came to be known as the Nakba (the "disaster"), was what most affected the trends and characteristics of the Jewish-Arab divide within the borders of the State of Israel. The slogan adopted among the country's Arab citizens, who were called "Israeli Arabs" (or, variously, "the Arab sector," "1948 Arabs," "internal Arabs," or "Israeli Palestinians"), since the 1948 war is "The day of your independence—the day of our calamity."

The Arab population within the borders of the State of Israel were supposed to become citizens of the state immediately and be accorded equal rights and duties. In the spirit of the Declaration of Independence, the state should have worked on the development of the country for the benefit of all its inhabitants; to act according to the principles of freedom, justice, and peace; to maintain full social and political equality of rights for all its citizens without distinction of religion, race, or gender; and to guarantee freedom of religion, conscience, language, education, and culture. However, from 1949 to 1967, the state adopted a clearly discriminatory policy against its Arab citizens based on a national-religious foundation. The official policy of the Israeli establishment during this period widened the Jewish-Arab divide in the country considerably.

The first and immediate sign of this policy was the imposition of a military administration on areas with a concentration of Arabs. Simultaneously, in Arab settlements that remained half-empty, the authorities worked to concentrate the Arab population, and in cases where the settlements were near the border, such as Iqrit and Bir'am, the authorities pushed the Arab residents across it.

Yair Bauml concluded that the selective enforcement of military rule on the Arab population was a result of the ruling establishment considering the Arab citizens a security risk and a fifth column due to their ethnic affiliation, the manner of their geographical distribution, and the rate of their demographic growth. Leaders such as David Ben-Gurion and Yigal Alon claimed that Israel's Arabs identified with its enemies and therefore posed a danger in terms of espionage, terrorism, and sabotage. In addition to the mechanisms of the military government, which excluded the Arab citizens from the circles of public life in Israel, the mechanisms of Shabak and the Israel Police were activated against the same "security threat," even though there were no recorded attempts by Arab citizens to act against the state or its Jewish citizens.[11]

Bauml's conclusion was based, among other things, on a statement made in early 1958 by Issar Harel, one of the founders of the Israeli intelligence apparatus, which illustrates the establishment's perception of its Arab citizens and includes an express threat to destroy citizens due to their ethnic origin:

> In light of the dangers from the outside, we must burden them. . . . We need to instill in the minds of the Israeli Arabs . . . that if there is a rebellion or mutiny or non-cooperation that seeks to harm the existence of the state, the Israeli Arabs will be destroyed first. That is, the Israeli Arabs—and, first of all, their leadership—will be destroyed before the State of Israel is damaged. They have been living with this fear for all these years, and they should know that this fear is very tangible.[12]

This mindset of a senior member of the security establishment was transferred to lower ranks as well as to the general public. In such an atmosphere of persistent suspicion toward Arabs, the national cleavage between the parties was seen in reality, such as in the Kfar Qasem massacre on October 29, 1956, the first day of Operation Kadesh. On the same day, the IDF's Central Command ordered a curfew on the Arab villages near the triangular border with Jordan and Syria in preparation for war to break out with Jordan and ordered anyone who broke the curfew to be shot. The unit operating in Kfar Qasem followed its orders to the letter, and its soldiers shot dead forty-five residents returning from work, including nine women and seventeen children. Another four people were killed in the village itself. Despite the attempts made by the authorities to conceal the incident, the massacre became widely known, and the state had no choice but to prosecute eleven police officers and soldiers who were involved. Some of those involved were sentenced to prison terms, but in most cases, the sentences were reduced.[13]

Simultaneously with the application of military rule, the State of Israel made extensive use of legislation in order to restrict the movement of the Arab population in its territory. In 1950, the Knesset enacted the Absentees' Property Law, which gave the state possession of the assets of people who fled during the 1948 war. The office that enforced this law was the custodian of absentee assets. In the state's early years, the Israeli authorities used this law to seize the properties and holy lands (*waqf*) of refugees and displaced persons. This law was also enforced against Arabs who were considered "present absentees"—that is, who stayed within the borders of the State of Israel but not in their original settlements or who left the country (voluntarily or involuntarily) and then returned. It is estimated that of the 156,000 Arabs within the country in 1949, about 46,000 were "present absentees."[14]

Along with the military rule and the Absentees' Property Law, the Israeli establishment promoted another piece of legislation that contributed to the Jewish-Arab cleavage. In 1950, the Knesset enacted the Development Authority (Transfer of Assets) Law, by virtue of which the Development Authority was established and tasked with managing the lands entrusted to the custodian of absentee assets and the lands expropriated by the Real Estate Acquisition (Authorization of Operations and Compensation) Law enacted in 1953. This law retroactively regulated land confiscation. The law did state that financial compensation would be paid to people whose lands were expropriated, but in most cases, the compensation was significantly lower than the value of the expropriated lands. In cases where Arab citizens refused compensation in order not to cooperate with the authorities, pressure was exerted on them by conditioning the lease of state lands and granting building permits with an agreement to receive the compensation set by the state.[15]

The land laws in the 1950s and 1960s transferred most of the control over the land and water sources to the state. Although the Israeli establishment only held about 13.5 percent of the land in 1949, by the time the legislation was fully implemented, it controlled no less than 93 percent and also held most of the country's water sources. "The land policy and the regional planning policy in Israel at that time were an integral part of the control mechanism of the Israeli establishment over the Arab minority and a central pillar in the Judaization of the country and the establishment of the Israeli ethnocratic society, driven by the Zionist concept that holds that Israel is a territory and a country that belongs to the Jewish people and only to them."[16] This is an essential manifestation of a Jewish takeover, on a national and religious basis, of valuable resources in an area mostly (two-thirds) defined as desert. This situation created deliberate discrimination between the Jewish majority and the non-Jewish minority, who were forced, against their will, to break the law through illegal construction.

Simultaneously with the land legislation, the Knesset also enacted the Citizenship Law and the Law of Return. The Law of Return (1950) granted immediate citizenship to people arriving in Israel, but only to Jews. The Citizenship Law (1952) granted automatic citizenship to all Jews who lived within the state's borders but only to 60,000 of the fewer than 160,000 Arabs. The remaining Arabs who stayed in Israel had to start a naturalization process that lasted several years. The law intended to make it very easy for Jews to obtain citizenship and as difficult as possible for Arabs to be granted citizenship. The goal was to reduce the number of Arabs in Israel.[17]

These laws had a direct impact on the quality of life of the Arab minority. Over time, the Arab population grew, and the conditions in Arab localities deteriorated. The lack of building permits not only increased illegal construction but also created overcrowded living conditions and decreased sanitation conditions. The inability of the Arab population in those years to use the land for agriculture—a primary source of livelihood—created considerable frustration within the Arab sector and raised unemployment rates (in the absence of alternative professions and a paucity of opportunities to integrate into the public sector). It was only in 1958 that the Histadrut opened its doors to Arab members, thereby expanding their employment options, but in practice, most Arab workers found themselves at the bottom of the employment ladder in Israel, and many of them worked as day laborers.

Security became another factor in the deepening rift. After the establishment of the State of Israel, where "the whole country is a front, the whole nation is an army," most Arab citizens were given exemption from military service, with the exception of the Circassians, Druze, and some Bedouins. The failure to draft Arabs into the IDF perpetuated their status—rightly or wrongly—as "enemies of the state," and as a result, many in the Jewish public justified their continued discrimination. Unable to provide military (or national or civil) service, Arabs were denied the ability to enter Israeli society and suffered from a policy of exclusion. Their difficulty was not only in finding a job but also in exclusion from benefits awarded to military veterans in the areas of taxation, mortgages, school fees, and unemployment. In other words, their inability to enlist in the army, even though it was justified as a move to prevent Arab citizens from fighting against their brothers across the border, was a significant factor in the exclusion of Arabs from social, economic, and administrative life. As a result, the Jewish-Arab divide in the country deepened even further.

The Israeli establishment's fear of an Arab rebellion, as testified by Issar Harel, translated into the establishment of control mechanisms—covert and overt. The most obvious of these mechanisms, contributing to the rift until its dissolution in 1992, was the Office of the Advisor for Arab Affairs in the Prime Minister's Office. The bureau was an institutional buffer between the Arab citizen, a member of the minority, and the government ministries, which were supposed to provide services without any mediation. Alongside this bureau, another operated secretly—the Central Committee for Security, a small forum established solely for the purpose of dealing with Arab citizens' affairs and dictating their moves to the military government. A third mechanism was the Committee for Arab Affairs, established by Mapai in 1957, which was the body that formulated practical policies, not only of the party but also of the government and the Histadrut, concerning the Arabs in Israel. Official bodies of this type do not exist in any democracy in the world, let alone in any liberal democracy, and their very establishment deepened the rift between Jews and Arabs. Moreover, most of their decisions harmed the Arab population on all levels.[18]

The Jewish-Arab divide in the 1950s found expression not only in security and civil aspects but also in political aspects. Mapai, the ruling party, decided not to include Arab members. Instead, it established satellite lists through local and traditional Arab leaders, who maintained ties with the members of the military government in order to minimize the damage from the government to the Arab population. Before each election, the ruling party gave favors to the heads of the Arab public and thus bought their vote while preserving the rift through the security and legislative processes. In doing so, the Israeli establishment also preserved a rift between the traditional Arab leadership and the leaders of the Communist Party, which was perceived as radical in those years, and, from 1959, between the traditional leadership and the leaders of the Al-Ard movement.[19]

The party that acted most significantly at that time to reduce the Jewish-Arab divide was the Israeli Communist Party (Maki), established in 1948 as a continuation of the Palestine Communist Party from the British Mandate period. The Arab public supported Maki due to its hostility to the Zionist idea, its opposition to the policies of the Israeli establishment, its pro-Arab attitude toward the Arab national question, and the national aspects of the Arab population in Israel. Maki was also the only national leadership framework that remained after most of the Arab leadership fled the country in the 1948 war. The party managed to position itself as responsible (a sort of guardian) for the problems of the disadvantaged Arab minority. Later, in the mid-1960s, the party split: The "Jewish faction" recognized the existence of two national movements in the region—Zionist and Arab—and became the New Communist List (Rakah), while the "Arab faction" adopted a distinctly pro-Arab approach.

It is important to remember that other factors worked to narrow the Jewish-Arab cleavage in those years, mainly by striving to bring about the abolition of the military government. The acceptance of the Arab workers into the Histadrut created a situation where more Arabs were allowed to enter Jewish localities and forced the government as early as 1959 to ease the enforcement of the military government regulations. In 1960–1961, various parties, including Herut, Mapam, the General Zionists, and Maki, submitted proposals for order and called for the abolition of the military government. It was a rare political cooperation between parties from all areas of the political spectrum that sought to strike down Ben-Gurion and, at the same time, to promote an agenda that reflected ideas of liberalism (Herut) and socialism (Mapam), as well as an effort to improve Israel's image as a democratic country that did not need a military government. At that time, civil society also began to speak out, and a lively discussion arose in Israeli society regarding the existence of the military government, which found its expression in press articles and petitions to abolish it.[20]

Levi Eshkol, who replaced Ben-Gurion as prime minister, also believed that the Arab citizens constituted a security risk but claimed that there was no connection between the Arab-Israeli conflict and the military government. He worked hard to ease the impositions on society caused by the military government to make it "seeing yet invisible" and minimize the signs of discrimination and deprivation as much as possible. In 1965, Eshkol openly stated that his government aimed to abolish the military government, which was a stain on Israeli democracy and was no longer needed. In a special speech, he stated that the military government would be abolished as of December 1, 1966. In practice, the military government was abolished only in 1968 after an interim period in which the army's powers to enforce movement restrictions against Arab citizens were transferred to the Israel Police.[21]

From the Six-Day War to Land Day: The Deepening of the Jewish-Arab Divide

The June 1967 war had many consequences in intra-Israeli, regional, and international circles. For the present purpose of mapping the divisions in Israeli society, including the Jewish-Arab divide, the war had a direct and significant impact on the formation of a non-Israeli identity among the Arab minority. One of the keys to the development of this identity was the separation of the physical border that prevented direct contact between Israeli Arabs and Palestinians living in the West Bank and Gaza Strip. The abolition of the military government, the removal of movement restrictions, and Israeli control over the entire territory created a new geopolitical reality in which direct contact was established between the populations on both sides of the border that was erased after June 1967.

Within the political arena in Israel, the post-1967 split manifested itself in several arenas:

1. The division between Jewish and Arab members of the Communist Party was completed.

2. The Arab voter, who since 1949 had voted for Zionist parties for fear of being persecuted, transferred political support to the Arab stream of the Communist Party.

3. Rakah spread ideas of Palestinian nationalism among the Arab public in Israel. In this sense, the communist Arab stream decided in favor of nationalism, partly due to the influence of external moves, such as the establishment of the PLO.[22]

The Palestinian national awakening in the ranks of Israeli Arabs received its political expression in the early 1970s. In 1972, the Sons of the Land movement (Abna' al-Balad) was established in Umm al-Fahem. This movement called for the Palestinian people's right to self-determination to also apply to Arabs in Israel. Additionally, it called for the promise that any future negotiation for ending the conflict between Israel and the Palestinians discuss the status of the Israeli Arab. The movement denied the historical right of the Jewish people to the Land of Israel, did not recognize the right of the State of Israel to exist, and believed that the "Zionist enemy" must be fought in every possible way. This position not only expressed uncompromising support for Palestinian demands but also sharpened the national divide because the Sons of the Land were not ready for any compromise that would allow the continued physical presence of Israel as a sovereign state.[23]

The national divide that widened in the early 1970s was also expressed in the official Israeli policy of land expropriation for public purposes. In 1974, the Israeli Arabs founded the National Committee of the Heads of the Arab Local Councils in order to improve the living conditions of the minority population. Among other things, they wanted to reduce the extent of land expropriation. About a year later, in 1975, the National Committee for the Protection of the Lands was founded by Rakah and Arab students.[24]

The attempts of these bodies to negotiate with the authorities and prevent the expropriation of the land were unsuccessful. After several cases on a relatively small scale in 1975, the Israeli government ordered, in early 1976, through a decree published by the Israel Lands Administration, extensive land expropriation in the Galilee for the purpose of expanding the city of Karmiel. The expropriation included about twenty thousand *dunams*, of which about a third was in the area of Deir Hanna, 'Arrabeh, and Sakhnin. In response, the leaders of the Arab public announced a general strike in the Arab sector on March 30, 1976. In a press release on this subject, they said,

> We believe that the real interest of the State of Israel for all its residents, the Jews and the Arabs, is not consistent with the policy of expropriation and dispossession of the Arab citizens from their lands. The rest of the lands left in the hands of the Arab residents do not satisfy the basic needs for living, such as the construction of buildings, areas for public use, and not even for cemeteries, not to mention areas for agriculture as a place of livelihood for the workers of the land.[25]

Following the announcement of the strike in the Arab sector, the government imposed a curfew on March 29, 1976, on the settlements of Sakhnin, Arraba, Deir Hana, Tur'an, Tamra, and Kabul. The next day, there were demonstrations, mainly in Sakhnin, Arraba, and Deir Hana, which quickly turned violent and included blocking roads and throwing stones and Molotov cocktails. The Israel Police, unable to contain the incident, sought the help of the IDF. By the end of the day, six demonstrators had been killed. The events of Land Day in 1976 opened a deep rift in Jewish-Arab relations in Israel. Land expropriation stopped for a long time, but the wounds did not heal. Israeli Arabs became increasingly involved in contacts with Palestinians in the West Bank and the Gaza Strip, a reality that sharpened the polarity of the national divide. In academic conceptualizations, this process received the expression "palastination."[26]

Narrowing the Cleavage, 1976–1987: From Land Day to the Outbreak of the First Intifada

The change of government in May 1977 raised the question of the new government's attitude toward the Arab minority in the public agenda. We have already seen in previous chapters that there were no real ideological differences between the currents of Zionism concerning the Arab question, including in their attitudes toward Israeli Arabs. Mapai's official policy until 1977 proved this claim in full, and it was only natural to wonder how Likud (in its early incarnation, freedom was promoted) would behave toward the Arab minority. In his message to the Knesset on June 20, 1977, Begin stated, "We do not want to dispossess and will not dispossess any Arab resident of his land. Jews and Arabs, Druze and Circassians can live together in this country, and they should live together in peace, mutual respect, equal rights, elections, and socio-economic progress."[27]

One of the first test stations for the impact of the new political reality on the relations between Jews and Arabs was the official program to extend Jewish localities in the Galilee. This wide-ranging program was formulated in 1979–1980 and became known to the public by its unofficial name, The Galilee Jewry Program. As part of this plan, a large number of small Jewish settlements called *mitzpim* ("lookouts") were established in the Galilee. The stated goal was to deploy a Jewish population in the mountainous Galilee to increase the proportion of the Jewish population in this region and to prevent a succession of Arab villages on state land.

Regarding the Jewish-Arab cleavage, Avraham Dor has pointed out that implementing the mitzpim program led to radicalization among the Arab public and created a wave of nationalism in the villages of the Galilee against the Israeli government. At the same time, Arabs in Israel identified with Arabs of the West Bank and the Gaza Strip. The peace treaty with Egypt, which was signed in 1979 and led to the possibility of promoting a solution to the Palestinian problem by creating Palestinian self-government (autonomy), also led to similar ideas among the Arabs of the Galilee, who saw in the new reality an opportunity to strive for a similar solution. In this sense, the promotion of the idea of irredenta to the Israeli Arabs in the Galilee (including on the basis of a claim that the Galilee has an Arab demographic majority) deepened the suspicion of the Israeli establishment toward the separatist tendencies of the minority, and from here to the preservation of the national divide, the distance was short.

Security officials in Israel recommended that the government expand the project of establishing the Jewish mitzpim in central Galilee, including near the settlements that were the focus of violence on Land Day in 1976. Apparently, implementing the lookout program was expected to lead to further flare-ups from the Arab minority. However, this did not happen. As for the Israeli authorities, there seems to have been an attempt to avoid reescalation. From 1976 onward, the state used mainly state land to expand Jewish localities instead of confiscating Arab-owned private lands.[28]

The mitzpim program affected the Jewish-Arab divide in Israel in general and in the Galilee in particular. In 2003, Mohammad Kana'an, the head of Majd al-Krum's local council and the spokesman for the monitoring committee of the Arab local authorities, said that this program caused feelings of deprivation among the Arab population in this region because the Arab sector did not receive equal treatment and measures to those received by the Jewish lookouts. The program's implementation had been very beneficial to the latter's Jewish residents, but the economic situation of their Arab neighbors had not improved because the Jews did their shopping in Karmiel, not in the nearby Arab settlements. Moreover, he claimed that the lookout program annexed Arab lands to the outline plan of the Jewish Misgav Regional Council. In practice, the loss of land caused the residents of the nearby Arab settlements to expect to build illegal constructions within the settlements and thus found themselves in confrontations with the state's enforcement authorities.[29]

October 1982 marked another milestone in Jewish-Arab relations in the country with the establishment of the Supreme Monitoring Committee for Arab Affairs in Israel, which was intended to serve as a super-framework for the state's various Arab public bodies. The committee was established following the massacre of Palestinians in the Sabra and Shatila refugee camps in September 1982. It sought to reflect the national identity of the Arab elite in Israel, and indeed, the establishment of the Supreme Monitoring Committee was seen by the Israeli establishment as an act of defiance as it aspired to represent the Arabs as a national minority.[30] The national governments did not recognize the committee on its national agenda, but the state maintained contacts with the National Committee of Arab Mayors and took advantage of the fact that this body was headed by Ibrahim Nimer Hussain, who also headed the Supreme Monitoring Committee, to conduct dialogue with the Arab public on the civilian level.[31]

The First Lebanon War, which broke out in June 1982, led to a change in the political behavior patterns of the Arab citizens in Israel. Along with the decrease in their general turnout in elections, the deep anger among the Arab population as a result of the massacre in the refugee camps in Lebanon led to a combined civil and national protest that included strikes, demonstrations (some of them violent), mourning processions, and mass funerals in the Arab sector. All of these deepened the Jewish-Arab rift, and the prevailing feeling in the Arab sector in the mid-1980s was that "their country was fighting against their people."[32]

A Paradigmatic Change in the State's Relationship with its Arab Citizens, 1987–2000: From the First Intifada to the 2000 Riots

The First Intifada, which broke out in 1987, directly affected the Jewish-Arab rift within the borders of the State of Israel. For the first time since the establishment of the state, Israel—under the unity government until 1988 and then under the Likud government—found itself rethinking its course in relation to the Arab minority in Israel. This was a consequence of the fear of the violence in Judea, Samaria, and the Gaza Strip spilling over into the territories of the Green Line and the presence of liberal right-wing elements whispering in the ear of Prime Minister Yitzhak Shamir.

In practice, during the years of the First Intifada, there were several bloody incidents that further deepened the rift between Jews and Arabs in Israel. In May 1990, following the massacre carried out by Ami Popper at the Rose Garden Junction near Rishon Lezion, the Supreme Monitoring

Committee announced a strike in the Arab sector and three days of mourning. These events spread to several places, especially in the Galilee and the Triangle, and developed into riots in which young Arabs, some of them concealing their faces, waved PLO flags, threw stones and Molotov cocktails, blocked roads, and engaged in clashes on the Temple Mount. In October 1990, after violent clashes between the police and Palestinian youths on the Temple Mount in which twenty Arabs were killed, including an Israeli resident of Tamra, more riots occurred in the Galilee and the Triangle, where dozens of Arab civilians were injured.[33]

However, the majority of the Arab public opposed copying the operation patterns of West Bank and the Gaza Strip residents in the territories of Israel and were content to identify with Palestinians within the framework of Israeli law. Elie Rekhess, Adel Manna, and Majid al-Haj found that the reason for this was the unwillingness of the Arab citizens in Israel to risk their achievements in the civil sphere. They also concluded that as the years of the intifada lengthened, the Green Line grew stronger among the Arab citizens of Israel as a clear political border between them and the Palestinians in the West Bank and the Gaza Strip.[34]

The understanding that there was a need for an orderly civil policy toward the Arab minority received political expression as early as 1990. While civil servants were busy putting together plans to promote the Arab sector, a political crisis developed that led to the dissolution of the unity government in 1990. Shimon Peres tried to establish a minority government under his leadership with a significant political partnership between Labor and the Hadash movement, whose members were members of the Arab minority. It was politically unprecedented when the two parties (Labor and Hadash) signed an agreement, which included general commitments to promote the equality of Arab citizens, such as "The government will carry out, immediately, an arrangement for the distribution of debts of the Arab local authorities and will approve a plan for the establishment of a sewage system in the Arab villages. For this purpose, an amount of NIS 40 million per year will be allocated."[35]

In the run-up to the elections to the thirteenth Knesset, Yitzhak Rabin, Labor's candidate for prime minister, chose to adopt a positive policy toward the Arab minority. One of the senior members of his party, Moshe Shachal, who traveled with him to an election rally in Nazareth (an Arab city), was quoted many years later saying that he told Rabin during the trip that he would not be able to win the hearts of the Arabs because of his statements from the intifada period about breaking the arms and legs of Palestinians. Shachal then said,

Rabin insisted and I told him: It might be that if a Zionist leader stood up and said, "We are to blame for the situation where there are gaps, we are the ones to blame"—maybe that would help. Rabin said that he would not be able to say such a thing! We arrived in Nazareth, and he surprised me. He got on stage and said: "We were in power for 29 years, and we are guilty of discrimination. I apologize, and I intend to act to eradicate discrimination." Thousands of people stood and applauded him enthusiastically.[36]

The thirteenth Knesset elections put Labor in power, but the results required a political safety net that included five MKs from Hadash. Beyond this being a precedent, which allowed the government to move forward in the political process vis-à-vis the Palestinians, it was also a sign of the readiness to reach an agreement with an Arab party for the first time. Rabin's government served for three years until he was assassinated. In this period, the decades-long gaps between the Jewish majority group and the Arab minority group began to close. The narrowing of the Jewish-Arab divide during the Rabin government, beyond the influence of the Oslo Accords, was manifested in the fact that the government took real steps: eliminating discrimination in child allowances between Jews and Arabs, allocating large sums to Arab local authorities, and changing the discourse and rhetoric regarding Arab citizens.[37]

In 2018, Thabet Abu Rass, joint CEO of the Abraham Initiatives for integration and equality between Jews and Arabs, analyzed the policy of the Rabin government toward the Arab minority. He defined Rabin as the most courageous Israeli leader because he recognized the importance of the Arab public, gave legitimacy to the Arab voice, was not ashamed of and did not hesitate to cooperate with the Arab voice, and planted a feeling among the Arab citizens that they were being considered. In addition, Rabin strove to establish peace between the people to which the Arab citizens belong and the state of which they are citizens. According to him, the Arab public forgave Rabin for his statements from the intifada period because he created an atmosphere of euphoria among the Arabs in Israel.[38]

Rabin's assassination in November 1995 and the wave of Palestinian terror attacks in early 1996 raised fear in the Arab sector that the government's policy toward the Arab population would once again be focused on security issues. Benjamin Netanyahu's narrow victory in the elections to the fourteenth Knesset increased this concern. Although the first Netanyahu government did not include in its basic guidelines a reference to the Arab minority in Israel, the prime minister adopted the policy of the outgoing government. In 1996 to 1999, the government gave preference to the budgets of education and local authorities in the Arab sector, including the Bedouin settlements. In 1997, a government minister participated in the annual commemoration of the Kfar Qasem massacre victims for the first time. On the other hand, the Netanyahu government tightened the enforcement of demolition orders for illegal buildings in the Arab sector and closed off an area of approximately five hundred *dunams* in the al-Roha lands in Wadi Ara, defining this as a "fire zone"—a case that provoked much violence on the part of the Arab residents.

Paradoxically, in the 1990s, when the continuous efforts by Israeli government to improve the situation of the Arab minority were evident, internal developments within the Arab public deepened the rift between Jews and Arabs. During this period, Arabs' radicalization was evident on the political map both from the conservative-Islamic direction and from the secular-liberal direction.

Since the mid-1980s, the Islamic Movement had increased its political activity—first at the municipal level and then at the national level. After the signing of the Oslo Accords between Israel and the PLO, the debate within the movement intensified regarding the course of action it should take. Despite the explicit ideology of the Muslim Brotherhood, the members of the Islamic Movement found themselves between two poles. On the one hand was a separatist current that did not recognize the State of Israel and strove to establish an Islamic caliphate in Palestine. On the other hand was a more reserved approach that supported integration into state institutions to improve the situation of the Arab citizen. These differences of opinion led to the split of the Islamic Movement in 1996. The "southern" faction, led by Sheikh Ibrahim Sarsour, recognized the State of Israel and advocated integration into the Israeli political system, while the "northern" faction, led by Sheikh Raed Salah and Sheikh Kamal al-Khatib, denied the existence of the state.[39]

The separatist approach of the northern faction and its nonrecognition of the State of Israel translated into a permanent challenge to the government authorities. After the Western Wall Tunnel riots in September 1996, the faction initiated a mass rally in Umm al-Fahem under the title "Al-Aqsa is in danger." Salah and his colleagues took advantage of the event for wild incitement against the State of Israel, its institutions, and its leadership. This separatist-incitement line was repeated regularly in an event that became an annual tradition in the Arab sector. In September 1998, after the expropriation of the al-Roha lands, the northern faction established a body called the Committee for the Protection of the al-Roha Lands, which initiated the establishment of protest tents near the organization of mass prayers and eventually developed into violent and large-scale riots. In March 1999, Salah called for people to "get out of the patterns of reaction and move to initiative and confrontation with the authorities in order to obtain rights for the Arab minority in Israel." A year later, during the Land Day events in Baqa al-Gharbiya, he said, "The Arab public is not violent, but if violence is forced upon us, we will be more violent."[40]

Parallel to the Muslim current's activity, the National Democratic Alliance (Balad) was established in 1995, led by Azmi Bishara. The party took a secular, national-Arab, and anti-Zionist line that was expressed, among other ways, in the call to make the State of Israel a state for all its citizens, to separate religion from the state, to cancel the state's recognition of Zionist institutions, to declare the Arabs a national minority, and to put an end to the deprivation of Arab citizens in the country.[41]

Balad's ideology and activity expressed not only the Arab public's rift with the Jewish public but a gap of real disagreements, to the point of a rupture, in the Arab public's leadership. Balad presented a separatist vision that was not acceptable to either the Islamic Movement or public figures who supported a political solution to the Palestinian question that would leave Israel as the state of the Jewish people. This led to the dissolution of a political partnership within the sector, and at the same time, Bishara made sure to cultivate a public image of himself as an Arab nationalist, regularly attacking, criticizing, and condemning Israel. He took an extreme line and did not hesitate to speak out strongly against the State of Israel to the extent that he considered it an enemy. For example, after the IDF's withdrawal from Lebanon in May 2000, he said, "Hezbollah won, and for the first time since 1967, we tasted victory. It is Hezbollah's right to be proud of its achievement and humiliate Israel. . . . Israel suffered defeat after defeat and was forced to leave southern Lebanon. This is the truth. . . . Lebanon, the weakest of the Arab countries, has presented a tiny model. If we look deeply at it, we can draw the necessary conclusions for success and victory."[42] The situation of the Jewish-Arab divide in Israel in the second half of the 1990s highlights the real influence that the separatist elements—the Islamic Movement and Balad—had on the Arab sector's state of mind. The actions of the Israeli establishment to reduce this rift were taken for granted. The Orr Commission (formally, the National Commission of Inquiry into the Clashes Between Security Forces and Israeli Citizens in October 2000) was set up to make recommendations for intervention to the government and did so by analyzing surveys. The surveys conducted in the Arab sector in the second half of the 1990s illustrated how wide the Jewish-Arab divide had become in the country. They also showed a correlation between the number of violent incidents at the end of that decade and the principled support for breaking the law as a means of political struggle.[43]

A Sign of Calm, 2000–2009: The Rift Between Jews and Arabs from the Orr Commission Until the End of the Olmert Government

The sequence of events in the Arab sector in 1998–2000 is a good reflection of the deepening of the Jewish-Arab rift and the trend of escalation. Besides the issue of the al-Roha lands, there were many other violent events between 1998 and 2000:

1. The demolition of houses in Umm al-Sahali (near Shfar'am) in April 1998, which led to violent demonstrations and roadblocks near Shfar'am and Nazareth.

2. The demolition of the house of an Arab resident in Lod in June 1999, which provoked violent protests by residents of Lod and Ramla in which Arab MKs also participated.

3. The demonstrations of hundreds of Arab citizens in front of the prime minister's office protesting the discrimination against Arab local authorities (November–December 1999).

4. Violent protests in March 2000 against the placement of a cellular antenna in Usafiyya, during which the police even used live ammunition and in which police officers were injured.

5. Violent riots during the Land Day events of March 2000. In the city of Sakhnin, an elderly woman died of smoke inhalation after being shot by police officers.

6. Violent protests by Arab students at the University of Haifa and the Hebrew University in April 2000.

7. The riot of Arabs in Shfar'am during the Independence Day events of 1999.

8. Violent demonstrations in September 2000 caused by clashes concerning the closing of a quarry in Nazareth-Illit.[44]

The deepening of the Jewish-Arab rift in the second half of the 1990s reached a peak in October 2000 after Ariel Sharon, the head of the opposition, visited the Temple Mount on September 28, 2000. This gave the signal for a burst of violent events in the West Bank and the Gaza Strip and among the Arab sector in Israel. Four years of the Islamic Movement and Balad's campaigns of incitement reached a boiling point when Abdel Malek al-Dahamsha, an MK from the Islamic Movement, called to "save al-Aqsa." For two weeks, Israeli Arabs rioted in seventy locations and clashed with police and security forces. In the wave of riots that swept Israel, fourteen people were killed, including twelve Arab, Palestinian, and Jewish citizens. This was the culmination of a rift that turned into a bloody rupture.[45]

The Orr Commission's report did not ignore the Jewish-Arab cleavage. Along with its historical analysis, it did not spare criticism of both sides: It placed responsibility for the divide being maintained both on the establishment, which for years had disadvantaged the Arab minority in favor of the Jewish majority, and on the Arab leadership (with an emphasis on its radical elements), who incited violence at the heart of the riots. In conclusion, the committee determined that the events of October 2000 worsened Jewish-Arab relations in the country and increased the suspicion and hostility between the two communities.[46]

In the weeks, months, and even years that followed, the deepening rift between Jews and Arabs as a result of the October 2000 events was very evident. The level of interaction between Jews and Arabs in the country has decreased significantly, which is reflected mainly in fewer Jews going to shop in Arab cities and Arabs in Jewish cities, a significant decrease in the number of Jews who traveled in Wadi Ara, the dismissal of many Arab workers from Jewish-owned workplaces, and the sharp decrease of activities in which Jews and Arabs coexist.[47]

Public opinion polls conducted among the Jewish public after the October 2000 events revealed another dimension of the divide. For example, in a survey conducted among approximately seven hundred Israeli Jews by the Department of Political Science at the University of Haifa, it was found that 60.7 percent believed that "the government should encourage the immigration of Arab citizens outside the country," 34 percent claimed that "the economic situation in the country is getting worse because the Arabs are taking Jews' jobs," and 22.4 percent identified with the statement that the leader of Kach (a radical Orthodox movement), Rabbi Meir Kahana, "could have been a good leader for the Jewish people today."

This radicalization trend was also reflected in the public-political arena. In a 2004 report by the Arab Musawa Center, it was highlighted that after October 2000, more Jewish politicians spoke out in favor of expelling Arabs from the country, such as Minister of Transporation Avigdor Lieberman's plan for the "separation of nations," Minister of Finance Benjamin Netanyahu's statement that "the problem is the country's demographics are rooted in the Arabs of Israel," and Minister of Internal Security Tzachi Hanegbi's call to the Jewish residents of the Negev to "take sticks and drive out Bedouin invaders."[48]

At the same time, however, the Israeli government made moves to narrow the rift. One of the most significant was its decision on September 14, 2003, to establish a committee of ministers to implement the conclusions of the Orr Commission. This new committee (the Lapid Committee) published a number of recommendations in May 2004, some of which had already been put into practice. The committee decided that a permanent committee of ministers should be established to deal with the affairs of the Arab sector, establish an authority to promote minorities, foster values of Jewish-Arab cooperation, integrate the Arab public into the civil service, and speed up the drafting of a master plan for the Arab settlements. The committee's recommendations were approved by the Israeli government on June 13, 2004.[49]

Another step toward narrowing the Jewish-Arab divide was reflected in the discussions and conclusions of the Committee for Establishing a National Civil Service (the Ivri Committee). This committee dealt with the general public who do not serve in the IDF. In early 2005, the committee recommended a civil service framework for the Arab sector as an alternative to military service that would allow Arab youths to contribute to their community, society, and country. The committee stated that it believed this process would create positive consequences for the status of the Arab citizens in the country and their relationship with the Jewish public. The committee's recommendations were approved by Ehud Olmert's government on February 18, 2007.[50]

These moves of Ariel Sharon's two governments (2001–2006) to soften the rift between Jews and Arabs continued under Olmert's government (2006–2009). However, this activity in the civil sphere had to confront an escalating security situation: the Second Lebanon War in the summer of 2006 and Operation Cast Lead in the Gaza Strip in December 2008. In the Second Lebanon War, nineteen of the forty-four civilians killed by Hezbollah's rocket fire were Arab citizens. In general, the Arab public showed restraint during the war and did not act against the state. As for Operation Cast Lead, Israel's security forces arrested hundreds of Israeli Arabs who violated the public order, but beyond that, no incidents of violence or terrorism on the part of Israeli Arabs were recorded.[51]

The most significant event during the Olmert government regarding the Jewish-Arab cleavage was the prime minister's conference for the Arab sector convened in Haifa on July 10, 2008. Discussions on interior, education, and economic issues were held with government representatives—Minister of Education Yuli Tamir, Minister of the Interior Meir Shitrit, and Minister of Science, Culture, and Sports Ghaleb Majadala (an Israeli Arab)—as well as heads of Arab authorities, representatives of the Israel Democracy Institute, and education, economics, and finance personnel from the Arab sector. At the conference's concluding session, Olmert said, "Israeli Arabs are not a strategic threat; they are citizens with equal rights in the State of Israel. You have always been part of the state and always will be." Olmert detailed how his government prioritized the Arab sector localities in the implementation of the New Horizon educational reform and government subsidies for land for veterans from the non-Jewish sector. He stated that he supported establishing an Arab city in the Galilee. He expressed pride that the first Arab minister was serving in his government and that there had been an increase in the number of Arabs employed in the civil service. Finally, Olmert said that he hoped that the discourse from at the conference would lead to the erasure of expressions of racism in Israeli society and form the basis for improving relations between Arabs and Jews: "I believe that today we have written a chapter of great significance, and I hope that it will be a historical turning point, which will lead to the improvement of the status of the Arabs of Israel in the country."[52] This was the culmination of a government effort that lasted almost eight years, designed to narrow the gap between Jews and Arabs and expand cooperation in many civil fields to overcome the scars left by the severe violence of October 2000.

Netanyahu Governments, 2009–2021: Widening the National-Religious Divide, Narrowing the Civil Divide

In the first half of 2009, Likud returned to power under Netanyahu's leadership. Its basic guidelines did not explicitly mention Arab citizens but stated that "the government will preserve the country's Jewish character and heritage and at the same time respect the religions and traditions of the members of other religions in the country, in accordance with the values of the Declaration of Independence."[53]

In practice, the dozen years during which Netanyahu headed the Israeli government (2009–2021) were characterized by official policies that deepened the divide between Jews and Arabs and highlighted the religious and national differences between the groups. On the other hand, the Netanyahu governments worked to reduce the gap between the Jewish majority and the Arab minority on the civil level.

In the twelve years of Netanyahu's continuous rule, Israel was caught up in escalating security concerns in the Palestinian arena, such as the Gaza flotilla raid and the Israeli Naval Forces' thwarted boarding of the Turkish ship *Mavi Marmara* (May 2010), Operation Pillar of Defense (November 2012), and Operation Protective Edge (July–August 2014). Despite this, it was not the security reality that dictated the attitude of the Israeli establishment toward the Arab minority but primarily the composition of the ruling coalition in those years. This was a period when the (artificial) identities of "right" and "left" dissolved almost completely and the faith-state divide opened up, as we saw in chapter 3. The religious camp, whose power grew significantly in those years (except between 2013 and 2015), worked for legislation that would emphasize the image of Israel as a Jewish state and reduce public space for the Arab minority.

Not all of the laws designed to strengthen Israel's Jewish character were ultimately approved by the Knesset plenum, but the parliamentary and public discussions sparked a media storm that deepened the Jewish-Arab divide. For example, a series of loyalty laws submitted by various members of the Knesset intended to refine the question of the loyalty of all guests of the State of Israel as a Jewish (and democratic) state. In essence, the bills required, each in its own way, declarations of loyalty to the State of Israel at various points in a citizen's life: at the time of naturalization, at the time of swearing-in as a civil servant or MK, when applying for licenses or certificates of various types (identity card, passport, driver's license), or when applying for government funding to various entities. Although they did not pass in the end, these bills sought to create a representation according to which an Arab citizen is disloyal to the state until they prove their loyalty.[54]

Another law that sought to discriminate against the non-Jewish minority was the Acceptance Committees Law. This was designed to allow small settlements to operate acceptance committees and thus filter candidates who wished to purchase a house in the settlement. Although this law did not specifically mention Arab citizens, it was clear that it intended to enshrine in the primary legislation a norm that was in real danger following the verdict of the Supreme Court in *Ka'adan v. Israel Land Administration* (which allowed Arabs to live in settlements with a Jewish character). This law underwent some softening, but the law that eventually passed the third reading in 2011 was one that targeted the Arab population.[55]

In the same year, the Knesset passed Amendment 40 to the Basic Budget Law, also known as the Nakba Law. This law established that a body recieving budgets from the state might be subject to financial sanctions if it spends money that, in its essence, constitutes: (1) a negation of the existence of the State of Israel as a Jewish and democratic state; (2) an incitement to racism, violence or terrorism, or support for armed struggle and terrorism against the State of Israel; (3) marking Independence Day or the day of the establishment of the state as a day of mourning; or (4) an act of defacement or physical humiliation that harms the honor of the country's flag or symbol. The law, in its initial form, which was first proposed in 2009, included a punishment of up to three years in prison for those who celebrated Independence Day as a day of mourning or sorrow, but it was softened following sharp public criticism.[56]

In 2015, the Knesset tabled the bill known as the Muezzin Bill, which sought to limit the use of muezzins' loudspeakers in mosques in the early hours of the morning. This bill passed a preliminary reading in 2017, and it was clear that its purpose was to harm the Muslim population in Israel through its religious symbols. When the legislation reached an impasse, what remained was the existing law to prevent noise hazards. However, in 2018, a government committee recommended tightening the legislation on noise hazards and suggested giving the police the authority to raid mosques and confiscate loudspeakers.[57]

At the same time, the Knesset enacted the Kaminitz Law—an amendment to the Planning and Construction Law that allowed for administrative enforcement, without legal proceedings, against construction offenses and made the punishment for these offenses worse. In the Arab sector, the Kaminitz Law is seen as targeting the Arab population. An amendment to the law passed the third reading in April 2017. It was supported by the factions that a few years later became factions that made up the religious bloc.[58]

The most prominent piece of anti-Arab legislation during this period was the enactment of Basic Law: Israel—Nation State of the Jewish People, better known as the Nationality Law. This law was finally approved on July 19, 2018, during the tenure of the twentieth Knesset. It states that the State of Israel is the nation-state of the Jewish people, in which their natural right to self-determination is a right that is unique to the Jewish people. The Basic Law enshrines the status of the symbol of the State of Israel, the Israeli flag; "HaTikva" ("The Hope") as the state anthem; the Hebrew calendar; Jewish holidays and their dates; and Hebrew as the state language. The law also allows the state to encourage Jewish settlement, sees Jerusalem as the capital of Israel, and considers Arabic not an official language but a language with a special status.[59]

The approval of the Nationality Law provoked severe reactions among Arab Jews. Youssuf Jabarin, an Israeli Arab, reflected this mindset in his article "Deepening Exclusion: On the Proposal for a Basic Law: Israel—Nation State of the Jewish People":

> It seems that the bill contains very bad news for the Arab citizens of Israel and for society as a whole. First, because it seeks to decide on the value of and ideological discussions on a future constitution in Israel through a coup d'état—without a significant public discussion on the subject, and with the risk of deepening the Jewish-Arab divide in the country. Second, the bill creates and deepens, in a clear and striking manner, inequality between Jews and Arabs in Israel and even stipulates it at the constitutional level. Under these circumstances, the legal norm itself is biased in favor of the majority group in the constitutional layer of the country. As the bill shows, this discrimination is not limited to symbolic areas only, such as the definition of the state and its symbols, but worse than that—it invades areas that go to the root of the legal status of any minority in a given society: immigration and citizenship, culture, heritage, and religion. This discrimination creates a formal bias in the country's constitutional norm that erodes the status of Arab citizens.[60]

Mohammad Watad, also an Israeli Arab, pointed out that the Nationality Law does not mention, even with one word, the fact that Israel is a democratic country, which is supposed to grant equality to all its citizens:

> The words are written mainly in light of the legislator's (deliberate?) disregard, within the Nationality Law, of the country's democratic identity. In my opinion, the definition of the state

as Jewish and democratic gives the Jews of the world, wherever they are Jews, a golden key that allows them to enter the house (Israel) almost automatically. However, inside the house, full equality must prevail between all the citizens of the country. In addition, as a Jewish entity, Israel is a country whose main official holidays are Jewish holidays and whose official language is Hebrew. However, this should not mean that the existence of a native and large national minority, the Arab minority, must be ignored—a minority holding full Israeli citizenship.[61]

Anti-Arab legislation was not the only method used to make the Jew-Arab cleavage even worse. Unusual statements by the heads of state also contributed, including from Netanyahu's on the morning of the twentieth Knesset (March 2015) election: "The Arabs are flocking to the polling stations, and the Israeli left is funding their buses and transportation to the polling stations." Later, Netanyahu posted the following status on his Facebook page: "The right-wing government is in danger. Arab voters are moving to the polls in large numbers, and left-wing associations are bringing them in buses."[62] The reaction to his words was extremely sharp, including in the foreign media. *The New York Times*, for example, wrote in an editorial that Netanyahu was referring to the Arabs of Israel as enemies and that this was demagoguery that exacerbated the anger between Jews and Arabs.[63]

In contrast to deepening the national and religious dividing line, Netanyahu's administration since 2009 has adopted policies to continue closing the divide between the majority and minority in civil issues. In this framework, the Israeli establishment made a series of significant moves, one of the most prominent being Resolution No. 922 of December 30, 2015, known as Government Activity for the Economic Development of Minority Populations in 2016–2020 or the Five-Year Development Plan for Arab Society. This constituted a decision to allocate NIS 15 billion to the Arab sector, of which almost NIS 6 billion went to the Arab education system. This plan had two overarching goals: the economic development of the Arab population and its integration into the Israeli economy and society, and reducing the gaps between the Arab population and the general population. The program focused mainly on the areas of housing, transportation, education, higher education, employment, and strengthening the Arab local authorities.[64]

Another event worthy of note came at the end of the term of Netanyahu's fifth government. On January 13, 2021, during his visit to a health fund clinic in Nazareth as a guest of Mayor Ali Salem, as part of his election campaign Netanyahu apologized for his statements from 2015:

> This is an opportunity to start a new era in the relationship between us and the Arab citizens of the State of Israel, an era of respect and equality, personal respect, opportunities, and power. Whoever says that we remembered the Arabs only because of the elections is either lying or doesn't know the facts. If Jews and Arabs can dance together in the streets of Dubai, they can also dance together in the State of Israel. A new era begins today—of prosperity, integration, and security.[65]

However, the vast majority of the Arab MKs rejected Netanyahu's words. The chairman of the Joint List, Ayman Odeh, wrote on Twitter:

> Netanyahu's great escape from justice brought him to Nazareth in another attempt to divide Arab society and divide us into good and bad. There would be something pitiful about it if it didn't bring with it huge police forces that beat protesters and journalists. If this is what your reconciliation attempts look like, you'd better stay home. Before Netanyahu's arrival, the police cleaned Nazareth of the remnants of democracy. They used violence on demonstrators and dragged members of the Knesset and journalists away. Before Netanyahu even opened his mouth, he immediately reminded everyone that the most immediate threat to Arab citizens is his continued tenure.[66]

At the end of the second decade of the twenty-first century, the long-term efforts of the Netanyahu government to reduce civil disparities found a partner: Mansour Abbas, chairman of the Ra'am party and deputy chairman of the southern faction of the Islamic Movement. Abbas, born in 1974, was previously a resident dentist in Maghar, a city with a mixed Muslim-Druze population, and one of the leaders of the Wasatiyyah current in the Islamic Movement, which advocates a moderate line. At the end of 2020, when the election campaign for the twenty-fourth Knesset was already in high gear, he expressed his ambition to form a government to achieve results for the Arab sector. He even emphasized that his membership in the Islamic Movement, which is a conservative religious movement, gave him more in common with ultra-Orthodox Jewish parties:

A practice has become established here: the Arab Knesset members want to overthrow every government and dissolve every Knesset. We sat this week. I told them: Stop! Why? What awaits you? Let's think. When I act to serve my public, to prevent crime and murder in the sector, I act as a statesman, not as an automaton. What do I actually want from Netanyahu? Budgets and legislation. If I receive them, what do I care about giving him what he needs?[67]

Abbas expressed his readiness to narrow Israel's Jewish-Arab divide in a speech he delivered from the stage of the Knesset as part a Holocaust commemoration event in April 2020:

> Today I stand and say a prayer from the Koran for the upliftment of the souls of six million Jews who perished in the Holocaust in World War II. As a Palestinian Arab and a religious Muslim, I have empathy for the pain and suffering over the years of the Holocaust survivors and the families of those who perished. I stand here and express solidarity with the Jewish people, here and around the world. The people chosen by the Nazis as a target for mass extermination and genocide. And I say here: Never. I bow my head before the heroism of women and men who went out in the Warsaw Ghetto uprising against the death sentence and the feeling of despair in order to maintain a human image.[68]

The Jewish-Arab divide, consisting of national, religious, and civil aspects, erupted again in May 2021. The security escalation in the Palestinian arena led to severe violence of Israeli Arabs in the mixed cities (Haifa, Jaffa, Acre, Lod, Ramla) in the Galilee and Negev. In the background were also the Arab minority's feelings of deprivation in civil matters, despite the government's effort to reduce these gaps. In these events, three civilians were killed and hundreds were injured.

The riots in May 2021 gave even stronger expression to the new, complex reality: the Jewish-Arab divide in the national and religious spheres can worsen while the divide in the civil sphere narrows. They also illustrated that it is a conditional rift, which is exposed in its entirety during periods of tension between Arabs and Jews on national or religious grounds but dims in periods of calm.

After May 2021: The Deceptive Divide—Between Political Partnership and a Journey Back in Time

On June 13, 2022, the thirty-sixth Knesset was sworn in (the Bennett-Lapid government). For the first time in Israel's history, the coalition included an Arab party. At the time of this coalition's establishment, Ra'am, under Abbas, was performing a balancing act between the statehood and faith camps (most religious political forces remained outside the coalition). The change government of Naftali Bennett and Yair Lapid worked to reduce the Jewish-Arab divide on the civilian level but without acting in parallel on the national-religious level. When Bennett was asked in an interview if Ra'am is a faction that supports terrorism, he answered,

> First of all, no, not Abbas. For two years, Netanyahu has embraced him; in fact, he made Mansour Abbas tip the scales in Israel. . . . I really never imagined in a thousand years that I would sit with Mansour Abbas, I never considered it. The political constraints brought this about. During the war and disturbances [the May 2021 riots], something grabbed me. Mansour Abbas came to the city of Lod, to the synagogue, in the middle of the tensest moments, and said: "I want to help." . . . I saw a decent human being, I saw a brave leader, it must be said. Now, time will tell, I don't know how to be an Arab. But when he reaches out and says something very simple: I want to take care of the civil aspect of the Israeli Arabs. If you look at the coalition agreements that we will publish, you won't find a single mention of the word "national."[69]

In December 2021, Abbas said,

> The State of Israel was born as a Jewish state. This is the decision of the people, and the question is not what the identity of the state is, it was born that way and it will remain that way. . . . The question is what is the status of the Arab citizen in the Jewish state of Israel. That is the question. Therefore, the challenge now is not only facing Mansour Abbas but facing the public and the Jewish citizen. . . . There is no doubt that we are at the beginning of a new era, and I say this cautiously and hope that the process will be successful and the partnership at

the coalition level will be a trend for more different partnerships in the economy, industry, and more. . . . We are at the beginning of the partnership, but I believe in it—you cannot wait for change without creating a new reality. We have always demanded change without stepping forward. Ra'am have come and said, "Let's make a partnership that will bring about change."[70]

The Bennett-Lapid government did not last long. Its minimal parliamentary majority, heterogeneous composition, and internal political pressures prevented it from promoting an agenda, including passing laws. In June 2022, Bennett resigned as prime minister, handing over the position to his senior partner in the government, Yair Lapid, who served only a few months until the elections held on November 1—the fifth set of elections in about three years.

On December 29, 2022, the thirty-seventh Knesset was sworn in. At the time of writing, the government's tenure has not yet lasted six months. However, two main trends are evident, although they may change in due course. Although narrowing the Jewish-Arab divide on the civil level, mainly while directing large budgets to the Arab sector, is a continuing trend, it seems that the government is not doing the same for the religious-national level. Considerable parts of the components of this government, particularly the religious Zionist MKs, hold concepts of Jewish supremacy, which involves the exclusion of non-Jewish citizens.

The legal reforms that the government began promoting in January 2023, reforms whose purpose is to change the balance of power between the governing authorities while strengthening the executive and legislative and weakening the judiciary, carry a real danger of significantly expanding the Jewish-Arab divide in the State of Israel. The reforms' opponents claim that, if passed, Israel will no longer be a democratic country or an illiberal democracy; in any event, it will no longer be able to be a Jewish and democratic country. If this does occur, the divide is expected to deepen or even take on an unprecedented form.

Summary

This chapter dealt with the Jewish-Arab divide, which many see as the main divide that has crossed Israeli society since 1948 and, in many ways, even before. The fact that the Israeli-Arab conflict in general and the Israeli-

Palestinian conflict in particular are not yet fully resolved is enough to support the existence of the divide.

The rift in relations between Jews and non-Jews (or Arabs) within the boundaries of the State of Israel studied in this chapter regularly revolves around three areas: religious, national, and civil. There are two main reasons for the rift in religious terms. First, it is the result of a decision by the Israeli establishment to allow religious freedom for all sects and religions with regard to personal status, marriage and burial laws, prayer arrangements in holy places, and holidays. Second, when a clash occurred between the vision of the Jewish state and the vision to establish an Islamic caliphate, the Israeli establishment did not resolve the ideological divide but thwarted the activities of the Islamic Movement, including taking punitive measures against those who violated the law. The culmination of this split was the outlawing of the northern faction of the movement in 2015.

The national divide encompasses the identity differences between the Jewish majority and the non-Jewish minority. This cleavage stems from the overlap, in the Jewish case, between religion and nationality on a primordial basis. This overlap produced the term "Am Yisrael" (People of Israel) as a synonym for Jews. By definition, these terms do not allow the entry of non-Jews into this Jewish collective community. Indeed, in the reality that has developed since 1948, the non-Jewish population has found itself with multiple identities—Israeli, Palestinian, Arab, Muslim, Christian, Druze, or Circassian. This situation has created a hybrid identity for most of the non-Jewish population in Israel that combines various elements of nationalism and citizenship.

The civil aspect of the rift has undergone a change. Since the 1990s, it has become an integral and essential part of Israeli policy and the identity of Israeli Arabs. Until 1990, the Israeli establishment focused on thwarting security threats from among the Israeli Arabs, but in recent decades, the focus has included an integrated policy to improve the quality of life for Arab citizens. This directly affected the perception of the identity of the Arab minority in Israel and sharpened the dividing lines between Israeli citizenship and non-Jewish nationalism. Moreover, the public characteristics of Jewish identity—the state flag, the national anthem, the menorah, and so on—have no meaning for Israel's non-Jewish citizens. On the other hand, the fact that they hold an identity card and an Israeli passport gives them a civil status equal to that of Jews. For many, this situation created a hybrid identity of nationality (Arab, Palestinian, or combined) and citizenship, whether they are Muslim, Christian, or belong to another religion.

Chapter 5

The Internal Arab Rift

This chapter discusses the divisions within Arab society in Israel, which is a minority society in a country that defines itself as Jewish and democratic. During the preparation of this chapter, I had to decide whether to include an analysis of the divisions in the Palestinian system (between the Palestinian Authority/Fatah and Hamas) because of the effect this rift has on the Israeli system. The reason for this hesitation is that I found that most of the Israeli public uses the word "Arabs" without distinguishing between the various subgroups concerning their definition and identity. Eventually, I chose to focus on the Arab society in Israel for two reasons. First, it alone consists of a heterogeneous fabric of religions, ethnicities, and sociopolitical ideas, which we will present below. Second, in the past two decades the realization of some of these sociopolitical ideas created patterns of action, ranging from carrying out terrorist activities to entering the coalition government in 2021–2022. This pattern will allow us to outline the developments of identities and divisions within Arab society in Israel and point to a plurality of identities. It also expresses the challenges for and difficulties of the Arab public to adopt a clear identity that would allow a choice between absolute separatism and the use of violence to achieve their interests and cooperation with the Jewish majority, as chosen, for example, by the Joint Arab List in 2015 and Ra'am in 2021.

As presented in chapter 1, the non-Jewish minority in Israel constitutes about a fifth of the total population. It is a heterogeneous minority consisting of Muslims, Christians, Bedouins, Druze, Circassians, Ahmadis, Baha'is, and other small groups. The relationship between the social and political power factors within it cannot be analyzed without direct references to life in a country whose character differs in religion and nationalism. These differences had and still have a direct impact on ideologies and patterns of action that developed within this sector.

Since the establishment of the State of Israel in 1948, many political frameworks have emerged within the Arab sector to influence the agenda of the minority population and its relationship with the Israeli establishment.[1] The very fact of the large number of political frameworks points to diverse ideas regarding the reality in which the non-Jewish minority (or the Arab minority, as it is commonly called) lives and the actions that must be taken to improve it. The focus on patterns of action and ideology is not accidental: It makes it possible to learn about trends of separatism, integration, and turning to protest or violence to promote civil, religious, or national issues. All of these trends have an impact not only on the relationship of the Arab minority with the Israeli establishment and the Jewish majority but also on the relationship between the political parties within the Arab sector. This chapter's main argument is that the political system of the Arab minority in Israel has regularly been split since they became a minority in 1948. This internal split exists despite a shared historical ethos, and the political attempt to end this split in 2015 was also unsuccessful. The political turmoil in Israel since March 2019 widened the rift even within the Arab society in Israel and created a serious social and political crisis.[2]

The Historiographical Background

A historiographical analysis of the literature dealing with the Arab minority leads to several important insights regarding the issue of identity and the rift. In 1974, the American sociologist Seymour Lipset accepted that there was a paucity of studies dealing with the Arab citizens of Israel and claimed that almost no academic research had been done concerning this group's educational problems or social mobility.[3] At that time, Sammy Smooha and Ora Cibolsky sought to map the number of academic studies written on the Arab citizens of Israel, divided by research discipline, including history, sociology, psychology, and others. They identified 245 publications from 1948 to 1975 that met scientific standards, including masters' and doctoral theses, but of these, nearly 70 percent were published after 1970.[4] One possible conclusion is that research into the Arab minority in Israel was scarce in the first decades after the establishment of the state. This research situation also raises an obvious question regarding the quality of the studies, the extent of their political bias, and attempts to characterize the identity of the Israeli Arab. Did this minority community become Israeli and feel Israeli because they received citizenship? Did they have or did they develop an Arab or Palestinian national identity? Are they secular or religious? Are they educated or uneducated? Aziz Haidar, for example, claims "the majority of Palestinians in Israel identified with pan-Arabism, which flourished from the late 1950s to the mid-1960s and was identified with the rule of Gamal Abdel Nasser, but between the two frames of reference—the Arab national and the Israeli civil—no contradictions arose, because the one belonging to the Arab side had no practical dimension."[5] This sentence raises more questios than answers. For instance, Haider is already using the term "Palestinians," a term they did not use in public statements in those years. They even used this term, Haider emphasizes, because they supported pan-Arabism. If so, were they Palestinians, Arabs, or Israelis? Haider's text goes on to strengthen this argument when he writes that the "Arab Front, the Arab national organization at the beginning of Israel, was founded" in July 1958. Why did they not adopt a name that also included the term "Palestinians"? If they had, we could call them Palestinian Arabs, which is a double identity but not necessarily contradictory. The problem is not only semantic. It is also essential. If they considered themselves Palestinians, they did not call for the establishment of a Palestinian state in place of Israel, with which they could identify on an ethnic, linguistic, and territorial basis. The founders of al-Ard (The Land), which arose in 1959, also adopted an Arab rather than Palestinian identity and sought through the name to emphasize the connection to the homeland, to present a position that did not recognize the State of Israel, and to establish a political framework based solely on the purity of Arabs.[6]

From the publications available until the beginning of the 1980s, it can be learned that researchers who wanted to follow the social, political, economic, and cultural transformations among the Arab citizens of Israel closely and examine their relationship with the Israeli government did so, for the most part, through descriptions and analyses of a prominent and central characteristic: the conduct of the Israeli establishment since 1948. In the view of various researchers, this policy had a decisive effect on the life of the Arab minority in Israel, on its identity, and on its choice of an approach that seeks to integrate or, alternatively, to separate.[7] Arab researchers have proposed a concept according to which Israel carried out a "colonialist" takeover of the "Palestine territories" and excluded the Arab population from the political and public sphere, an activity that had an effect not only on the Jewish-Arab divide but also on the Arab identity, which was perceived as inferior to that of the majority population.[8]

Political Frameworks as an Expression of Division and a Reflection of Identity

The academic literature offers several ways to map the political powers who consider themselves part of the leadership of the Arab minority in Israel. Since 1948, many research frameworks have arisen (and dissolved) to express the political identities and ideas of the Arab minority in Israel. However, these frameworks also reflected differences of opinion and gave expression to different identities—religious, secular, separatist, integrative, national, and civil.

Yitzhak Reiter proposed three approaches to the political division of power in the Arab sector that developed on the historical timeline, during which political awareness increased among the members of the Arab sector. As a result, new frameworks emerged that sought to implement different ideologies.

The first approach divides the political map of the Arab minority into two camps that existed instead of the state until the mid-1970s. The first camp was called the moderate camp, which included Arab public figures who were members of Jewish-Zionist parties, such as Yosef Khamis, Rostam Bastuni, and Abd el-Aziz el-Zoubi. Other public figures from the Arab sector belonged to satellite parties and served in the second (1951) and third (1955) Knessets, such as Saif el-Din el-Zoubi, Jaber Mu'adi, and Masaad Kassis, who were members of the Democratic List for Israeli Arabs. This camp developed a concept centered on the Arab minority's acceptance as an ethnic and cultural minority living in a Jewish state. The civil affiliation was clear, as was the ethnic (Arab) one, but there is no evidence to suggest they developed a Palestinian (or other) national identity. The second camp was the national-radical camp, which in those years included political groups such as the Communist Party, in which there were Jews (including Meir Vilner, who signed the Declaration of Independence), Hadash (formerly known as Rakah), the Sons of the Land, the Progressive List for Peace (Ramal), and al-Ard. This camp, or at least part of it, did not accept the political reality in the Middle East, opposed the existence of the State of Israel, and did not reconcile with Israel's Zionist character.[9]

The validity of this division expired in the early 1970s. New ideas that expressed new identities led to the growth of new frameworks, and as a result, Reiter's second approach constituted three different camps. The first, the moderate camp, referred to Arab figures who were active within Jewish-Zionist parties and reconciled with the existence of the State of Israel. The second camp was the nationalist camp, led in those years by Ramal, who strove to abolish the current character of the State of Israel and sought to root a Palestinian national identity among the Arab minority in Israel. The third camp was the extreme nationalist, which included Arabs formerly in al-Ard and Sons of the Land who wished to establish a Palestinian state on all the territories of Mandatory Palestine.

Reiter's third approach developed in the late 1980s and included four camps. The first was the obligators, who accepted the existing situation in which the Jewish-Zionist character of the state was preserved. The dissenters camp included those who ranged between the Zionist establishment and the opposition, such as the Communist Party. This camp did not reject the nature of the state but strove to advancethe interests of the Arab minority through electoral power. Both the obligators and dissenters sought to promote civil issues, and they also indirectly adopted an element of Israeli civil identity. The third camp was the dissidents, who accepted the state's existence but waged a struggle to introduce fundamental changes to its character through organizing in non-Zionist or anti-Zionist parties, such as Ramal. The fourth camp was the deceivers, which included movements like the Sons of the Land. Their guiding ideology was that of the Popular Front for the Liberation of Palestine (PFLP), and they rejected the existence of the State of Israel. Both the dissidents and the decievers rejected the element of Israeli identity and sought to strengthen Palestinian, Arab, or a combined identity, which reflected not only identities but also a divide. As we will see in this chapter, these dividing lines continue in similar outlines even today.

As'ad Ghanem, a member of the Arab minority in Israel, proposed a fourfold political division according to the distinctions of ideology, basis of organization, and degree of radicalism:

a) The Israeli Arab current, which accepts the existing situation and was represented in the past (1988) by the Arab Democratic Party (ADP) of Abdulwahab Darawshe and currently by Arab activists in Zionist parties (e.g., Na'el Zu'ebi, who was on the Likud list for the twenty-fifth Knesset in November 2022).

b) The communist current, which is interested in the organization of the state on a binational basis as a strategic choice and whose main activity is in the national sphere rather than in promoting a communist agenda. This current has an identity consisting of Palestinian nationalism and Israeli citizenship.

c) The nationalist current, which derives its concept from the Arab national and Palestinian movements and is interested in autonomy for Arab citizens of Israel. Its major political power is Balad, which had representatives in the Knesset from 1996 to 2022. In the 1980s, the Sons of the Land movement formed part of this camp.

d) The Islamic current, which is based on religious values and principles and calls for the state and society to be organized on an Islamic basis. However, this current's supporters do not neglect other elements of identity, including Arabness, Palestinianism, or Israeli citizenship. The current is represented by the Islamic Movement, which was established in 1972.[10]

A third way to partition the Arab political power factors is to examine their patterns of action vis-à-vis the establishment, which are derived not only from ideology but also from collective identity. These can range from ignorance, indifference, and dialogue to protest and violence. In the first decade after the events of October 2000, it was possible to discern two camps, according to this parameter. The first camp was the deceivers, who sought to deny contact with the establishment. This camp included the northern faction of the Islamic Movement, the Sons of the Land, and Balad, despite its seat in the Knesset. The second camp was the negotiators, so-called because of their willingness to negotiate with the Israeli establishment. This camp included the National Committee for Heads of Local Arab Authorities, the communist current, and the southern faction of the Islamic Movement.[11]

Prominent Characteristics of the Arab Minority in Israel

Researchers of different backgrounds and origins—Israeli Arabs, Palestinians, Israelis, and others—agree on a number of unique characteristics of the Arab citizens of Israel that distinguish them from the Jewish majority group. The Arabs in Israel are a native population that consider themselves, historically, under the hegemony of a majority group, a significant part of which was not born in Israel when it was proclaimed in 1948. As a rule, the native character of a minority strengthens its self-awareness and the validity of its claims to a great extent beyond those of minorities emerging, for example, from the assimilation of immigrants into welfare societies to improve their situation. The same is true in the case of the Arab minority in Israel. The value of steadfastness (*sumud*)—that is, the determined clinging to the inheritance of ancestors in the face of challenges posed by the Jewish majority, which they perceive as a society of immigrants—is highly ranked in the world of the Arab minority. This feeling, which is shared by most of the Arab public in Israel, does not necessarily bridge ideological gaps—national, civil, religious, pan-Arab—nor different patterns of action taken over the years.

The transition from a majority group to a minority community is one of the significant results of a severe defeat suffered by the Arabs in their war against the Jewish settlement in 1948. The very existence of the state within which they find themselves a minority is a constant reminder of their stinging downfall, or, as one of their leaders put it, "The state was built on the ruins of the Palestinian community." The decisive victory that the Zionist movement achieved in the struggle for the establishment of the state had a direct impact on the life of the Arab minority in Israel. The Zionist ideals of settlement and kibbutzim were the organizing principles of the Jewish state. The actual implementation of this policy meant taking over most of the land in the country and clearing a place for the masses of Jewish immigrants who came to Israel. The Jewish majority saw programs like Jews of the Galilee as legitimate goals of the State of Israel, while the Arab minority faced the reality of land expropriations, "absent-present," and building restrictions, and therefore saw the state as representing interests and fulfilling a vision that was not theirs and that violated their rights. The Arabs also had difficulty accepting the definition of Israel as the state of the entire Jewish people, a definition that gave Jewish immigrants and citizens rights that Arab citizens did not enjoy. This situation gave the minority the feeling that Israeli democracy was ethnic and served only the Jewish majority. This understanding led to an increase in Arabs' protests against the background of their inferior status, and, in some cases, these protests received violent expressions.[12]

The question of the identity of the Arab minority in Israel, which was directly affected by contact with the Jewish majority, has led since 1948 to the establishment of diverse political parties. Those frameworks not only sought to promote an agenda for the Arab minority in aspects of nationality, religion, and citizenship but also reflected deep divisions that were (and are) present within Arab society. On the historical timeline, there was one attempt to connect all the political factors into one framework: the Joint Arab List in 2015. However, this attempt, which was an unprecedented political success, lasted only four years before the joint framework fell apart.

The Communist Party

The roots of the Communist Party were planted in 1919 when a group of Jewish left-wing activists founded the Socialist Workers' Party. Four years later, after overcoming differences of opinion and divisions, the activists united the ranks and founded the Palestinian Communist Party (PCP).[13] From the mid-1920s, Arab members joined this party, and thus it became a political body whose members belonged to various ethnic and national groups. This fact has been important throughout history as it has created a constant tension between the unifying communist idea and the ethno-national differences that have distinguished and separated its members. The Jews were the majority in the Communist Party from 1919 until the mid-1960s, when an ideological rift opened up between its members. This internal cleavage affected the methods of action between the Jewish and Arab members and, later, led to the dissolution of the structural partnership, but not the ideological one.

The establishment of the State of Israel forced the Communist Party to adapt to a new political reality: The party soon became the only significant political force among the Arab minority in Israel. There were several reasons for this. First, the communist platform defended the interests of the weaker sections in society, including the minority population. Second, the party provided the Arab minority with explanations for its new situation and, at the same time, presented possible solutions based on class equality. Third, the party maneuvered between communism and nationalism according to the events of the time, thereby maintaining its strongholds of support in the Arab sector. Fourth, the party made sure to reach most homes in the Arab sector through propaganda activities, including publishing three newspapers and resuming activity with its local branches throughout the country. Fifth, it was a legitimate political party, the only one in the Arab sector, which operated within the rules of the parliamentary game.[14]

The constant tension between choosing nationalism and maintaining a communist ideology accompanied the party even after the establishment of the State of Israel. As long as the nationalist and communist currents shared a common interest, their differences were pushed aside. When the camps responded to political developments in the region, as happened, for example, in the union between Egypt and Syria in February 1958, the friction led to a serious escalation between its Jewish and non-Jewish (Muslims and Christians) members. The national camp, based on the Arab members of the party, such as Emile Habibi, Tawfik Toubi, Tawfiq Ziad, Hana Nakara, and Amin Jarjoura, encouraged violent actions in order to promote and maximize the interests of the party and the Arab minority.[15]

The internal rift within the Communist Party became official after the June 1967 war. The Arab members, who had seceded to form the New Communist List (Rakah), deepened their ties with the Soviet Union and their identification with the pro-Arab line held by Moscow. Thereafter, the party continued to adhere to its traditional principles: the establishment of a Palestinian state alongside the State of Israel within the borders of June 1967, the right of return for the Palestinian refugees who left the country during the 1948 war, opposition to war as a means of resolving the conflict between the two national movements, and the participation of Jews in the party.

From the 1980s onward, the communist current found itself in a constant struggle with the new forces that arose in the Arab sector, showing not only a plurality of identities in theminority population but also rifts arising from ideological disagreements regarding action vis-à-vis the Israeli establishment. This struggle is being waged on several levels. On the national level, the communists are fighting with other political currents for Arab votes in national elections. In the regional arena, a fight broke out over the character of the Supreme Monitoring Committee (established in 1982). At the local level, there are struggles over the systems for municipal elections, the quality of the National Committee of the Heads of Arab Localities, and the methods used in its struggle against the government on national and civil issues.

Al-Ard Movement

The first seeds of the al-Ard movement appeared as early as 1959, when Arab students at the Hebrew University in Jerusalem were influenced by the atmosphere in the Arab world and especially by the national line demonstrated by the ruler of Egypt, Gamal Abdel Nasser. In July 1959, they founded a new political movement called Usrat al-Ard (The Land Family), consisting of prominent Christians, including Mansour Kardoush, Habib

Khaougi, Sabri Jiryis, and Shukri Khazan. The movement was registered as a book publishing and importing company before presenting itself in 1964 as a form of opposition to the State of Israel.[16]

At first, the movement operated in three directions. First, preservation of the new framework on the purity of Arabism. In contrast to the communists, the members of al-Ard were not interested in integrating Jews because they saw Israel as an entity that should not be recognized. Second, the struggle against the traditional political formation of the Arab minority, which the founders of al-Ard saw as suiting the needs of old-generation leaders rather than the minority. Third, activities undertaken against the communists, identified as a strong political force within the Arab sector that needed to be crushed. One of the first manifestations of this was adopting a separatist line that called on the Arab public to boycott the Knesset elections in 1965. This was the first political split within Arab society, and it reflected the awakening of a new generation—young people in their twenties who sought to shape a new reality for the minority population in Israel.

From 1959, the movement began to publish statements characterized by militant and inflammatory lines against the state that expressed consistent support for the United Arab Republic. Al-Ard's newspapers, as of 1959, were not published regularly, and each issue was even given a different name in order to avoid the need to contact the authorities to obtain an operating license. The editors harshly criticized the Israeli government, using offensive expressions to refer to the heads of state, and demanded that the land be returned to its owners. For example, Na'im Makhool, one of al-Ard's founders, wrote that "the land is ours and it will move from under the feet of the oppressors."[17]

In the second issue, the Arab public was called to boycott the general elections for the fourth Knesset. In an opinion piece titled "The Believer Will Not Be Stung Twice from the Same Den," contempt was expressed for the Arab parties associated with Zionist parties, thus giving expression to the rift within the Arab minority society.[18] In the December issue, an article compared the situation of Arabs who remained in Israel after the disaster (the Nakba) with conditions in the Nazi concentration. The prime minister at the time, David Ben-Gurion, was called "soft-hearted." In another article, Anis Shokoor, a student at the Hebrew University, wrote, "Live and let others live, maybe you will live." These messages reflected a new political idea, and the communist movement had reservations.[19]

After a lengthy legal battle in which both the ideology of al-Ard and the state, which saw the movement as a threat, were exposed, the minister of defense signed a decree in November 1964 to outlaw al-Ard. This order also resulted in the dissolution of the company established by al-Ard's members. Some of its members tried to form a new party called the Arab Socialist List in preparation for the Knesset elections in 1965, but the Central Election Committee disqualified the list on the grounds that it was a continuation of al-Ard. This brought an end to the movement, but not to the activity of its members in other settings. Some of its leaders left Israel, others retired to their homes, and a few tried to contact Palestinian terrorist organizations but were caught and imprisoned.

After the June 1967 war, the General Security Service thwarted attempts by al-Ard members to establish Fatah terror cells within the borders of the State of Israel. Six Arab citizens of Israel were arrested during the suppression operation.[20] In the 1980s and 1990s, new political movements arose that, from an ideological point of view, were a continuation of al-Ard and contributed to preserving the internal divide in Arab society.

The Sons of the Land

The Sons of the Land movement was founded in 1972 by a group of educated young people with liberal professions and headed by the lawyer Mohammed Kiwan, a resident of Umm al-Fahem. The movement did not publish a cohesive platform and relied on the strength of local groups in Kfar Tira, where the Bnei Tira (Sons of Tira) group was founded: al-Nahda (The Revival) in Taybeh and al-Sawt (The Voice) in Nazareth. The Sons of the Land entered the political scene in the municipal elections in 1973. Lists of the movement ran in several localities on similar platforms, but it only managed to have representatives elected to the local councils in Umm al-Fahm and Taybeh.[21]

The Sons of the Land's ideological line was based on the following ideas: rejection of the sovereignty of the State of Israel over the entire territory of Palestine, full identification with the PLO, and acceptance of the platform of the PFLP. In addition, the movement believed the Jewish people had no right to self-determination and that it must strive to establish a secular democratic state in all territories of Palestine within its pre-1948 borders. The way to achieve the goal was defined as an "armed Palestinian revolution," in which all parts of the Palestinian people—in the territories and in the State of Israel—would participate. The movement's leaders wrote the slogan "Al-Khalil [Hebron] and the Galilee are the same" on their flag to emphasize the national identity shared by the population on both sides of the Green Line.

This platform was contrary to the path of the communist current and expressed fundamental differences regarding the path for the Arab minority in Israel.

The movement's deceptive and separatist line, which did not recognize the existence of the State of Israel, was clearly expressed in its nonparticipation in the Knesset election system. An internal rift developed around this issue, and three camps were formed within the Sons of the Land as early as the 1970s. They all agreed on the principles of the movement's ideology (the liberation of Palestine) but differed on the means of its realization.[22] One camp, led by Hassan Jabareen and Hassan Aghbaria, supported the struggle by running in the Knesset elections, believing this would serve the movement's goals. A second camp, led by Raja Aghbaria, rejected the idea of a parliamentary struggle outright because participating would be a recognition of the Zionist entity. The third camp sought a middle way between the two opposing approaches and, in the end, found itself largely engulfed by the camp supporting parliamentary contests. This internal cleavage weakened the sociopolitical power of the Sons of the Land from the late 1980s. The fact that new political forces also emerged at his time made it even more difficult for the movement to garner popular support.

The Islamic Movement

Regarding the rift within the Arab society in Israel, until now we have discussed secular movements concerned with civil and national issues. However, within the Arab sector, there are also strong social forces that seek to promote a religious, traditional, and conservative agenda. Since 1972, the Islamic Movement has been the significant power factor in this regard. Its attitudes toward Israel and the political forces within the Arab population have also contributed to the deepening of the internal rift in this society.

The first organization of an Islamic political movement in the Land of Israel in the modern era arose under the direct influence of the Muslim Brotherhood, founded in Egypt by Hassan al-Banna in 1928. In the midst of the Arab Revolt that took place in 1936–1939, al-Banna's brother visited Palestine/the Land of Israel and laid the foundation for organized Islamic activity there. According to various estimates, the Muslim Brotherhood had twenty-five branches and about twenty thousand members in Palestine by 1946.[23]

The growth of the Islamic Movement among the Arab citizens of Israel is also related to the Islamic wave that gained momentum in the

Middle East in the 1970s, which was reflected in the revolution in Iran in February 1979. During these years, there was a phenomenon of conversion to Islam and the adoption of the slogan "Islam is the solution." The figure behind this activity was Sheikh Abdullah Nimer Darwish from Kfar Qasem, and he was joined by other activists, the most prominent of whom were Sheikh Raed Salah of Umm al-Fahem and Sheikh Kamal al-Khatib from Kafr Kanna, who absorbed the values of Islam during their studies at the Islamic College in Hebron. In 1979, Darwish gathered dozens of converts around him in an underground framework called Usrat al-Jihad (the Family of Jihad) and translated as holy warriors.[24] Its members stockpiled weapons, burned fields, and murdered an Arab in Umm al-Fahm whom they suspected of collaborating with the authorities. The group's leaders were captured in 1981 and imprisoned for various prison terms. This was the first tangible manifestation of their involvement in violent activities against the state.

After their release from prison in 1983 and 1984, the group's members changed their pattern of action. Darwish realized that the method of jihad would not bring the hoped-for objectives and ruled that the movement should act within a legal framework that would be expressed in several areas. The first area was strengthening of *da'wah*, which meant preaching for education according to the values of Islam. During these years, this activity was carried out mainly among the younger generation as part of the long-term effort to win their hearts. The national institutions of the *da'wah* mechanism included health services (general clinics, dental clinics, and milk drop stations), welfare services, and charity meals and fundraisers for people in need.[25]

The Islamic Movement established a network of associations across the country to carry out their diverse activities. This was a new pattern of activity for the Arab population in Israel. The goal was not only to act in the spirit of Islamic values while differentiating between the community and the state but also to increase the number of supporters returning to the Islamic religion while drawing power away from secular political forces such as Rakah and Sons of the Land. The secular-religious divide within Arab society became a permanent element in the conduct of all political actors, and it directly and regularly affects the voting percentages and patterns of Arabs in general elections. The political participation of Arab citizens and the distribution of their votes show that the divide exists not only in the political arena but also inside Arab society.

The 1980s were marked by a tightening of ties between the Islamic Movement and the Islamic camp in the West Bank and the Gaza Strip (known as of December 1987 as Hamas). Before the general elections for the fourteenth Knesset in 1996, a sharp and principled disagreement emerged within the Islamic Movement over whether to compile a list on its behalf to run in the elections. This dispute was a turning point in the movement's development. Darwish ruled in favor of forming a list, paving the way for a split in the movement and the formation of two factions: one, led by him, was known as the southern faction due to the location of a stronghold in Kfar Qasem, and the other, led by Salah, was known as the northern faction due to its center being in Umm al-Fahem.

The internal rift within the Islamic Movement has never been bridged. The northern faction was outlawed in 2015 and continues to champion separatist positions, the nonrecognition of the State of Israel as a Jewish state, and rejection of Zionism. The southern faction chose a more pragmatic approach (*wasatiyyah*, "moderation"), and it regularly participates in Knesset elections, supports dialogue with the Israeli establishment, and works to promote civil issues for the Arab minority in Israel. This reality has created a permanent rift within the religious camp, the first internal Arab-Muslim cleavage within the non-Jewish minority in Israel. The second rift is between the religious camp and the secular one to which secular Muslims and Christians belong.

Balad

The National Democratic Alliance (known in Hebrew as Brit Leumit Demokratit, or Balad) was founded in 1995 by a group of Arab, Christian, and Muslim left-wing activists headed by Azmi Bishara, together with former members of Sons of the Land, the Communist Party, and the Progressive List for Peace, as well as social activists from other marginal groups among the Arab minority.[26]

Ahead of the elections for the fourteenth Knesset in 1996, Balad's list joined that of the Communist Party. Despite their ideological differences, political interests prevailed: Balad, as a newly founded body, sought to use the established organizational structure of the communists to increase its odds of entering the Knesset, while the communists hoped to increase their political power by joining with a new political body. Bishara was elected to the Knesset after finishing fourth on the list. After the elections, there was a rift between the parties (inter alia because of financial disputes), and since then, Balad has competed in every election and won two or three seats in the Knesset. In the 2015 elections, it was part of the Joint Arab List, and after that disbanded, it ran as an independent list. In the elections for the twenty-fifth Knesset in November 2022, Balad did not pass the threshold percentage, and for the first time since 1996, it has no representation in the Knesset.

Balad's platform defines the party as a "patriotic Palestinian national party" that strives for a just and comprehensive solution to the Palestinian question. Balad's premise is that the Arab citizens of Israel are discriminated against by the government, both as individuals and as a collective. These two attitudes reflect national and civic affairs and are entirely different from the ideology of the Islamic Movement, which is looking for an Islamic caliphate across Palestine.

The solution offered by the party is to highlight the component of Arab (not necessarily Palestinian) nationalism and present it as a basis for the unification and organization of the Arab public in Israel. It aims to make Israel a "state of all its citizens," as opposed to what it defines as "a state with a Jewish character." Balad demands that the Arab population be recognized as a national minority and be granted collective national rights and full civil equality. Other prominent elements in the party's platform include fighting for the cultivation of Arab nationalism, organizing the Arab public as a collective with equal rights to the Jewish public, providing cultural and institutional autonomy to the Arab citizens of Israel, and expressing solidarity with the Palestinian struggle. In the past, this identification has more than once led to open expressions of support for terrorist organizations and blunt condemnations of the government's policy.[27]

Balad's view relies on UN resolutions in relation to minorities' rights. The party supports autonomy in all areas of life:

a) Education: Balad strives to establish an Arab university and let Arab schools manage themselves, determine study programs, and appoint teachers independently.

b) Religion: Balad strives to appoint Sharia judges (*kadim*) and manage endowment assets.

c) Communication: Balad seeks to allow the opening of independent radio and television stations and open communication in relation to other civic areas such as health and welfare.

This position was also expressed in its political platform: "The Arab minority is entitled to participate actively in the decision-making processes that concern it. The state will not make decisions of far-reaching significance regarding Arabs' lives without the active participation (in the decision-making process) of the Arabs as a nation. The Arab minority has the right to reject any decision made without its active participation or against its legitimate interests and rights."[28] This platform is still valid today and illustrates the gap with other conceptual frameworks not only in theory and vision but also in practice.

If the Sons of the Land/communist current and the southern faction of the Islamic Movement are included in the pragmatic camp and the Islamic Movement's northern faction is viewed as the separatist camp, then Balad is situated between these two poles. It formed a permanent part of the Israeli parliament from 1996 until 2022.

Alongside its parliamentary activity to promote national and civil issues, Balad worked to realize a series of separate projects, including the weekly publication of *Fasl al-Makal* (*The Decisive Things*), which, in the second half of the 1990s, distributed approximately twenty thousand copies and gave a platform to the party's ideology. Balad also established a nonprofit organization called the Arab Culture Association, which operated summer camps and conducted tours of abandoned villages for teenagers. Party members worked to enhance Palestinian and Arab nationalism among the younger generation. The Baladuna association (Our Homeland) organized exhibitions related to the Palestinian struggle and conducted fundraising campaigns for the Palestinians. Between 2015 and 2019, when it was part of the Joint Arab List, Balad focused its activities on national issues in contrast to the other member parties and mainly invested its time in promoting civil issues. The differences in attitudes created an internal rift within the Joint List.

The Joint Arab List

Negotiations for the formation of the Joint Arab List began in December 2014 and ended shortly before the last day to register electoral lists at the end of January 2015. Under this acute time pressure, the parties had to democratically approve the measure and agree on a joint program and a list of candidates. With these two important issues needing answers, the Hadash movement (the communists-socialists), which was most hesitant to join the Joint List, had the upper hand. Not only was it the biggest faction, it also had the most common and comprehensive social, political, and economic programs. This negotiation among the Arab parties resulted from a series of political and social developments that happened within Israeli politics and the Arab minority. The inevitable result was a Joint Arab List geared toward the general elections for the Knesset in March 2015.

First, the law changed the electoral threshold from 2 percent to 3.25 percent. The original bill was submitted to the Knesset by Yisrael Beiteinu (Israel Our Home), a right-wing party, in order to reduce the number of parties in the Knesset and increase the government's ability to govern.[29] However, the Arab parties within the nineteenth Knesset (and other minor Jewish parties) claimed that the new law was a political maneuver to reduce the likelihood of reelection. In practice, the new law did reduce the odds of the Arab lists (Hadash/communist, Balad, Ra'am-Ta'al) passing the higher threshold. Therefore, their leaders decided to consolidate the Joint List. It should be noted that the fear that not one Arab list would pass the electoral threshold was genuine. Over the years, and especially after the events of October 2000, there had been a steady decline in the number of Arab voters in the elections.[30]

The second reason was social pressure within the Arab sector for joint candidacy. A survey showed that 85 percent of the Arab interviewees supported the Arab parties running in a joint list. The Arab population wanted a list that would advance civil issues first, alongside Palestinian national goals, even though the Arab population was aware of internal ideological differences between the political forces. Another survey was conducted in December 2014 by StatNet,[31] three months before the elections, in which 48 percent of seven hundred interviewees noted their disappointment with Arab MKs' performance regarding the civil affairs of the Arab population. Another survey in the same month found that 83 percent of Arabs surveyed indicated a preference for one list of candidates. The findings of these surveys are reinforced by a content analysis of Arab social media networks in 2013. At this time, more highly educated Arabs shared their political and social thoughts, calling for unity within the Arab society. As Manal Harib put it, "Since 2013, there has been a noticeable trend of a steep rise in the involvement of young Arab civilians in politics on the Internet and on social networks. Through the extensive use of Facebook, these young people built campaigns to influence public opinion and succeeded in leading the Arabs on the street in Israel and in the Arab parties to large demonstrations and protests about programs and laws on the public agenda in Israel, such as the National Law."[32] Third, a group of young, educated Arabs created a new Facebook page titled United Arabs (*muttahidoon* in Arabic) and stated they would only vote for a unified list. The fact that this Facebook page received thousands of "likes" within a few hours was one of the triggers for consolidating a joint political list. This activity on social networks and the findings of the surveys were a watershed for the Israeli Arab leadership. Arab politicians were aware of a steady decline in voter turnout and feared that low rates in the 2015 elections would keep them outside the Knesset.

The fourth factor that accelerated the Arab parties' decision to compete on the Joint List was the widening rift between Jews and Arabs since 2009. A series of new bills submitted to the Knesset, mostly by right-wing politicians who became part of the ruling coalition headed by Netanyahu after the 2009 elections, sought to exclude the Arab population from public life and enhance the Jewish character of the state. The prevailing mood within Arab society was a sense of real threat to Arabs as a minority group. Arabs shared their fears about this threat to their Palestinian national identity and their personal and collective rights as Israeli citizens. These worries, from 2009 on, encouraged Arab politicians to join forces in order to protect the rights of the minority. In practice, the new joint list stressed that the decision to combine forces was a political response to racism and an expression of national-political unity.[33]

Despite their common political platform, statements made by Arab parties' spokespersons on the eve of the elections in 2015 pointed to fundamental disagreements that made it difficult to achieve true unity. Moreover, most of the Joint List's political activity on the eve of the elections was done separately by the parties.[34] For instance, Awad Abdelfattah, then the general secretary of Balad, stated that the Joint List might work closely with the Palestinian leadership in Ramallah to achieve Palestinian national goals. He did not mention civil affairs, which were part of the Joint List's platform and constituted a critical issue for the Arab citizens of Israel. Ja'afar Farah, an Israeli Arab and a prominent activist for minority rights, argues that the decision to form the Joint List was defensive—that is, to protect Arab representation in the Knesset.[35]

Afterward: Joint but Split

The Joint Arab List became the new home for communists, socialists, liberals, and the religious. Some members are Christians, others are Druze, and the majority are Muslims. In addition, the Joint List has women such as Hanin Zoabi (Balad) and Aida Touma-Suleiman (Hadash) in key positions. Notable religious Muslim members opposed their inclusion but had to accept it in order to survive politically. From any perspective, it was a heterogenous political alignment, reflecting the variety of internal Arab ideologies rather than unity.

The common goal of all the parties who joined the list was to be represented in the Knesset, except for those who did not recognize the State of Israel (Sons of the Land and the northern branch of the Islamic Movement). However, this political supermarket had the potential to expose conflicts, disagreements, and tensions among Arab MKs, even in situations where Arab unity was required to face the challenges of a Jewish-majority government controlled by a right-wing coalition.

Examining the Arab MKs' activity in the Knesset from 2015 to 2019 in national, civil, and religious affairs, including parliamentary activities, statements to the media, and participation in public events and protests, is useful for delineating differences of opinion and priorities within the Joint Arab List. National issues refer to the Palestinian arena and include both initial activities and responses to Israeli policy.

MEETINGS WITH THE PALESTINIAN LEADERSHIP IN RAMALLAH

Abu Mazen, president of the Palestinian Authority, decided to enhance ties with left-wing Jewish parties and the Arab minority in Israel. Surprisingly, only Balad members, headed by Mtanes Shehadeh, the party's general secretary, accepted the invitation in February 2017. Other MKs from the Joint List did not visit the presidential compound (the Mukataa) in Ramallah.[36] They did not explain their position publicly, but a reasonable inference is that they preferred to promote civil affairs over national ones.

VISITS TO TERRORISTS' FAMILIES

On February 3, 2016, Jamal Zahalka, Hanin Zoabi, and Basel Ghattas, three Balad MKs from the Joint Arab List, met in East Jerusalem with families of terrorists. Other MKs from the Joint List did not accompany them. This visit led to harsh criticism. Zahalka had to explain that the terrorists, who died during their attacks on Jews, civilians, and security forces, were victims of the Israeli occupation.[37] Balad's members in the Joint List remained silent, not wanting to worsen the disagreements and knowing such a meeting broke Israeli law. The only public comment came from Ayman Odeh, the chair of the Joint List and leader of Hadash, who said the meeting intended to discuss MKs providing assistance in transferring the terrorists' bodies to the

Palestinians.³⁸ Zahalka responded by saying that Odeh "is the chair of the Joint List, but he is certainly not the leader of the Arabs."³⁹

Assistance to Palestinian Terrorists or Prisoners

In December 2016, Balad MK Basel Ghattas was photographed smuggling envelopes containing twelve cell phones and other objects to security prisoners in Ktzi'ot Prison in southern Israel.
He used his parliamentary immunity to pass through the prison gates without his possessions being examined. Two days later, the Knesset removed his immunity, and he was arrested. On January 2, 2017, the Knesset Ethics Committee decided to ban Ghattas from Knesset committees and plenum sessions, with the exception of votes, for half a year. At this point, the Joint List denounced the decision, claiming that "it is a harsh and unprecedented punishment."⁴⁰ On March 16, 2017, Ghattas signed a plea bargain, according to which he would resign from the Knesset and serve two years in prison, and was convicted of moral turpitude. As early as December 2016, Odeh said publicly that he could not believe Ghattas would perform an illegal act like assisting Palestinian security prisoners. In response, Ghattas accused Odeh of "lacking any pride or self-esteem." Ghattas made it clear that the Joint List did not need what he called "agents of the racists."⁴¹ These mutual accusations were not just indicative of a personal rivalry: They expressed an ideological gap between perceptions of the Arab population's identity, as well as its positions toward the Jewish majority and the Palestinian matter.

Responses to Terror Attacks Carried Out by Israeli Arabs

On July 14, 2017, three Israeli Arabs opened fire on police officers on the Temple Mount (Noble Sanctuary), killing two Druze officers. As a rule, the Arab struggle to improve its minority situation did not include using terror against the State of Israel. Moreover, when Israeli Arabs committed acts of terror, most Arab political entities condemned them. This was the case in July 2017, but the Joint List was not able to formulate a unified communiqué, and its MKs issued separate statements of condemnation.⁴²

Contact with the Arab World

There were bitter public differences of opinion among the members of the Joint List regarding the ongoing civil war in Syria. Odeh refused to condemn

Assad's regime after it used chemical weapons against civilians, explaining that he did not believe Assad used these weapons in Idlib and Douma. In response, Talab Abu Arar, representing Ra'am, declared that "Odeh is not representing the Joint List."[43] It is worth mentioning that in the Arab sector, there is a fierce debate between supporters of the Assad regime and its opponents. This debate is conducted not only between members of the Joint List and in the Knesset but also in the press and on social media.[44] In April 2015, the Arab League headquarters sent an invitation to the Joint Arab List to discuss the interaction between the Arab world and the Arab minority in Israel. Odeh announced that the Joint List had rejected the invitation due to a desire to focus on internal (i.e., civilian) issues. He admitted the Joint List had different views on the situation in the Arab world, particularly regarding Syria and Yemen, adding that its members had not succeeded in forming a unified position on these issues.[45]

The Joint Arab List: The Split

The four circumstances that catalyzed a Joint Arab List before 2015 remained valid in 2019. When Netanyahu decided to call early elections for the Knesset, the political system within the Arab sector moved into action. The prevailing premise within the Arab minority was that the Joint List would compete again as a party that represented the entire minority. Despite different ideologies and personal rivalries, the joint activity of Arab MKs was a positive sign that Arab leaders could work together.

However, as early as November 2018, the engineer Salman Abu Ahmad announced that he was "considering the option of establishing a new party with Ali Salem, Nazareth's mayor, called Wasat (New Arab Horizon)."[46] At the same time, cracks between the Joint List's MKs were made public. Arab MKs expressed their will to maintain the Joint List as a political power, but on January 8, 2019, Ta'al leader Ahmad Tibi asked the Knesset procedurel committee to remove his party from the Joint List, legally provided for by the law. A few days later, Tibi explained his move to split the Joint List, attributing it to several internal Arab reasons:[47]

   a) In 2015, he had not been enthusiastic about forming a joint list. According to his version of events, he agreed for two reasons: his underst]anding that the new threshold may have left Arab parties outside of the Knesset and his awareness of the Arab public asking for the various political frames to merge. He claimed that his consent involved giving up political power since his party received fewer MKs than its support on the streets suggested it could.

b) During the Joint List's activity, his party made the most significant concessions compared to the others. In particular, he mentioned Balad and the Islamic Movement, which threatened to dismantle the partnership due to disagreements about internal rotation between the Arab candidates. His party was the only one that fulfilled its commitment and carried out the rotation in accordance with agreements signed on the eve of the elections in 2015.

c) There were too many disagreements among MKs on the Joint List to achieve a unified position on national and civil issues. Indirectly, he accused Odeh of being responsible for the failure to create unity among the list's members. Still, in the end, Tibi chose to compete in a joint list with Odeh in the 2019 elections as this connection would increase the number of mandates his party would receive.

d) While increasing the international community's awareness of the situation of the Arab minority, Tibi reduced the success of the Joint List. However, he mentioned that he had been raising awareness long before the list was founded. Tibi sought to achieve two goals in this regard: hint to his leadership rivals that he had considerable political experience and persuade Arab voters to vote for a man with experience.

In response, Tibi was attacked by colleagues both within and outside the Joint List. According to Balad's secretary general, Mtanes Shehadeh, "Tibi's decision to dismantle the Joint List was expected, especially in view of his attempts in recent weeks to squeeze more seats from the other parties. During his years of service in the Knesset, he never ran on an independent list and did not stand the test of the voter." Odeh refrained from attacking Tibi and stated, "The one who wants to see the Joint List dismantled, most of all, is Netanyahu. Anyone who wants to divide and rule between Arabs and Arabs is the extreme right. I am proud to be part of a party that knows how to put ideology before personal interests."[48] Odeh's effort to reduce

Arab internal conflicts was authentic, despite already knowing that there was no real chance of keeping the Joint List together as one political unit.

Tibi's political maneuver symbolized old and traditional politics within the Arab sector. In an age when social networks are platforms for the free expression of opinions, a discourse emerged quickly in which Arab society expressed its dissatisfaction with a polity that prefers personal interests. In February, Khaled Awad wrote about the dismantling of the old ideologies of communism, Islamism, and nationalism among the Arab minority. None of that is relevant nowadays—only personal aspirations are, as Tibi demonstrated. Moreover, Awad claimed that Tibi's party, Ta'al, has no ideology at all.[49] Trying to explain his decision, Tibi concluded that both personal rivalry and political ego influenced him significantly.

A survey by StatNet published a month before the elections found that 34 percent of respondents saw Tibi as solely responsible for the dismantling of the Joint List, and another 18 percent placed joint responsibility on Tibi and Odeh.[50] The criticism against Tibi was also reflected on social media, including a Facebook page that defamed him on a daily basis. Tibi filed a complaint with the Central Elections Committee, alleging that he was being slandered. The committee chairman accepted the petition and ordered the closure of the Facebook account on the grounds that its operators were spreading lies and inciting slander against Tibi, which was liable to influence voters' discretion.[51]

The list's dissolution became official on February 22, 2019, when Tibi and Odeh founded the Hadash-Ta'al List, and Balad, a secular party that seeks to advance the agenda of a "state of all its citizens," found itself in an unnatural partnership with Ra'am, a religious party. The official dismantling of the Joint List turned the election campaign for the twenty-first Knesset (April 2019) in the Arab sector into a battle of mutual slander between the two leading lists: Hadash-Ta'al and Balad-Ra'am. The two sides distributed videos and information insulting each other, and this charged public discourse created a negative atmosphere on the street on the eve of the elections. Quite a few residents expressed their sense of disgust at the behavior of their candidates, arguing that they were busy addressing their personal issues and were not attentive to the needs of the Arab public.

Between mid-2019 and mid-2021, Arab politicians tried to keep the political form of the Join Arab List alive, though without success. Despite its impressive success in the elections held in March 2020 (fifteen seats) and the public's evident will for one Arab party, the Joint List did not last long. Ahead of the elections for the twenty-fourth Knesset scheduled for

March 2021, Mansour Abbas, the leader of Ra'am, the party with roots in the Muslim Brotherhood, also withdrew. Representatives of Hadash, Ta'al, and Balad claimed that Abbas had planned this for a long time because he did not commit to witholding his recommendation of Netanyahu for prime minister. At this point, the Jewish-Arab and Arab-Arab divides coalesced. Abbas, for his part, claimed that he was withdrawing due to a dispute about religious issues that Ra'am wanted to promote but his partners disapproved of.[52] The differences of opinion and ideology favored an independent run for Ra'am, although the decision was also influenced by an assessment that Ra'am could obtain a high number of votes if it ran separately.

The election result was very bad for the Arab minority community: a drop from fifteen to ten seats. This could have caused a political dispute. However, for the first time since the establishment of the state, the internal Arab rift also brought about a change in the balance of power to the detriment of the Joint List. It remained in opposition, but Ra'am formed part of the coalition of the change government led by Naftali Bennett and Yair Lapid.

In the general elections held in November 2022, the Arab lists again received ten seats at the Knesset: five for the list that included the communists and Ta'al, and five for Ra'am. Balad had withdrawn from the Joint List for political and ideological reasons but did not pass the electoral threshold percentage.

The result is that at the beginning of 2023, there were three camps in Arab society, as there have always been: religious, national, and liberal Israeli. The gaps between them are too great. The personal rivalries are extremely bitter, and their inability to unite over time to promote and improve Arab citizens' quality of life has become a permanent reality.

Summary

This chapter examined the divisions within Arab society in Israel from a historical point of view. These divisions have existed consistently since 1948 and are influenced not only by developments within the Arab minority society but also by external events, including the policies of the Israeli establishment, the attitude of the Jewish majority, and developments in the Palestinian arena and the Arab and Muslim world. These developments led to complex identities—personal and collective—and the perpetuation of political frameworks that promoted different ideas, which ranged from distinctly liberal to traditional religious values, to address civil, national, and religious issues, and each Arab party did so according to its own ideology and priorities. It was only in 2015 that an unnatural political connection was created between political power factors, which itself happened because of external reasons that reduced their chances of passing the electoral threshold to enter the Knesset individually.

The Arab public is aware of the Arab parties' ideological and political divisions. As of 2023, it can be determined that this public is fed up with opportunistic politicians. The Arab people would prefer that their elected officials focus on civic issues that improve their quality of life and want to see tangible results as quickly as possible. When disputes increase, the public punishes the politicians and refrains from voting. Arab public figures are aware of this phenomenon, yet they have failed to consolidate conceptual unity and shared action patterns that would benefit their people. This reality preserves multiple personal and group identities and, at the same time, traditional divisions within this population. All of this has regularly been reflected in conflicts and disputes between Arab parties that chose to engage with the State of Israel.

Since the 1960s, political separatists that did not recognize Israel as a political entity acted against parties willing to engage with Israel. These separatists included the al-Ard movement, the Sons of the Land, Balad (to an extent), and the northern faction of the Islamic Movement. It is worth considering that these factions did not just deny the existence of Israel as a state (or as a Jewish state in the case of Balad). Moreover, they also strove to erode the public and political power of those Arab parties that recognize Israel. This situation created ideological blocs within Arab society, which still exist, even if the Israeli establishment chose to outlaw them, as happened with al-Ard (1965) and the northern faction of the Islamic Movement (2015).

Ultimately, the Arab minority, like the Jewish majority, is heterogeneous in its views and seeks a common identity and vision. This is a complex challenge not only because of the political disputes but also because of the different priorities of the younger generation, which is, for example, bolder, more demanding, and embraces elements of modern society much more readily than previous generations.

Conclusion

This book has aimed to present the reader with an analysis of Israeli society as it stands in the middle of 2023. The focus was on the divisions that, to the best of my understanding, have had the most impact on the various identities that have developed in the Jewish majority and Arab minority societies.

Israel was founded as a multicultural and multi-identity society, and it remains so even today. The attempt to produce the new Israeli—including through the melting pot of the IDF as the People's Army—failed or, at most, only partially succeeded. From the beginning, this pot did not intend to unite all Israeli citizens under the same identity because it excluded the non-Jewish or Arab population. If the Jewish-Arab rift (as analyzed in chapter 4) was the only rift in Israeli society, it could be defined as an ethnic-national rift. In practice, the number of rifts is greater, and the analysis of four of them in this book allows us to draw several conclusions.

First, Israel is a society without a shared vision for all its citizens. This is true for both the majority group and the minority group. The ongoing political crisis in Israel (2018–2023) culminated in five election campaigns in less than four years and resulted in the largest social protest since 1948. This protest crossed two camps within the Jewish majority group and raises a question regarding the dividing line between Jews and non-Jews, because the latter are a minority but they take part in protests. Regarding the Jewish majority group, the research suggests seeing this as an identity war between a religious camp, which wants a state with a conservative Jewish character, and a statehood camp, whose religion is liberal democracy. The conservative-liberal divide finds expression in the political, legal, and public arena. As of now, there is no leader who will lay down a shared vision for all groups in Israeli society.

Second, the faith-state rift is the cleavage that most threatens the cohesion of the Jewish majority group (about 74 percent of the total population). It is about more than politics; it is about the identity of the state and the society. People who serve in the Knesset and in the government have a nationalist ideology. They do not recognize non-Jews' right to equal rights. They strive to turn Israel into a conservative state and, if possible, into a halacha state according to the laws of the Torah. In 2023/2024, they no longer hide their faith and sectarian vision and try, despite difficulties, to increase the power and involvement of religion in state affairs.

Third, the present research suggests, as insights or conlusions, three reasons for the worsening of the faith/religion-state divide since the beginning of the twenty-first century. Firstly, the religious camp recognizes a demographic change in its favor and no longer behaves as a minority uniting several groups (ultra-Orthodox, religious Zionists, ultra-nationalists, Messianic Jews, racists). Secondly, some of the leaders of this camp, such as Simcha Rothman, believe that the right-wing camp will remain the electoral majority and that the political map in Israel is unlikely to change in the coming years. Thirdly, despite the security reality of terrorist threats or low-intensity combat, Israel has not been in a conventional military campaign with an Arab army since the October 1973 war. This perception, and the fact that Israel has signed a series of peace/normalization agreements with Arab countries, has significantly reduced the external threat to Israel's continued existence. In the absence of a real existential threat (despite statements by politicians on the subject for instrumental reasons), there has been a loosening of the cohesion of Israeli society (which mobilizes and coalesces around the flag in times of localized escalation). Such a consciousness in a reasonable security reality, without a sense of existential threat, creates a softer media and political ground for dealing with internal issues such as the image of the state.

This third insight, about the absence of an existential threat, may raise in readers a question about the validity of this argument after October 7, 2023, the date when Hamas terrorists invaded Israeli territory. The conclusion, a year into the war, is that that the threats of Hamas (and also Hezbollah in light of the war of attrition in the northern part of Israel) do not constitute an existential threat to Israel. On the other hand, domestically, the divisions within the Jewish majority group not only failed to diminish—they worsened. This has several prominent manifestations, such as new attempts by the religious camp to carry out legal reform (conservative in essence); complete refusal of the ultra-Orthodox group (12 percent of the population) to take part in the public effort and enlist in the army (despite the urgent need for manpower); the continued refusal of the minister of justice to appoint a president to the Supreme Court; hostility and hatred of Jews toward Arabs and Arabs toward Jews; and a debate within the government about the goals of the war and the exit strategy both on the southern front and on the northern front. This reality leads to a particularly bleak conclusion: The Jews, as a majority group, know how to fight side by side against an external enemy on the battlefield, but find it difficult to live side by side.

Fourth, the split between the right and left is an imaginary divide that is frequently exploited for political needs and gains. Two main reasons explain its non-existence. The first is that all currents of Zionism presented very similar ideas, perhaps even identical, regarding the vision of the Jewish state and its territory (the Land of Israel). They disagreed about the place of religion, but this is not a left-right divide. This variable could have put religious Zionism on the right side of the ideological map, but it is not sufficient in itself. The economic variable of the model presented in chapter 2 demonstrates the opposite: Ultra-Orthodox parties, only some of which are Zionist, declare their support for the right wing, but in practice, their policies are those of a socialist state. The second reason deals with the practical aspects. All Israeli governments—whether wrongly identified with the right or the left—have agreed to territorial compromises in exchange for a peace settlement or a political settlement with an Arab entity: Menachem Begin (Likud, right-wing) did so in 1977 with Egypt, Yitzhak Rabin (Labor, left-wing) did so in 1993 with the PLO in the Oslo Accords, Benjamin Netanyahu (Likud) continued the implementation of the Oslo Accords in 1996–1999, and Ariel Sharon (Likud) carried out the unilateral disengagement from the Gaza Strip in 2005.

Finally, the Jewish-Arab divide is a conditional emotional-perceptual divide. It is based on a national conflict between two groups who have found themselves living in the same sovereign area since 1948. The relationship between the two sides—the Jewish majority and the non-Jewish minority living in Israel—is characterized by mutual distrust, a result of factors analyzed in chapter 4. This rift is unique because it is conditioned by security escalations that occur either within the State of Israel or in the territories of Judea, Samaria, or the Gaza Strip, all inhabited by people whose national identity is the same as that of most Israeli Arabs. Whenever such an escalation occurs, the Jewish population uses the term "Arab" to define the terrorist threats to security forces, civilians, and the home front. The fact that there are also Israeli Arab citizens who have been killed or injured as a result of terror attacks does not diminish the strength of the divide during waves of terrorism. At the same time, this is an artificial divide because, in normal times, Jews and Arabs, Israeli citizens, live side by side and frequently interact in work, studies, culture, sports, and recreation. In 2021, this rift closed slightly (it is too early to determine whether the change was temporary or permanent) when an Arab party formed part of the coalition that presided over the country for eighteen months (June 2021–December 2022). However, at the time of writing (early 2023), there is still a Jewish-Arab divide in the political and media fields, and at the same time the common life of Jews and Arabs also continues to exist.

The Arab-Arab divide is authentic, has deep roots, and cannot be bridged ideologically. The attempt to connect different ideas regarding the situation of the minority compared to the majority and the minority community's quality of life lasted only a few years (2015–2019) and fell apart due to political rivalries. The glass ceiling for the image of the State of Israel as a Jewish state was broken with the entry of Mansour Abbas into the Bennett-Lapid coalition in order to improve the situation of the Arab minority. In doing so, he deepened the internal Arab rift because he won political support at the expense of his opponents, who have traditionally avoided joining the Israeli government. Looking ahead, this rift is not expected to close, and it may even widen if in future general elections an Arab list is required to establish a coalition that will govern Israel.

Notes

Chapter 1

1. Shaul Tchernichovsky, "Man Is Nothing but . . . ," Ben Yehuda Project, https://benyehuda.org/read/2722 [Hebrew].

2. Assaf Shapira, *Citizenship: A Theoretical and Historical Review* (Israel Democracy Institute, 2010) [Hebrew].

3. Roger Brubaker and Frederick Cooper, "Beyond 'Identity,'" *Theory and Society* 29, no. 1 (2000): 19.

4. Helen Spencer-Oatey, "Theories of Identity and the Analysis of Face," *Journal of Pragmatics* 39, no. 4 (2007): 639–56.

5. Pew Research Center, *Pew-Templeton Global Religious Futures Project*, https://www.pewresearch.org/topic/religion/religious-demographics/pew-templeton-global-religious-futures-project/.

6. David Buckingham, "Introducing Identity," in *Youth, Identity, and Digital Media*, ed. David Buckingham (MIT Press, 2008), 1–2.

7. Bernd Simon, *Identity in Modern Society: A Social Psychological Perspective* (Blackwell, 2004), 1–4.

8. Brubaker and Cooper, "Beyond 'Identity.'"

9. Charles Tilly, "Citizenship, Identity and Social History," *International Review of Social History* 40, S3 (1995): 1–17.

10. Simon, *Identity in Modern Society*, 3.

11. Antony Easthope, "Bhabha, Hybridity and Identity," *Textual Practice* 12, no. 2 (1998): 341–48.

12. Néstor García-Canclini, "Hybridity," in *International Encyclopedia of the Social & Behavioral Sciences*, 2nd ed. (Elsevier, 2015).

13. Nikos Papastergiadis, "Hybridity and Ambivalence: Places and Flows in Contemporary Art and Culture," *Theory, Culture & Society* 22, no. 4 (2005): 40.

14. Keri E. Iyall Smith and Patricia Leavy, *Hybrid Identities: Theoretical and Empirical Examinations* (Brill, 2008).

15. Hamish Telford, "The Federal Spending Power in Canada: Nation-Building or Nation-Destroying?," *Publius* 33, no. 1 (2003): 23–44.

16. Gloria T. Beckley and Paul Burstein, "Religious Pluralism, Equal Opportunity and the State," *Western Political Quarterly* 44, no. 1 (1991): 185–208.

17. Sammy Smooha, "Ethnic Democracy: Israel as a Prototype," in *Zionism: A Contemporary Polemic*, eds. Pinchas Ginosar and Avi Bareli (Ben-Gurion Heritage Center, 1996), 277–311.

18. Chaim Kaufman, "Possible and Impossible Solutions to Ethnic Civil Wars," *International Security* 20, no. 4 (1996): 137–38.

19. Angela Ordóñez-Carabaño and María Prieto-Ursúa, "Forgiving a Genocide: Reconciliation Processes Between Hutu and Tutsi in Rwanda," *Journal of Cross-Cultural Psychology* 52, no. 5 (2021): 427–48.

20. Kevin Deegan-Krause, "New Dimensions of Political Cleavage," in *The Oxford Handbook of Political Behavior*, eds. Russell J. Dalton and Hans-Dieter Klingemann (Oxford University Press, 2006), 538–56.

21. Seymour Martin Lipset and Stein Rokkan, eds., *Party Systems and Voter Alignments: Cross-National Perspectives* (Free Press, 1967).

22. Lipset and Rokkan, eds., 3.

23. Clem Brooks et al., "Cleavage-Based Voting Behavior in Cross-National Perspective: Evidence from Six Postwar Democracies," *Social Science Research* 35, no. 1 (2006): 91.

24. Israel Central Bureau of Statistics, "The Population of Ethiopian Origin in Israel: Selected Data Published on the Occasion of the Sigd Festival 2021," November 1, 2021, https://www.cbs.gov.il/en/mediarelease/pages/2021/the-population-of-ethiopian-origin-in-israel-selected-data-on-the-occasion-of-the-sigd-festival-2021.aspx.

25. Israel Central Bureau of Statistics, "Persons Aged 20 and Over, by Religiosity and by Selected Characteristics," December 5, 2021, https://www.cbs.gov.il/he/publications/LochutTlushim/שנתון%20לוחות/st28_06x.pdf.

Chapter 2

1. Hans Kohn, *The Idea of Nationalism: A Study in Its Origins and Background* (Macmillan, 1944), 205.

2. Asher Arian and Michal Shamir, "The Primarily Political Functions of the Left-Right Continuum," *Comparative Politics* 15, no. 2 (1983): 139.

3. Yehuda Gottholf, "Right and Left in a Divided Generation," *Balances* 2 (1977): 126 [Hebrew].

4. Ed Rooksby, "The Relationship Between Liberalism and Socialism," *Science & Society* 76, no. 4 (2012): 497.

5. Jeremy Waldron, "Theoretical Foundations of Liberalism," *Philosophical Quarterly* 37, no. 147 (1987): 130.

6. Rooksby, "The Relationship Between Liberalism and Socialism," 501–2.

7. Rooksby, 498.

8. Avraham Levinson, *Ahad Ha'am and His Teachings*, Ben Yehuda Project, https://benyehuda.org/read/4166 [Hebrew].

9. Einat Ramon, "Cultural Zionism as an Alternative to Reforming the Ahad Ha'am Writings," *Iyunim Bitkumat Israel* 14 (2014): 104–40 [Hebrew].

10. Cited in Yossi Goldstein, *Ahad Ha'am and Herzl* (Zalman Shazar Center, 2011) [Hebrew].

11. Yael Weiler Israel, "Religion, Nationalism and the New Gospel: Rabbi Dr. Yehuda Aryeh Leon Bivas, the Forerunner of Zionism," in *A Time for Mercy: Rabbi Zvi Hirsch Kalisher and the Awakening to Zion*, ed. Asaf Yedidya (Yad Yitzhak Ben Zvi, 2015) [Hebrew], 50–69.

12. Knesset, *Benjamin Ze'ev Herzl, 1860–1904*, https://main.knesset.gov.il/About/commemoration/pages/herzl.aspx [Hebrew].

13. Yehuda Reinhart, "The Confrontation Between Zionism and Traditionalism Before the First World War," *Iyunim Bitkumat Israel* 3 (1993): 366–79 [Hebrew].

14. Theodor Herzl, *The Jewish Question: Diaries, 1895–1898* (Mosad Bialik, 1997), 1:119–20 [Hebrew].

15. Dov Borochov, *Writings* (United Kibbutz, 1955), 36–37.

16. Gideon Katz, "The Secular Element in Aharon David Gordon's Thought," *Iyunim Bitkumat Israel* 11 (2001): 466–67 [Hebrew].

17. Elhanan Oren, "From the Transfer Proposal, 1937–1938, to Retrospective Transfer, 1947–1948," *Iyunim Bitkumat Israel* 7 (1997): 76–77 [Hebrew].

18. David Ben Gurion, *Letters to Pola and the Children* (Am Oved, 1968), 211.

19. Quoted in Benny Morris, "And Books and Scrolls in Normal Old Age: A New Look at Marxian Zionist Documents," *Alpim* 12 (1996), https://www.sharett.org.il/cgi-webaxy/sal/sal.pl?lang=he&ID=880900_sharett_new&act=show&dbid=library&dataid=1486 [Hebrew].

20. Aharon Yaffe, *Lines for the Redemption Process of the Bet Shean Valley* (Jewish National Fund, 1992), 52–59, https://www.kkl.org.il/files/karka/35/karka-35-1992-10.pdf [Hebrew].

21. Gadi Hitman and Libi Moskovitz, "Two Went Together Unless They Were Meant to Be: Herut and Mapam Parties and Their Relation to the Military Government," *National Resilience, Politics and Society* 1, no. 1 (2019): 35–58 [Hebrew].

22. Institute for Israeli-Palestinian Conflict Research, "'There Is the Question of the Arabs and the Question of the Jews': Government Discussion on the Future of the West Bank, August 20, 1967," https://www.akevot.org.il/en/article/question-of-arabs-and-question-of-jews/.

23. Institute for Israeli-Palestinian Conflict Research, "'There Is the Question.'"

138 | Notes to Chapter 3

24. "The Story of the Settlement," *kedumim.org.il*, https://kedumim.org.il/.

25. Jewish Telegraphic Agency, "Dayan: Better to Hold Sharm El-Sheikh Without Peace Than Peace Without This Area," *JTA Daily News Bulletin*, February 18, 1971, 2, http://pdfs.jta.org/1971/1971-02-18_033.pdf.

26. Arian and Shamir, "The Primarily Political Functions of the Left-Right Continuum," 139–58.

27. Benny Neuberger, "Between Ideology and Sociology: The Parties in Israel 1950–2000," *State and Society* 1 (2001): 79–87 [Hebrew].

28. Yeshayahu Aviad, "Reflections on a Jewish State," in *Religious Zionism: An Anthology*, ed. Yosef Tirosh (World Zionist Organization, 1975), 128–47.

29. Eliezer Papo, *Sefer Pele Yoetz* [*The Land of Israel*] (Beine, 1870), 33.

30. Ehud Luz, *Parallels Meet: Religion and Nationalism in the Early Zionist Movement in Eastern Europe, 1882–1904* (Am Oved, 1985), 304 [Hebrew].

31. Zvi Yehuda Kook, "Psalm 19," *yeshiva.org.il*, https://www.yeshiva.org.il/midrash/2022 [Hebrew].

32. Shlomo Goren, "Problems of a Religious State," in *Religious Zionism: An Anthology*, ed. Yosef Tirosh (World Zionist Organization, 1975), 180–87.

33. Shifra Mishlov, "The Zionist View of Rabbi Goren," *Israel* 20 (2012): 85–87, 91–92 [Hebrew].

34. Ze'ev Jabotinsky, "Left Jordan," *Doar Hayom*, April 11, 1930, https://www.nli.org.il/he/newspapers/dhy/1930/04/11/01/article/7/ [Hebrew].

35. Aryeh Naor, *Ze'ev Jabotinsky's Constitutional Outline for the Jewish State in the Land of Israel*, 75, https://in.bgu.ac.il/bgi/iyunim/DocLib3/zeev3a.pdf.

36. *Doar Hayom*, April 12, 1930.

37. Colin Shindler, *The Rise of the Israeli Right: From Odessa to Hebron* (Cambridge University Press, 2015).

38. Ze'ev Jabotinsky, *Plytonim* (Eri Jabotinsky, 1954), 86 [Hebrew].

39. Ze'ev Jabotinsky, *Basa'ar* (Eri Jabotinsky, 1953), 16 [Hebrew].

40. Eliezer Don-Yehiya, "Between Nationalism and Religion: The Change in Jabotinsky's Attitude Towards the Religious Tradition," *Studies in the Israel Uprising* (2004), 160.

Chapter 3

1. Moti Karpel, "Indeed, There Is No Right and There Is No Left," *Makor-rishom*, April 28, 2019, https://www.makorrishon.co.il/opinion/134957/ [Hebrew].

2. Max Weber, *Essays in Sociology*, trans., ed., and introd. Hans Gerth and Charles Wright Mills (Oxford University Press, 1946).

3. John P. Nettl, "The State as a Conceptual Variable," *World Politics* 20, no. 4 (1968): 559–92.

4. Yossi Goldstein, *Between Zion and Zionism: The History of the Zionist Movement, 1881–1914* (Open University Press, 2015) [Hebrew].

5. Theodor Herzl, *The Jewish State* (Zionist Library, 1972), 65 [Hebrew].

6. Chaim Weizmann, *Essays and Work* (Shoken, 1949), 449–50 [Hebrew].

7. Avraham Yitzhak HaCohen Kook, *Orot Yisrael* (Yedioth Ahronoth, 2019), chap. 6 [Hebrew].

8. Michael Duchan, "A Religious Zionist Cannot Vote for Identity," *Kipa*, April 4, 2019, https://www.kipa.co.il/חדשות/דעות/אדם-ציוני-דתי-לא-יכול-להצביע-זהות/ [Hebrew].

9. Israel Democracy Institute, *On Democracy, Equality and Individual Rights* (Israel Democracy Institute, 2012), https://www.idi.org.il/books/2803 [Hebrew].

10. Provisional Government of Israel, "Declaration of Independence, May 14, 1948," https://main.knesset.gov.il/en/about/pages/declaration.aspx.

11. Provisional Government of Israel, "Declaration of Independence, May 14, 1948."

12. Eldad Naor, "The War of Independence in the Eyes of the Orthodox, According to Agudat Yisrael Diary Published in Jerusalem (March–April 1948)," *Study of Orthodox Jews* 5 (2018): 94–131 [Hebrew].

13. Yehuda Elitzur, *The Borders of the Land in the Israeli Tradition*, https://www.daat.ac.il/daat/tanach/tora/gvul-eli-1.htm [Hebrew].

14. The Law of Return, 1950.

15. Anita Shapira, *Ben Gurion: The Character of a Leader* (Am Oved, 2015), 158 [Hebrew].

16. The General Zionists were initially formed in the European diaspora, evolving in the Land of Israel and in the State of Israel. They had a central liberal ideological concept and existed from the early 1930s to the 1960s, when they merged with the Liberal Party, which itself merged into what is now Likud. See Amir Goldstein, "The Decline of the General Zionists and the Failure of the Liberal Alternative, 1959–1961," *Iyunim Bitkumat Israel* 16 (2006): 296 [Hebrew].

17. Ariel Finkelstein, "Graduates of State-Religious Education in the Labor Market: A Preliminary Overview," Ne'emanei Torah Va'Avodah, August 2017, https://toravoda.org.il/בוגרי-החינוך-הממלכתי-דתי-בשוק-העבודה/; Yair Sheleg, ed., *From the Training Supervisor to the Locomotive Driver? Religious Zionism and Israeli Society* (Israel Democracy Institute, 2019) [Hebrew].

18. Roi Mendel and Yron Druckman, "The History of the Exemption: From Ben Gurion and Begin to the Tal Law," *Ynet*, June 15, 2012, https://www.ynet.co.il/articles/0,7340,L-4242559,00.html [Hebrew].

19. Kook, "Psalm 19."

20. Kook, "Psalm 19."

21. The Israeli government's announcement of the annexation of East Jerusalem was made by virtue of Section 11b of the Government and Judicial Procedures Ordinance, 1948; Basic Law: Jerusalem the Capital of Israel, 1980; Golan Heights Law, 1981.

22. Michael Bruno and Stanley Fischer, "The Inflationary Process in Israel: Shocks and Accommodation," in *The Israeli Economy: Maturing Through Crises*, ed. Yoram Ben-Porath (Harvard University Press, 1986), 347–71.

23. Dan Giladi, *Israel's Economy: Handing the Shock-Stabilization and Its Success, 1985–1989* (Ministry of Education, Public Service Information Center, 1998).

24. Moshe Hellinger and Isaac Hershkowitz, *Obedience and Disobedience in Religious Zionism: From Gush Emunim to the Price Tag Attacks* (Israel Democracy Institute, 2015), 24–68.

25. Hellinger and Hershkowitz, 35–40.

26. Merav Arlozorov, "Is Israel Degenerating into a Birth Race—of War Through the Womb?," *The Marker*, December 30, 2022, https://www.themarker.com/opinion/2022-12-30/ty-article/.premium/00000185-5d44-d68b-a7ef-7dec7dab0000 [Hebrew].

27. Justice Aharon Barak, in the judgment of *United Mizrahi Bank v. Migdal Cooperative Village*, November 9, 1995.

28. Evelyn Gordon, "The Creeping Delegitimization of Peaceful Protest," *Azure Online* 7 (1999), https://azure.org.il/article.php?id=314.

29. Nadav Shragai, *Mount of Contention: The Struggle for the Temple Mount, Jews and Muslims, Religion and Politics Since 1967* (Keter, 1995), 110.

30. Yaniv Pohorils, "The National Demographer: There Is No Jewish Majority Between the Jordan and the Sea," *Ynet*, October 4, 2016, https://www.ynet.co.il/articles/0,7340,L-4860863,00.html [Hebrew].

31. Kobi Nachshoni, "'Modern Pinchas': Yigal Amir's Halachic Move to Justify Murder," *Ynet*, November 1, 2019, https://www.ynet.co.il/articles/0,7340,L-5617285,00.html [Hebrew].

32. Peninei Halakhah, Likkutim 2, 11:13–14.

33. Dvir Kariv, *Yitzhak Rabin's Assassination: The Untold Story* (Teper, 2015) [Hebrew].

34. Cited in Moshe Gorli, "Rabin's Murder: Between the Responsibility of the Religious Fanatic and the Responsibility of the Right and Netanyahu," *Calcalist*, October 18, 2021, https://www.calcalist.co.il/local_news/article/bjofxnirk [Hebrew].

35. "Rabin's Murder: 'We Were Beaten Because We Wore a Kippa," *Ynet*, November 4, 2014, https://www.ynet.co.il/articles/0,7340,L-4588068,00.html [Hebrew].

36. Avner Hofstein, "The Counselor Who Divided Israel," *Zeman Israel*, August 30, 2022, https://www.zman.co.il/336195/popup/ [Hebrew].

37. "Netanyahu in 2003: 'Increased Child Allowances Will Bring Us to Collapse'; Netanyahu in 2015: 'Allowances Were Increased,'" *Calcalist*, November 20, 2015, https://www.calcalist.co.il/local/articles/0,7340,L-3673988,00.html [Hebrew].

38. Yair Sheleg, *The Loss of Innocence: The Effect of Disengagement on Religious Zionism* (Israel Democracy Institute, 2015) [Hebrew].

39. Yanon Ben Ya'akov, "Rabbi Dov Lior: 'Democracy Is the Foreign Work of Our Generation.'" *Srugim*, July 3, 2011, https://www.srugim.co.il/20841 [Hebrew].

40. Haim Levinson, "Benny Katsober: Dismantling Democracy and Subordinating It to Judaism," *Haaretz*, January 8, 2012, https://www.haaretz.co.il/news/politics/2012-01-08/ty-article/0000017f-dbc2-db22-a17f-fff38df20000 [Hebrew].

41. "Billionaire Sheldon Adelson: It's Not Bad If Israel Isn't a Democracy," *Haaretz*, November 9, 2014, https://www.haaretz.co.il/news/world/america/2014-11-09/ty-article/0000017f-e64e-d97e-a37f-f76f69270000 [Hebrew].

42. Knesset, "Outgoing President Rivlin: 'The Various Tribes in Israeli Society Are Here to Stay. We Must Always Ensure That in the Natural Tension Between Kingdom and Tribalism, It Will Be the Kingdom That Overcomes Communal Tribalism,'" *Knesset News*, July 7, 2021, https://main.knesset.gov.il/News/PressReleases/pages/press07072021d.aspx [Hebrew].

43. A. R. Hoffman, "An Architect of Israel's Judicial Reform Warns of a Religious War in the Jewish State," *New York Sun*, March 31, 2023, https://www.nysun.com/article/an-architect-of-israels-judicial-reform-warns-of-a-religious-war-in-the-jewish-state.

44. Gilad Morg, "Four Years on the Way to the Indictment: This Is How the Netanyahu Cases Unfolded," *Ynet*, November 22, 2010, https://www.ynet.co.il/articles/0,7340,L-5630033,00.html [Hebrew]; Government of Israel, State Attorney's Office, "The Indictment against Prime Minister Benjamin Netanyahu Was Submitted to the District Court," January 28, 2020, https://www.gov.il/he/departments/news/28-1-2020-01 [Hebrew].

45. Basic Law: Israel—Nation State of the Jewish People.

46. Atara German, "Part of the Left: This Is What Will Be Done to the Person Who Leaves the Likud," *Makor Rishon*, December 13, 2020, https://www.makorrishon.co.il/opinion/292099 [Hebrew].

47. Shuki Friedman, "Religion and State: From Struggle to Dialogue," *Israel Institute for Democracy*, September 25, 2019, https://www.idi.org.il/articles/28710 [Hebrew]; Shmuel Rosner, "Do the Israelis Want a Jewish or a Democratic State?," *Kan 11*, January 17, 2023, https://www.kan.org.il/content/kan-news/opinions/243153/ [Hebrew].

48. Yascha Mounk, *The People vs. Democracy: Why Our Freedom Is in Danger and How to Save It* (Harvard University Press, 2018); Heino Nyyssönen and Jussi Metsälä, "Liberal Democracy and Its Current Illiberal Critique: The Emperor's New Clothes?," *Europe-Asia Studies* 73, no. 2 (2021): 273–90.

49. Andreas Schedler, *Electoral Authoritarianism: The Dynamics of Unfree Competition* (Lynne Reiner, 2006); Neil DeVotta, "From Civil War to Soft Authoritarianism: Sri Lanka in Comparative Perspective," *Global Change, Peace & Security* 22, no. 3: 331–43.

50. "And so in this sense the new state that we are constructing in Hungary is an illiberal state, a non-liberal state. It does not reject the fundamental princi-

ples of liberalism such as freedom, and I could list a few more, but it does not make this ideology the central element of state organisation, but instead includes a different, special, national approach." "Government of Hungary, Prime Minister Viktor Orbán's Speech at the 25th Bálványos Summer Free University and Student Camp," *kormany.hu*, July 30, 2014, https://2015-2019.kormany.hu/en/the-prime-minister/the-prime-minister-s-speeches/prime-minister-viktor-orban-s-speech-at-the-25th-balvanyos-summer-free-university-and-student-camp.

51. Fareed Zakaria, "What in the World: Turkey's Transition into an Illiberal Democracy," CNN, April 17, 2015, https://edition.cnn.com/videos/tv/2015/04/17/what-in-the-world-turkeys-transition-into-an-illiberal-democracy.cnn.

52. Marco Garrido, "The Ground for the Illiberal Turn in the Philippines," *Democratization* 29, no. 4 (2022): 673–91.

53. Joshua Pepper, "From Sector to People: Ultra-Orthodox Society in the Face of the Corona Crisis," *Hashiloach*, September 6, 2020, https://hashiloach.org.il/ [Hebrew].

54. Meir Elran, "The Mount Meron Disaster: A Deep Structural Change Is Required in the Israeli System," INSS, May 3, 2021, https://www.inss.org.il/he/publication/meron-stampede/ [Hebrew].

55. Globes, "What Is Your Position Regarding Civil Marriage, Public Transportation on Shabbat and Recruiting Ultra-Orthodox? The Answers in a Huge Survey by Globes," *Globes*, April 5, 2023, https://www.globes.co.il/news/article.aspx?did=1001443421 [Hebrew].

Chapter 4

1. Idan Avni, "'You Were Ready to Be Hurt for Everyone': Thousands Escorted Police Officer Amir Khoury to Rest," *Israel Hayom*, March 31, 2022, https://www.israelhayom.co.il/news/local/article/9615152 [Hebrew].

2. Yoav Itiel and Uri Sela, "Almost Lynched in Bat Yam: Members of the Minorities Were Driving in the City After the Fasting Started—the Crowd Overturned Their Car," *Walla*, October 5, 2022, https://news.walla.co.il/item/3533744 [Hebrew].

3. Rabbi Yehuda Bivas was the only one who believed that the Jews in the Land of Israel would have to take up arms, but he believed that this was necessary against the Ottomans. Yitzhak Molcho, "Rabbi Yehuda Bivas: Father of Political Zionism," *Hebron*, February 10, 2015, http://www.hebron.org.il/history/97 [Hebrew].

4. Shlomo Avineri, "Herzl's Altneuland: A View of Israeli Society," *Israel Academy of Sciences*, 2013, https://www.academy.ac.il/SystemFiles/21552.pdf [Hebrew].

5. Ahad Ha'am, "Truth from the Land of Israel," Ben Yehuda Project, https://benyehuda.org/read/1153 [Hebrew].

6. Shabtai Teveth, "Ben-Gurion and the Arab Question," *Cathedra* 43 (1987): 52–68 [Hebrew].

7. Uri Milstein, "Ben Gurion's Strategy: Transfer for the Arabs," *News1*, February 4, 2018, https://www.news1.co.il/ [Hebrew].

8. Ze'ev Jabotinsky, "Us and the Arabs: The Iron Wall," *Razvit*, November 4, 1923, http://www.jabotinsky.org/ [Hebrew].

9. Naor, *Ze'ev Jabotinsky's Constitutional Outline, for the Jewish State in the Land of Israel*, 51–92, https://in.bgu.ac.il/bgi/iyunim/DocLib3/zeev3a.pdf.

10. Hillel Cohen, *Good Arabs* (Keter, 2006), 10 [Hebrew].

11. Yair Bauml, "Principles of the Policy of Discrimination Against the Arabs in Israel, 1948–1968," *Iyunim Bitkumat Israel* 16 (2006): 395–397 [Hebrew].

12. Bauml, 398.

13. Ruvik Rosenthal, ed., *Kfar Qasem: Events and Myth* (Hakibbutz Hameuchad, 2000) [Hebrew].

14. Absentee Property Law, 1950.

15. David A. Wesley, *State Practices and Zionist Images: Shaping Economic Development in Arab Towns in Israel* (Berghahn Books, 2013), 113–14.

16. Bauml, "Principles of the Policy of Discrimination," 391–413.

17. Bauml, 396.

18. Bauml, 392–93.

19. Elie Rekhess and Eric Rodnitsky, eds., *Arab Society in Israel* (Abraham Foundation, 2009), 2–4 [Hebrew].

20. Gadi Hitman and Libi Moskovitz, "Two Went Together Unless They Were Meant to Be: Herut and Mapam Parties and Their Relation to the Military Government," *National Resilience, Politics and Society* 1, no. 1 (2019): 56–52 [Hebrew].

21. Yair Bauml, *The Military Government and the Process of Its Abolition, 1958–1968: c. The Changes in the Military Government from 1958 Until the Resignation of Ben-Gurion in June 1963*, https://lib.cet.ac.il/pages/item.asp?item=21357 [Hebrew].

22. Gideon Shilo, *The Israeli Arabs and the PLO* (Harry S. Truman Research Institute, 1982).

23. Ori Stendel, *The Arabs of Israel: Between Hammer and Anvil* (Akedmon, 1992), 253–58 [Hebrew].

24. Ra'anan Cohen, *Strangers in Their Home* (Dionon, 2006), 100–102 [Hebrew].

25. Israeli Communist Forum, *The First Land Day—March 30, 1976*, https://icf.org.il/?page_id=370 [Hebrew].

26. Sammy Smooha, "The Arab Minority in Israel: Radicalization or Politicization?," in *Israel: State and Society 1948–1988* (Studies in Contemporary Jewry 5), ed. Peter Y. Medding (Oxford University Press, 1989), 60–61.

27. Third session of the ninth Knesset, June 20, 1977.

28. Avraham Dor, "The Observatory Factory in the Galilee: Twenty Years Later," *Studies in National Defense* 6 (Haifa University, 2004), 7–14.

29. Dor, 59–62.

30. Gadi Hitman, *Israel and Its Arab Minority, 1948–2008: Dialogue, Protest, Violence* (Lexington Books, 2016), 130.

31. Stendel, *The Arabs of Israel*, 274–82.

32. Selection of Events in the Arab Sector, September–October 20–21, 1982 (prime minister's office), 4–6.

33. On the riots in May and October 1990, see the report of the Orr Committee, chap. 1, sect. 122–23.

34. Rekhess and Rodnitsky, *Arab Society in Israel*, 12–13.

35. For the official plan, see Israeli Minorities Ministry, *A Multi-Year Plan for the Development of the Arab Sector,* June 1990 [Hebrew]; "Agreement with Hadash: A Ministerial Committee That Will Work to Reduce the Disparities in the Arab Sector," *Haaretz*, June 5, 1990, cited in Vodi Awade, "The Arab Parties Have Been Recommending Candidates Since the 1980s, Without Success," *Sicha Mekomit*, October 11, 2022, https://www.mekomit.co.il/ [Hebrew].

36. Ron Gerlitz and Nidal Osman, "This Is How Rabin and Peres Built the Alliance with Hadash That Brought the Left to Power," *Sicha Mekomit,* February 25, 2015, https://www.mekomit.co.il/ [Hebrew].

37. Civil Right Association Report 1996, 8–9.

38. Thabet Abu Rass, "Between Peace and the Law of the Nation," *Molad: The Center for the Renewal of Democracy* (podcast), October 20, 2018, http://www.molad.org/articles/articlePrint.php?id=1351 [Hebrew].

39. Rana Eseed, "The Islamic Movement in Israel: Development and Key Features," *Journal of Welfare and Society* 4 (2019): 609–33 [Hebrew].

40. Rafa Abu Tarif, "Two Decades of Incitement, Hamas and Al-Aqsa," *Mida*, October 14, 2015, https://mida.org.il/2015/10/14/ [Hebrew].

41. For more about Balad, see chapter 5.

42. 213th session of the fifteenth Knesset, June 20, 2001.

43. State Commission of Inquiry into the Clashes Between Security Forces and Israeli Citizens in October 2000 (hereafter, the Orr Commission).

44. Orr Commission, sect. 126–36.

45. Hitman, *Israel and Its Arab Minority*, 192–95.

46. Orr Commission, conclusion.

47. Ori Nir, "Shock in the Laboratory," *Haaretz*, October 10, 2001 [Hebrew].

48. Yair Ettinger, "Center for Arab Rights: Ban Support for Transfer," *Haaretz*, June, 2, 2004 [Hebrew].

49. Government of Israel, Prime Minister's Office, "Report and Recommendations of the Committee of Ministers Regarding the 'Orr Committee' Report," Resolution No. 2015, June 13, 2004, https://www.gov.il/he/departments/policies/2004_des2015 [Hebrew].

50. Ivri Committee, *The Recommendations of the Committee for the Establishment of a National-Civil Service,* https://www.to-be.co.il/resource.aspx?resourceid=6103 [Hebrew].

51. Nir Yahav, "The Wound Opens Anew Every Day: The War in Which Israeli Arabs also Paid in Blood," *Walla*, July 23, 2016, https://news.walla.co.il/item/2976317 [Hebrew]; Jonathan Liss, Ofra Idelman, and Yoav Stern, "More Than 700 Arabs Have Been Arrested in Demonstrations in Israel Since the Beginning of the Operation in Gaza," *Haaretz*, January 18, 2009 [Hebrew].

52. Government of Israel, Prime Minister's Office, "The Prime Minister Participated in the Prime Minister's Conference for the Arab Sector Held in Haifa," Government of Israel, Prime Minister's Office, July 10, 2008, https://www.gov.il/he/departments/news/spokehaifa100708 [Hebrew].

53. Basic guidelines of the thirty-second government of the State of Israel headed by Benjamin Netanyahu, https://main.knesset.gov.il/mk/government/documents/kaveiyesod2009.pdf.

54. Amir Fuchs and Dana Blander, *Anti-Democratic Legislation in the 18th Knesset (2009–2013)* (Israel Democracy Institute, 2015), 17–18.

55. Fuchs and Blander, 22–23.

56. Fuchs and Blander, 33–42.

57. Knesset, Draft Bill for the Prevention of Hazards (Amendment: Prevention of Noise from a Public Address System in a Place of Worship), https://main.knesset.gov.il/activity/legislation/laws/pages/lawbill.aspx?t=lawsuggestionssearch&lawitemid=2009510 [Hebrew].

58. Building and Planning Law, Amendment No. 116.

59. Basic Law: Israel, Nation State of the Jewish People.

60. Youssuf Jabarin, "The Deepening of Exclusion: On the Draft Basic Law: The Nation State of the Jewish People," in *Conditional Citizenship: On Citizenship, Equality and Offensive Legislation*, eds. Youssuf Jabarin and Sarah Osetzki-Lazar (Pardes, 2016), 145–63 [Hebrew].

61. Mohammad Watad, "The Nationality Law and Relations Between the State of Israel and the Arab Public," *Hedim*, March 2019, https://www.inss.org.il/he/publication/ [Hebrew].

62. Ben Caspit, *Netanyahu: The Biography* (Yedioth Ahronoth, 2021), 9 [Hebrew]; Benjamin Netanyahu, "Right-Wing Rule Is in Danger," Facebook, March 17, 2015, https://www.facebook.com/268108602075/posts/10152778935532076 [Hebrew].

63. "An Israeli Election Turns Ugly," *New York Times*, March 17, 2015, https://www.nytimes.com/2015/03/18/opinion/an-israeli-election-turns-ugly.html.

64. Government of Israel, Prime Minister's Office, "The Government's Activity for Economic Development in the Minority Population in the Years 2016–2020," Resolution No. 922, December 30, 2015, https://www.gov.il/he/Departments/policies/2015_des922 [Hebrew].

65. Anna Brasky et al., "Netanyahu in Nazareth: 'A New Era of Prosperity, Integration and Security Begins Today,'" *Maariv*, January 13, 2021, https://www.maariv.co.il/news/politics/Article-814880 [Hebrew].

66. Brasky et al.

67. Amit Segal, "Ra'am Chairman: "If I Receive Budgets and Legislation from Netanyahu, What Do I Care About Giving Him What He Needs?," *Portal 12N*, November 13, 2020, https://www.mako.co.il/news-n12_magazine/2020_q4/Article-045312dcbabb571027.htm [Hebrew].

68. Hassan Shaalan and Moran Azoulai, "MK Abbas in the Plenum: The Holocaust Forces Us to Put Our Differences Aside," *Ynet*, April 21, 2020, https://www.ynet.co.il/articles/0,7340,L-5718607,00.html [Hebrew].

69. Amit Segal, "Prime Minister-Designate Bennett in an Exclusive Interview: 'I Told My Family That I Would Become the Most Hated Person in the Country,'" *Portal 12N*, June 3, 2021, https://www.mako.co.il/news-politics/2021_q2/Article-98a24f2b692d971027.htm [Hebrew].

70. Gad Peretz, "Mansour Abbas: The State of Israel Is a Jewish State and It Will Remain So. The Question Is What the Status of an Arab Citizen Is," *Globes*, December 21, 2021, https://www.globes.co.il/news/article.aspx?did=1001395413 [Hebrew].

Chapter 5

1. Twelve national political movements can be identified among the Arab citizens of Israel since 1948: the communist current in its various incarnations, the al-Ard movement, the Sons of the Land, the Progressive National Alliance, the Progressive List for Peace, the Arab Democratic Party, the Islamic Movement, Balad, the National Committee of the Heads of Arab Localities, the National Committee for the Protection of the Lands, the National Coordination Committee, and the Supreme Monitoring Committee.

2. Gadi Hitman, "From Separatism to Violence: A Typology of Interactions Between the Citizen and the State Establishment," *Cogent Social Sciences* 6, no. 1 (2020): a1832345.

3. Aziz Haidar and Elia Zuriek, "The Palestinians Seen Through the Israeli Cultural Paradigm," *Journal of Palestinian Studies* 16, no. 3 (1987): 68.

4. Sammy Smooha and Ora Cibulski, "Trends in Social Research on Arabs in Israel, 1948–1976," *Asian and African Studies* 12, no. 2 (1978): 263–78.

5. Aziz Haidar, "Introduction: Political Events in the Lives of the Arab Citizens of Israel," in *Political Aspects of the Lives of Arab Citizens in Israel*, ed. Aziz Haidar (Van Leer Institute Press, 2019), 8–9 [Hebrew].

6. Roni Shaked, "Between Al-Ard and Balad: In Search of National Identity," in *Political Aspects of the Lives of Arab Citizens in Israel*, 167–96 [Hebrew].

7. Sarah Ozacky-Lazar, "The Military Government as a Mechanism of Control Over the Arab Citizens, 1958–1948," *Ha-Mizrah Ha-Hadash* 43 (2002): 1–16 [Hebrew]; Yair Bauml, *A Blue and White Shadow* (Pardes, 2007) [Hebrew].

8. Elia T. Zureik, *The Palestinians in Israel: A Study in Internal Colonialism* (Routledge and Kegan Paul, 1979).

9. Yitzhak Reiter, "The Political Ideological System," in *Jews and Arabs in Israel*, ed. Rami Hochman (Hebrew University, 1988), 345–62 [Hebrew].

10. As'ad Ghanem, "Parties and Ideological Currents of the Palestinian-Arab Minority in Israel," *State and Society* 1, no. 1 (2001): 89–114 [Hebrew].

11. Gadi Hitman, "Israel's Arab Leadership in the Decade Attending the October 2000 events," *Israel Affairs* 19, no. 1 (2013): 121–38.

12. Orr Commission, 28.

13. Elie Rekhess, *Between Communism and Arab Nationalism: Rakkah and the Arab Minority in Israel (1965–1973)* (Tel Aviv University, 1993), 24 [Hebrew].

14. The three newspapers were *Al-Ittihad*, *Al-Ghad*, and *Al-Jadid*.

15. Rekhess, *Between Communism and Arab Nationalism*, 30–33.

16. Stendel, *The Arabs of Israel*, 234–39.

17. *Akhbar Al-Ard*, October 17, 1959, 4.

18. *Kalimat Al-Ard*, October 31, 1959, 4.

19. *Kifah Al-Ard*, December 7, 1959, 3.

20. *Maariv*, December 29, 1967.

21. Stendel, *The Arabs of Israel*, 258; Yitzhak Reiter and Reuven Aharoni, *The Political World of Israel's Arabs* (Institute for Israeli Arab Studies, 1993), 21 [Hebrew].

22. *Al-Awda*, October 29, 1983.

23. Raphael Israeli, *Muslim Fundamentalism in Israel* (Brassey's, 1993).

24. Nachman Tal, "The Islamic Movement in Israel," *Strategic Update* 2, no. 4 (2000): 10–15.

25. Israeli, *Muslim Fundamentalism in Israel*, 26.

26. Balad, Homepage, https://www.altajamoa.org/.

27. Balad, Homepage.

28. Balad, Homepage.

29. Knesset Elections Law Bill, Amendment No. 61.

30. Aziz Haidar, "The Joint List in 2015 Elections: Establishment, Platform and Challenges," *Bayan* 5 (2015): 14–17 [Hebrew].

31. An Arab survey institution in Israel.

32. Manal Harib, "The Joint Arab List in the 2015 Elections: A Necessary Partnership," *Bayan* 4 (2015): 9–10 [Hebrew].

33. Hadash, "Hadash Candidates for the 21st Knesset," *hadash.org.il*, http://hadash.org.il/ [Hebrew].

34. Haidar, "The Joint List in 2015 Elections," 14–17.

35. Ja'afar Farah, "Political Participation of Arab Palestinian Society in Israel," *Mussawa Center*, 2015 [Hebrew].

36. Dalit Halevi, "Abu Mazem Met with a Delegation of the Balad Party," *Arutz Sheva*, February 20, 2017, https://www.inn.co.il/News/News.aspx/340523 [Hebrew].

37. Moran Azoulai et al., "MKs Met with Relatives of Terrorists: 'They Listened to Our Pain,'" *Ynet*, December 4, 2016, https://www.ynet.co.il/articles/0,7340,L-4762185,00.html [Hebrew].

38. Daphne Lial, "Prime Minister: 'The MKs Are Not Fit to Serve in the Knesset," *Mako*, February 4, 2016, https://www.mako.co.il/news-military/politics-q1_2016/Article-7f922a86cdca251004.htm [Hebrew].

39. Gidi Weitz and Jackie Khouryi, "The Balad MKs Do Not Regret It," *Haaretz*, March 10, 2016, https://www.haaretz.co.il/.premium-MAGAZINE-1.2878308.

40. "The Joint List Condemns the Decision to Remove MK Ghattas from the Knesset," *Bukja.net*, January 2, 2017, https://www.bukja.net/archives/647880 [Arabic].

41. Dana Weiss, "MK Odeh Admits to Accusations Against Ghattas," *Mako*, December 22, 2016, https://www.mako.co.il/news-channel2/Channel-2-Newscast-q4_2016/Article-c087567abd72951004.htm [Hebrew].

42. Jackie Khoury and Jonathan Liss, "The Members of the Joint List Failed to Draft a Joint Statement Following the Terror Attack," *Haaretz*, July 15, 2017, https://www.haaretz.co.il/news/politi/1.4257695 [Hebrew].

43. Taleb Abu 'Arar, "Odeh is Not Representing the Joint List," *Rotter.net*, April 10, 2018, https://www.rotter.net/forum/scoops1/464455/shtmal [Hebrew].

44. Khader Su'ad, "The Controversy in Arab Society Surrounding the Civil War in Syria," *Echoes*, March 2018, https://www.inss.org.il/he/publication/ [Hebrew].

45. Tamar Beeleeji, "The Joint List Turned Down the Arab League Invitation," *Times of Israel*, April 21, 2015.

46. Qassem Bakri, "Elections Season: A New Arab Party to Compete for Knesset Seats," *Arab48.com*, November 21, 2018, https://www.arab48.com/ [Arabic].

47. Miron Rapoport, "Following His Withdrawal from the Joint List, Tibi Declares: I Will Lead the Establishment of the Blocking Bloc," *Mekomit*, January 15, 2019, https://www.mekomit.co.il/ [Hebrew].

48. Hassan Shaalan, "MK Ahmed Tibi Quits the Joint List," *Ynet*, January 8, 2019, https://www.ynet.co.il/articles/0,7340,L-5442645,00.html [Hebrew].

49. Khaled Awad, "The 2019 Knesset Elections and the Misery of Arab Parties," *Panet*, February 25, 2019, https://www.panet.co.il/article/2501008 [Arabic].

50. Panet and Panorama, "Statnet Institute Poll: 52 Percent Believe That Tibi and Odeh Are Responsible for Dismantling the Joint List," *panet.co.il*, March 13, 2019, http://panet.co.il/article/2515882 [Arabic].

51. "The Elections Committee Decides to Close the Pages Inciting Against Al-Tibi and Gives Facebook 3 Days to Reveal the Identity of Its Managers," *Kul al-Arab*, March 28, 2019, https://www.alarab.com/Article/894731 [Arabic].

52. Arik Bender, "Hadash, Ta'al and Balad Will Run Together; Tibi: 'The Door Remains Open for Abbas,'" *Maariv*, February 4, 2021, https://www.maariv.co.il/news/politics/Article-819720 [Hebrew].

Bibliography

Abu 'Arar, Taleb. "Odeh Is Not Representing the Joint List." *Rotter.net*, April 10, 2018. https://x.com/kann_news/status/983701320191369217. [Hebrew].

Abu Rass, Thabet. "Between Peace and the Law of the Nation." *Molad: The Center for the Renewal of Democracy* (podcast). October 20, 2018. http://www.molad.org/articles/articlePrint.php?id=1351. [Hebrew].

Abu Tarif, Rafa. "Two Decades of Incitement, Hamas and Al-Aqsa." *Mida*, October 14, 2015. https://mida.org.il/2015/10/14/חמא-הסתה-של-עשורים-שני-האסלאמית-/התנועה. [Hebrew].

"An Israeli Election Turns Ugly." *New York Times*, March 17, 2015. https://www.nytimes.com/2015/03/18/opinion/an-israeli-election-turns-ugly.html.

Arian, Asher, and Michal Shamir. "The Primarily Political Functions of the Left-Right Continuum." *Comparative Politics* 15, no. 2 (1983): 139–58.

Arlozorov, Merav. "Is Israel Degenerating into a Birth Race—of War Through the Womb?" *The Marker*, December 30, 2022. https://www.themarker.com/opinion/2022-12-30/ty-article/.premium/00000185-5d44-d68b-a7ef-7dec7dab0000. [Hebrew].

Aviad, Yeshayahu. "Reflections on a Jewish State." In *Religious Zionism: An Anthology*, edited by Yosef Tirosh, 128–47. World Zionist Organization, 1975.

Avineri, Shlomo. "Herzl's Altneuland: A View of Israeli Society." *Israel Academy of Sciences*, 2013. https://www.academy.ac.il/SystemFiles/21552.pdf. [Hebrew].

Avni, Idan. "'You Were Ready to Be Hurt for Everyone': Thousands Escorted Police Officer Amir Khoury to Rest." *Israel Hayom*, March 31, 2022. https://www.israelhayom.co.il/news/local/article/9615152. [Hebrew].

Awad, Khaled. "The 2019 Knesset Elections and the Misery of Arab Parties." *Panet*, February 25, 2019. https://www.panet.co.il/article/2501008. [Arabic].

Awade, Vodi. "The Arab Parties Have Been Recommending Candidates Since the 1980s, Without Success." *Sicha Mekomit*, October 11, 2022. https://www.mekomit.co.il/תוגלפמה-תויברעה-ממליצות-עע-מעומדים-בכ-/. [Hebrew].

Azoulai, Moran, Shahar Hai, Telam Yahav, and Itmar Eichner. "MKs Met with Relatives of Terrorists: 'They Listened to Our pAin.'" *Ynet*, December 4, 2016. https://www.ynet.co.il/articles/0,7340,L-4762185,00.html. [Hebrew].

Bakri, Qassem. "Elections Season: A New Arab Party to Compete for Knesset Seats." *Arab48.com*, November 21, 2018. https://www.arab48.com/سياسة/محليات/2018/ 11/21/الكنيست-مقاعد-على-للمنافسة-جديد-حزب-الانتخابات-موسم. [Arabic.]

Bauml, Yair. *A Blue and White Shadow*. Pardes, 2007. [Hebrew].

Bauml, Yair. "Principles of the Policy of Discrimination Against the Arabs in Israel, 1948–1968." *Iyunim Bitkumat Israel* 16 (2006): 391–413. [Hebrew].

Bauml, Yair. "The Military Government and the Process of Its Abolition, 1958–1968: c. The Changes in the Military Government from 1958 until the Resignation of Ben-Gurion in June 1963." https://lib.cet.ac.il/pages/item.asp?item=21357. [Hebrew.]

Beckley, Gloria T., and Paul Burstein. "Religious Pluralism, Equal Opportunity and the State." *Western Political Quarterly* 44, no. 1 (1991): 185–208.

Beeleeji, Tamar. "The Joint List Turned Down the Arab League Invitation." *Times of Israel*, April 21, 2015.

Ben Gurion, David. *Letters to Pola and the Children*. Am Oved, 1968.

Ben Ya'akov, Yanon. "Rabbi Dov Lior: 'Democracy Is the Foreign Work of Our Generation.'" *Srugim*, July 3, 2011. https://www.srugim.co.il/20841--העבודה-זרההרב-דב-ליאור-הדמוקרטיה-היא. [Hebrew.]

Bender, Arik. "Hadash, Ta'al and Balad Will Run Together; Tibi: 'The Door remains Open for Abbas.'" *Maariv*, February 4, 2021. https://www.maariv.co.il/news/politics/Article-819720. [Hebrew.]

"Billionaire Sheldon Adelson: It's Not Bad If Israel Isn't a Democracy." *Haaretz*, November 9, 2014. https://www.haaretz.co.il/news/world/america/2014-11-09/ty-article/0000017f-e64e-d97e-a37f-f76f69270000. [Hebrew.]

Borochov, Dov. *Writings*. United Kibbutz, 1955.

Brasky, Anna, Alon Hachmon, Eric Bender, and Matan Wasserman. "Netanyahu in Nazareth: 'A New Era of Prosperity, Integration and Security Begins Today." *Maariv*, January 13, 2021. https://www.maariv.co.il/news/politics/Article-814880. [Hebrew.]

Brooks, Clem, Paul Nieuwbeerta, and Jeff Manza. "Cleavage-Based Voting Behavior in Cross-National Perspective: Evidence from Six Postwar Democracies." *Social Science Research* 35, no. 1 (2006): 88–128.

Brubaker, Roger, and Frederick Cooper. "Beyond 'Identity.'" *Theory and Society* 29, no. 1 (2000): 1–47.

Bruno, Michael, and Stanley Fischer. "The Inflationary Process in Israel: Shocks and Accommodation." In *The Israeli Economy: Maturing Through Crises*, edited by Yoram Ben-Porath, 347–71. Harvard University Press, 1986.

Buckingham, David. "Introducing Identity." In *Youth, Identity, and Digital Media*, edited by David Buckingham, 1–24. MIT Press, 2008.

Caspit, Ben. *Netanyahu: The Biography*. Rishon LeZion: Yedioth Ahronoth, 2021. [Hebrew.]
Cohen, Hillel. *Good Arabs*. Keter, 2006. [Hebrew.]
Cohen, Ra'anan. *Strangers in Their Home*. Dionon, 2006. [Hebrew.]
Deegan-Krause, Kevin. "New Dimensions of Political Cleavage." In *The Oxford Handbook of Political Behavior*, edited by Russell J. Dalton and Hans-Dieter Klingemann, 538–56. Oxford University Press, 2006.
DeVotta, Neil. "From Civil War to Soft Authoritarianism: Sri Lanka in Comparative Perspective." *Global Change, Peace & Security* 22, no. 3: 331–43.
Don-Yehiya, Eliezer. "Between Nationalism and Religion: The Change in Jabotinsky's Attitude Towards the Religious Tradition." *Studies in the Israel Uprising* (2004).
Dor, Avraham. "The Observatory Factory in the Galilee: Twenty Years Later." *Studies in National Defense 6*. Haifa University, 2004.
Duchan, Michael. "A Religious Zionist Cannot Vote for Identity." *Kipa*, April 4, 2019. https://www.kipa.co.il/חדשות/דעות-אדם-ציוני-דתי-לא-יכול-להצביע-זהות/. [Hebrew.]
Easthope, Antony. "Bhabha, Hybridity and Identity." *Textual Practice* 12, no. 2 (1998): 341–48.
Elitzur, Yehuda. *The Borders of the Land in the Israeli Tradition*. Accessed Nov. 20, 2024. https://www.daat.ac.il/daat/tanach/tora/gvul-eli-1.htm. [Hebrew.]
Elran, Meir. "The Mount Meron Disaster: A Deep Structural Change Is Required in the Israeli System." INSS, May 3, 2021. https://www.inss.org.il/he/publication/meron-stampede/. [Hebrew.]
Eseed, Rana. "The Islamic Movement in Israel: Development and Key Features." *Journal of Welfare and Society* 4 (2019): 609–33. [Hebrew.]
Ettinger, Yair. "Center for Arab Rights: Ban Support for Transfer." *Haaretz*, June, 2, 2004. [Hebrew.]
Farah, Ja'afar. "Political Participation of Arab Palestinian Society in Israel." Mussawa Center, 2015. [Hebrew.]
Finkelstein, Ariel. "Graduates of State-Religious Education in the Labor Market: A Preliminary Overview." Ne'emanei Torah Va'Avodah, August 2017. https://toravoda.org.il/החינוך-הממלכתי-דתי-בשוק-העבודהבוגרי-/.
Friedman, Shuki. "Religion and State: From Struggle to Dialogue." Israel Institute for Democracy, September 25, 2019. https://www.idi.org.il/articles/28710. [Hebrew.]
Fuchs, Amir, and Dana Blander. *Anti-Democratic Legislation in the 18th Knesset (2009–2013)*. Israel Democracy Institute, 2015.
García-Canclini, Néstor. "Hybridity." *International Encyclopedia of the Social & Behavioral Sciences*. 2nd ed. Elsevier, 2015.
Garrido, Marco. "The Ground for the Illiberal Turn in the Philippines." *Democratization* 29, no. 4 (2022): 673–91.
Gerlitz, Ron, and Nidal Osman. "This Is How Rabin and Pares Built the Alliance with Hadash Tthat Brought the Left to Power." *Sicha Mekomit*, February 25,

2015. https://www.mekomit.co.il/שהעלתה-חדש-עם-הברית-את-בנו-ופרס-רבין-כך/. [Hebrew.]

German, Atara. "Part of the Left: This Is What Will Be Done to the Person Who Leaves the Likud." *Makor Rishon*, December 13, 2020. https://www.makor-rishon.co.il/opinion/292099. [Hebrew.]

Ghanem, As'ad. "Parties and Ideological Currents of the Palestinian-Arab Minority in Israel." *State and Society* 1, no. 1 (2001): 89–114. [Hebrew.]

Giladi, Dan. *Israel's Economy: Handing the Shock-Stabilization and Its Success, 1985–1989*. Ministry of Education, Public Service Information Center, 1998.

Globes. "What Is Your Position Regarding Civil Marriage, Public Transportation on Shabbat and Recruiting Ultra-Orthodox? The Answers in a Huge Survey by *Globes*." *Globes*, April 5, 2023. https://www.globes.co.il/news/article.aspx?did=1001443421. [Hebrew.]

Goldstein, Amir. "The Decline of the General Zionists and the Failure of the Liberal Alternative, 1959–1961." *Iyunim Bitkumat Israel* 16 (2006): 293–342. [Hebrew.]

Goldstein, Yossi. *Ahad Ha'am and Herzl*. Zalman Shazar Center, 2011. [Hebrew.]

Goldstein, Yossi. *Between Zion and Zionism: The History of the Zionist Movement, 1881–1914*. Open University Press, 2015. [Hebrew.]

Gordon, Evelyn. "The Creeping Delegitimization of Peaceful Protest." *Azure Online* 7 (1999). https://azure.org.il/article.php?id=314.

Goren, Shlomo. "Problems of a Religious State." In *Religious Zionism: An Anthology*, edited by Yosef Tirosh, 180–87. World Zionist Organization, 1975.

Gorli, Moshe. "Rabin's Murder: Between the Responsibility of the Religious Fanatic and the Responsibility of the Right and Netanyahu." *Calcalist*, October 18, 2021. https://www.calcalist.co.il/local_news/article/bjofxnirk. [Hebrew.]

Gottholf, Yehuda. "Right and Left in a Divided Generation." *Balances* 2 (1977): 125–34. [Hebrew.]

Government of Hungary. "Prime Minister Viktor Orbán's Speech at the 25th Bálványos Summer Free University and Student Camp." *kormany.hu*, July 30, 2014. https://2015-2019.kormany.hu/en/the-prime-minister/the-prime-minister-s-speeches/prime-minister-viktor-orban-s-speech-at-the-25th-balvanyos-summer-free-university-and-student-camp.

Government of Israel, Prime Minister's Office. "Report and Recommendations of the Committee of Ministers Regarding the 'Orr Committee' Report." Resolution No. 2015, June 13, 2004. https://www.gov.il/he/departments/policies/2004_des2015. [Hebrew.]

Government of Israel, Prime Minister's Office. "The Government's Activity for Economic Development in the Minority Population in the Years 2016–2020." Resolution No. 922, December 30, 2015. https://www.gov.il/he/Departments/policies/2015_des922. [Hebrew.]

Government of Israel, Prime Minister's Office. "The Prime Minister Participated in the Prime Minister's Conference for the Arab Sector Held in Haifa." July 10, 2008. https://www.gov.il/he/departments/news/spokehaifa100708. [Hebrew.]

Government of Israel, State Attorney's Office. "The Indictment Against Prime Minister Benjamin Netanyahu Was Submitted to the District Court." January 28, 2020. https://www.gov.il/he/departments/news/28-1-2020-01. [Hebrew.]

Ha'am, Ahad. "Truth from the Land of Israel." Ben Yehuda Project. https://benyehuda.org/read/1153. [Hebrew.]

Hadash. "Hadash Candidates for the 21st Knesset." 2019. *Hadash.org.il*. http://hadash.org.il/הרשימה, 2019. [Hebrew.]

Haidar, Aziz. "Introduction: Political Events in the Lives of the Arab Citizens of Israel." In *Political Aspects of the Lives of Arab Citizens in Israel*, edited by Aziz Haidar, 7–18. Van Leer Institute Press, 2019. [Hebrew.]

Haidar, Aziz. "The Joint List in 2015 Elections: Establishment, Platform and Challenges." *Bayan* 5 (2015): 14–17. [Hebrew.]

Haidar, Aziz, and Elia Zuriek. "The Palestinians Seen Through the Israeli Cultural Paradigm." *Journal of Palestinian Studies* 16, no. 3 (1987): 68–86.

Halevi, Dalit. "Abu Mazem Met with a Delegation of the Balad Party." *Arutz Sheva*, February 20, 2017. https://www.inn.co.il/News/News.aspx/340523. [Hebrew.]

Harib, Manal. "The Joint Arab List in the 2015 Elections: A Necessary Partnership." *Bayan* 4 (2015): 9–10. [Hebrew.]

Hellinger, Moshe, and Isaac Hershkowitz. *Obedience and Disobedience in Religious Zionism: From Gush Emunim to the Price Tag Attacks*. Israel Democracy Institute, 2015. [Hebrew.]

Herzl, Theodor. *The Jewish Question: Diaries, 1895–1898*. Mosad Bialik, 1997. [Hebrew.]

Herzl, Theodor. *The Jewish State*. Zionist Library, 1972. [Hebrew.]

Hitman, Gadi. "From Separatism to Violence: A Typology of Interactions Between the Citizen and the State Establishment." *Cogent Social Sciences* 6, no. 1 (2020): a1832345.

Hitman, Gadi. "Israel's Arab Leadership in the Decade Attending the October 2000 Events." *Israel Affairs* 19, no. 1 (2013): 121–38.

Hitman, Gadi. *Israel and Its Arab Minority, 1948–2008: Dialogue, Protest, Violence*. Lexington Books, 2016.

Hitman, Gadi, and Libi Moskovitz. "Two Went Together Unless They Were Meant to Be: Herut and Mapam Parties and Their Relation to the Military Government." *National Resilience, Politics and Society* 1, no. 1 (2019): 35–58. [Hebrew.]

Hoffman, A. R. "An Architect of Israel's Judicial Reform Warns of a Religious War in the Jewish State." *New York Sun*, March 31, 2023. https://www.nysun.com/article/an-architect-of-israels-judicial-reform-warns-of-a-religious-war-in-the-jewish-state.

Hofstein, Avner. "The Counselor Who Divided Israel." *Zeman Israel*, August 30, 2022. https://www.zman.co.il/336195/popup/. [Hebrew.]

Institute for Israeli-Palestinian Conflict Research. "'There Is the Question of the Arabs and the Question of the Jews': Government Discussion on the Future of the West Bank, August 20, 1967." Institute for Israeli-

Palestinian Conflict Research. 2017. https://www.akevot.org.il/en/article/question-of-arabs-and-question-of-jews/.

Israel Central Bureau of Statistics. "The Christian Population in Israel: Data for Christmas 2021." December 21, 2021. https://www.cbs.gov.il/he/mediarelease/pages/2021/-לרגל-נתונים-בישראל-הנוצרית-האוכלוסייה2021-המולד-חג.aspx. [Hebrew.]

Israel Central Bureau of Statistics. "The Druze Population in Israel: Data for Ziyarat al-Nabi Shu'ayb 2022." April 24, 2022. https://www.cbs.gov.il/he/mediarelease/pages/2022/-נתונים-לקט-בישראל-הדרוזית-האוכלוסייה2022-שועייב-הנביא-חג-לרגל.aspx. [Hebrew.]

Israel Central Bureau of Statistics. "The Muslim Population in Israel: Data for Eid al-Adha 2022." July 6, 2022. https://www.cbs.gov.il/he/mediarelease/pages/2022/-האוכלוסייה2022-הקורבן-חג-לרגל-נתונים-בישראל-המוסלמית.aspx. [Hebrew.]

Israel Central Bureau of Statistics. "Persons Aged 20 and Over, by Religiosity and by Selected Characteristics." December 5, 2021. https://www.cbs.gov.il/he/publications/LochutTlushim/לוחות%20שנתון/st28_06x.pdf.

Israel Central Bureau of Statistics. "The Population of Ethiopian Origin in Israel: Selected Data Published on the Occasion of the Sigd Festival 2021." November 1, 2021. https://www.cbs.gov.il/en/mediarelease/pages/2021/the-population-of-ethiopian-origin-in-israel-selected-data-on-the-occasion-of-the-sigd-festival-2021.aspx.

Israeli Communist Forum. *The First Land Day—March 30, 1976*. https://icf.org.il/?page_id=370. [Hebrew.]

Israel Democracy Institute. *On Democracy, Equality and Individual Rights*. Israel Democracy Institute, 2012. https://www.idi.org.il/books/2803. [Hebrew.]

Israeli Minorities Ministry. *A Multi-Year Plan for the Development of the Arab Sector*. June 1990. [Hebrew.]

Israeli, Raphael. *Muslim Fundamentalism in Israel*. Brassey's, 1993.

Itiel, Yoav, and Uri Sela. "Almost a Lynching in Bat Yam: Members of the Minorities Were Driving in the City After the Fasting Started—the Crowd Overturned Their Car." *Walla*, October 5, 2022. https://news.walla.co.il/item/3533744. [Hebrew.]

Ivri Committee. *The Recommendations of the Committee for the Establishment of a National-Civil Service*. 2007. https://www.to-be.co.il/resource.aspx?resourceid=6103. [Hebrew.]

Iyall Smith, Keri E., and Patricia Leavy. *Hybrid Identities: Theoretical and Empirical Examinations*. Brill, 2008.

Jabarin, Youssuf. "The Deepening of Exclusion: On the Draft Basic Law: The Nation State of the Jewish People." In *Conditional Citizenship: On Citizenship, Equality and Offensive Legislation*, edited by Youssuf Jabarin and Sarah Osetzki-Lazar, 145–63. Pardes, 2016. [Hebrew.]

Jabotinsky, Ze'ev. *Basa'ar*. Eri Jabotinsky, 1953. [Hebrew.]

Jabotinsky, Ze'ev. "Left Jordan." *Doar Hayom*, April 11, 1930, https://www.nli.org.il/he/newspapers/dhy/1930/04/11/01/article/7/. [Hebrew.]

Jabotinsky, Ze'ev. *Plytonim*. Eri Jabotinsky, 1954. [Hebrew.]
Jabotinsky, Ze'ev. "Us and the Arabs: The Iron Wall." *Razvit*, November 4, 1923. http://www.jabotinsky.org/. [Hebrew.]
Jewish Telegraphic Agency. "Dayan: Better to Hold Sharm El-Sheikh Without Peace Than Peace Without This Area." *JTA Daily News Bulletin*, February 18, 1971, 2. http://pdfs.jta.org/1971/1971-02-18_033.pdf.
Kariv, Dvir. *Yitzhak Rabin's Assassination: The Untold Story*. Teper, 2015. [Hebrew.]
Karpel, Moti. "Indeed, There Is No Right and There Is No Left." *Makorrishom*, April 28, 2019. https://www.makorrishon.co.il/opinion/134957/. [Hebrew.]
Katz, Gideon. "The Secular Element in Aharon David Gordon's Thought." *Iyunim Bitkumat Israel* 11 (2001): 465–85. [Hebrew.]
Kaufman, Chaim. "Possible and Impossible Solutions to Ethnic Civil Wars." *International Security* 20, no. 4 (1996): 136–75.
Khoury, Jackie, and Jonathan Liss. "The Members of the Joint List Failed to Draft a Joint Statement Following the Terror Attack." *Haaretz*, July 15, 2017. https://www.haaretz.co.il/news/politi/1.4257695. [Hebrew.]
Knesset. *Benjamin Ze'ev Herzl, 1860–1904*. https://main.knesset.gov.il/About/commemoration/pages/herzl.aspx. [Hebrew.]
Knesset. "Outgoing President Rivlin: 'The Various Tribes in Israeli Society Are Here to Stay. We Must Always Ensure That in the Natural Tension Between Kingdom and Tribalism, It Will Be the Kingdom That Overcomes Communal Tribalism.'" *Knesset News*, July 7, 2021. https://main.knesset.gov.il/News/PressReleases/pages/press07072021d.aspx. [Hebrew.]
Kohn, Hans. *The Idea of Nationalism: A Study in Its Origins and Background*. Macmillan, 1944.
Kook, Avraham Yitzhak HaCohen. *Orot Yisrael*. Yedioth Ahronoth, 2019. [Hebrew.]
Kook, Zvi Yehuda. "Psalm 19." *Yeshiva.org.il*. https://www.yeshiva.org.il/midrash/2022. [Hebrew.]
Levinson, Avraham. *Ahad Ha'am and His Teachings*. Ben Yehuda Project. 2020. https://benyehuda.org/read/4166. [Hebrew.]
Levinson, Haim. "Benny Katsober: Dismantling Democracy and Subordinating It to Judaism." *Haaretz*, January 8, 2012. https://www.haaretz.co.il/news/politics/2012-01-08/ty-article/0000017f-dbc2-db22-a17f-fff38df20000. [Hebrew.]
Liel, Daphne. "Prime Minister: 'The MKs Are Not Fit to Serve in the Knesset.'" *Mako*, February 4, 2016. https://www.mako.co.il/news-military/politics-q1_2016/Article-7f922a86cdca251004.htm. [Hebrew.]
Lipset, Seymour Martin, and Stein Rokkan, eds. *Party Systems and Voter Alignments: Cross-National Perspectives*. Free Press, 1967.
Liss, Jonathan, Ofra Idelman, and Yoav Stern. "More than 700 Arabs Have Been Arrested in Demonstrations in Israel Since the Beginning of the Operation in Gaza." *Haaretz*, January 18, 2009. [Hebrew.]
Luz, Ehud. *Parallels Meet: Religion and Nationalism in the Early Zionist Movement in Eastern Europe, 1882–1904*. Am Oved, 1985. [Hebrew.]

Mendel, Roi, and Yron Druckman. "The History of the Exemption: From Ben Gurion and Begin to the Tal Law." *Ynet*, June 15, 2012. https://www.ynet.co.il/articles/0,7340,L-4242559,00.html. [Hebrew.]

Milstein, Uri. "Ben Gurion's Strategy: Transfer for the Arabs." *News1*, February 4, 2018. https://www.news1.co.il/. [Hebrew.]

Mishlov, Shifra. "The Zionist View of Rabbi Goren." *Israel* 20 (2012): 81–106. [Hebrew.]

Molcho, Yitzhak. "Rabbi Yehuda Bivas: Father of Political Zionism." *Hebron*, February 10, 2015. http://www.hebron.org.il/history/97. [Hebrew.]

Morg, Gilad. "Four Years on the Way to the Indictment: This Is How the Netanyahu Cases Unfolded." *Ynet*, November 22, 2010. https://www.ynet.co.il/articles/0,7340,L-5630033,00.html. [Hebrew.]

Morris, Benny. "And Books and Scrolls in Normal Old Age: A New Look at Marxian Zionist Documents." *Alfiim* 12 (1996). https://www.sharett.org.il/cgi-webaxy/sal/sal.pl?lang=he&ID=880900_sharett_new&act=show&dbid=library&dataid=1486. [Hebrew.]

Mounk, Yascha. *The People vs. Democracy: Why Our Freedom Is in Danger and How to Save It*. Harvard University Press, 2018.

Nachshoni, Kobi. "'Modern Pinchas': Yigal Amir's Halachic Move to Justify Murder." *Ynet*, November 1, 2019. https://www.ynet.co.il/articles/0,7340,L-5617285,00.html. [Hebrew.]

Naor, Aryeh. *Ze'ev Jabotinsky's Constitutional Outline for the Jewish State in the Land of Israel*. Iyunim bitkoomat Israel. https://in.bgu.ac.il/bgi/iyunim/DocLib3/zeev3a.pdf.

Naor, Eldad. "The War of Independence in the Eyes of the Orthodox, According to Agudat Yisrael Diary Published in Jerusalem (March–April 1948)." *Study of Orthodox Jews* 5 (2018): 94–131. [Hebrew.]

Netanyahu, Benjamin. "Right-Wing Rule Is in Danger." Facebook, March 17, 2015. https://www.facebook.com/268108602075/posts/10152778935532076. [Hebrew.]

"Netanyahu in 2003: 'Increased Child Allowances Will Bring Us to Collapse'; Netanyahu in 2015: 'Allowances Were Increased.'" *Calcalist*, November 20, 2015. https://www.calcalist.co.il/local/articles/0,7340,L-3673988,00.html. [Hebrew.]

Nettl, John P. "The State as a Conceptual Variable." *World Politics* 20, no. 4 (1968): 559–92.

Neuberger, Benny. "Between Ideology and Sociology: The Parties in Israel 1950–2000." *State and Society* 1 (2001): 79–87. [Hebrew.]

Nir, Ori. "Shock in the Laboratory." *Haaretz*, October 10, 2001. [Hebrew.]

Nyyssönen, Heino, and Jussi Metsälä. "Liberal Democracy and Its Current Illiberal Critique: The Emperor's New Clothes?" *Europe-Asia Studies* 73, no. 2 (2021): 273–90.

Ordóñez-Carabaño, Angela, and María Prieto-Ursúa. "Forgiving a Genocide: Reconciliation Processes Between Hutu and Tutsi in Rwanda." *Journal of Cross-Cultural Psychology* 52, no. 5 (2021): 427–48.

Oren, Elhanan. "From the Transfer Proposal, 1937–1938, to Retrospective Transfer, 1947–1948." *Iyunim Bitkumat Israel* 7 (1997): 75–85. [Hebrew.]

Ozacky-Lazar, Sarah. "The Military Government as a Mechanism of Control Over the Arab citizens, 1958–1948." *Ha-Mizrah Ha-Hadash* 43 (2002): 1–16. [Hebrew.]

Panet and Panorama. "Statnet Institute Poll: 52% Believe That Tibi and Odeh Are Responsible for Dismantling the Joint List." *panet.co.il*, March 13, 2019. http://panet.co.il/article/2515882. [Arabic.]

Papastergiadis, Nikos. "Hybridity and Ambivalence: Places and Flows in Contemporary Art and Culture." *Theory, Culture & Society* 22, no. 4 (2005): 39–64.

Papo, Eliezer. *Sefer Pele Yoetz* [*The Land of Israel*]. Beine, 1870.

Pepper, Joshua. "From Sector to People: Ultra-Orthodox Society in the Face of the Corona Crisis." *Hashiloach*, September 6, 2020. https://hashiloach.org.il/לנוכח-משבר-הקורונה-מגזר-לעם-החברה-החרדית/. [Hebrew.]

Peretz, Gad. "Mansour Abbas: The State of Israel is a Jewish State and It Will Remain So. The Question Is What the Status of an Arab Citizen Is." *Globes*, December 21, 2021. https://www.globes.co.il/news/article.aspx?did=1001395413. [Hebrew.]

Pew Research Center. *Pew-Templeton Global Religious Futures Project*. 2021. https://www.pewresearch.org/topic/religion/religious-demographics/pew-templeton-global-religious-futures-project/.

Pohorils, Yaniv. "The National Demographer: There Is No Jewish Majority Between the Jordan and the Sea." *Ynet*, October 4, 2016. https://www.ynet.co.il/articles/0,7340,L-4860863,00.html. [Hebrew.]

Provisional Government of Israel. "Declaration of Independence, May 14, 1948." 1948. https://main.knesset.gov.il/en/about/pages/declaration.aspx.

"Rabin's Murder: 'We Were Beaten because We Wore a Kippa.'" *Ynet*, November 4, 2014. https://www.ynet.co.il/articles/0,7340,L-4588068,00.html. [Hebrew.]

Ramon, Einat. "Cultural Zionism as an Alternative to Reforming the Ahad Ha'am Writings." *Iyunim Bitkumat Israel* 14 (2014): 104–40. [Hebrew.]

Rapoport, Miron. "Following His Withdrawal from the Joint List, Tibi Declares: I Will Lead the Establishment of the Blocking Bloc." *Mekomit*, January 15, 2019. https://www.mekomit.co.il/מ-באמצעות-חוסם-גוש-להקים-רוצה-טיבי-אחמד/. [Hebrew.]

Reinhart, Yehuda. "The Confrontation Between Zionism and Traditionalism Before the First World War." *Iyunim Bitkumat Israel* 3 (1993): 366–79. [Hebrew.]

Reiter, Yitzhak. "The Political Ideological System." In *Jews and Arabs in Israel*, edited by Rami Hochman, 345–62. Hebrew University, 1988. [Hebrew.]

Reiter, Yitzhak, and Reuven Aharoni. *The Political World of Israel's Arabs*. Institute for Israeli Arab Studies, 1993. [Hebrew.]

Rekhess, Elie. *Between Communism and Arab Nationalism: Rakkah and the Arab Minority in Israel (1965–1973)*. Tel Aviv University, 1993. [Hebrew.]

Rekhess, Elie, and Eric Rodnitsky, eds. *Arab Society in Israel*. Abraham Foundation, 2009. [Hebrew.]

Rooksby, Ed. "The Relationship Between iberalism and socialism." *Science & Society* 76, no. 4 (2012): 495–520.

Rosenthal, Ruvik, ed. *Kfar Qasem: Events and Myth*. Hakibbutz Hameuchad, 2000. [Hebrew.]

Rosner, Shmuel. "Do the Israelis want a Jewish or a democratic state?" *Kan 11*, January 17, 2023. https://www.kan.org.il/content/kan-news/opinions/243153/. [Hebrew.]

Schedler, Andreas. *Electoral Authoritarianism: The Dynamics of Unfree Competition*. Lynne Reiner, 2006.

Segal, Amit. "Prime Minister-designate Bennett in an Exclusive Interview: 'I Told My Family That I Would Become the Most Hated Person in the Country.'" *Portal 12N*, June 3, 2021. https://www.mako.co.il/news-politics/2021_q2/Article-98a24f2b692d971027.htm. [Hebrew.]

Segal, Amit. "Ra'am Chairman: "If I Receive Budgets and Legislation from Netanyahu, What Do I Care About Giving Him What He Needs?" *Portal 12N*, November 13, 2020. https://www.mako.co.il/news-n12_magazine/2020_q4/Article-045312dcbabb571027.htm. [Hebrew.]

Shaalan, Hassan. "MK Ahmed Tibi Quits the Joint List." *Ynet*, January 8, 2019. https://www.ynet.co.il/articles/0,7340,L-5442645,00.html. [Hebrew.]

Shaalan, Hassan, and Moran Azoulai. "MK Abbas in the Plenum: The Holocaust Forces Us to Put Our Differences Aside." *Ynet*, April 21, 2020. https://www.ynet.co.il/articles/0,7340,L-5718607,00.html. [Hebrew.]

Shaked, Roni. "Between Al-Ard and Balad: In Search of National Identity." In *Political Aspects of the Lives of Arab Citizens in Israel*, edited by Aziz Haidar, 167–96. Van Leer Institute Press, 2019. [Hebrew.]

Shapira, Anita. *Ben Gurion: The Character of a Leader*. Am Oved, 2015. [Hebrew.]

Shapira, Assaf. *Citizenship: A Theoretical and Historical Review*. Israel Democracy Institute, 2010. [Hebrew.]

Sheleg, Yair. *The Loss of Innocence: The Effect of Disengagement on Religious Zionism*. Israel Democracy Institute, 2015. [Hebrew.]

Sheleg, Yair, ed. *From the Training Supervisor to the Locomotive Driver? Religious Zionism and Israeli Society*. Israel Democracy Institute, 2019. [Hebrew.]

Shilo, Gideon. *The Israeli Arabs and the PLO*. Harry S. Truman Research Institute, 1982.

Shindler, Colin. *The Rise of the Israeli Right: From Odessa to Hebron*. Cambridge University Press, 2015.

Shragai, Nadav. *Mount of Contention: The Struggle for the Temple Mount, Jews and Muslims, Religion and Politics Since 1967*. Keter, 1995.
Simon, Bernd. *Identity in Modern Society: A Social Psychological Perspective*. Blackwell, 2004.
Smooha, Sammy. "Ethnic Democracy: Israel as a Prototype." In *Zionism: A Contemporary Polemic*, edited by Pinchas Ginosar and Avi Bareli, 277–311. Ben-Gurion Heritage Center, 1996.
Smooha, Sammy. "The Arab Minority in Israel: Radicalization or pOliticization?" In *Israel: State and Society 1948–1988* (Studies in Contemporary Jewry 5), edited by Peter Y. Medding, 59–88. Oxford University Press, 1989.
Smooha, Sammy, and Ora Cibulski. "Trends in Social Research on Arabs in Israel, 1948–1976." *Asian and African Studies* 12, no. 2 (1978): 263–78.
Spencer-Oatey, Helen. "Theories of Identity and the Analysis of Face." *Journal of Pragmatics* 39, no. 4 (2007): 639–56.
Stendel, Ori. *The Arabs of Israel: Between Hammer and Anvil*. Akedmon, 1992. [Hebrew.]
Su'ad, Khader. "The Controversy in Arab Society Surrounding the Civil War in Syria." *Echoes*, March 2018. https://www.inss.org.il/he/publication/-מלחמת-האזרחהמחלוקת-בחברה-הערבית-סביב/. [Hebrew.]
Tal, Nachman. "The Islamic Movement in Israel." *Strategic Update* 2, no. 4 (2000): 10–15.
Tchernichovsky, Shaul. "Man Is Nothing but . . ." Ben Yehuda Project. 2014. https://benyehuda.org/read/2722.
"The Elections Committee Decides to Close the Pages Inciting Against Al-Tibi and Gives Facebook 3 Days to Reveal the Identity of Its Managers." *Kul al-Arab*, March 28, 2019. https://www.alarab.com/Article/894731. [Arabic.]
"The Joint List Condemns the Decision to Remove MK Ghattas from the Knesset." *Bukja.net*, January 2, 2017. https://www.bukja.net/archives/647880. [Arabic.]
"The Story of the Settlement." *kedumim.org.il*. 2018. https://kedumim.org.il/סיפור-ההתיישבות/. [Hebrew.]
Telford, Hamish. "The Federal Spending Power in Canada: Nation-Building or Nation-Destroying?" *Publius* 33, no. 1 (2003): 23–44.
Teveth, Shabtai. "Ben-Gurion and the Arab Question." *Cathedra* 43 (1987): 52–68. [Hebrew.]
Tilly, Charles. "Citizenship, Identity and Social History." *International Review of Social History* 40, S3 (1995): 1–17.
Waldron, Jeremy. "Theoretical Foundations of Liberalism." *Philosophical Quarterly* 37, no. 147 (1987): 127–50.
Watad, Mohammad. "The Nationality Law and Relations Between the State of Israel and the Arab Public." *Hedim*, March 2019. https://www.inss.org.il/he/publication/מדינת-ישראל-והציבור-העחוק-הלאום-ויחסי-/. [Hebrew.]
Weber, Max. *Essays in Sociology*. Translated, edited, and introduction by Hans Gerth and Charles Wright Mills. Oxford University Press, 1946.

Weiler Israel, Yael. "Religion, Nationalism and the New Gospel: Rabbi Dr. Yehuda Aryeh Leon Bivas, the Forerunner of Zionism." In *A Time for Mercy: Rabbi Zvi Hirsch Kalischer and the Awakening to Zion*, edited by Asaf Yedidya, 50–69. Yad Yitzhak Ben Zvi, 2015. [Hebrew.]

Weiss, Dana. "MK Odeh Admits to Accusations Against Ghattas." *Mako*, December 22, 2016. https://www.mako.co.il/news-channel2/Channel-2-Newscast-q4_2016/Article-c087567abd72951004.htm. [Hebrew.]

Weitz, Gidi, and Jackie Khouryi. "The Balad MKs Do Not Regret It." *Haaretz*, March 10, 2016. https://www.haaretz.co.il/.premium-MAGAZINE-1.2878308.

Weizmann, Chaim. *Essays and Work*. Shoken, 1949. [Hebrew.]

Wesley, David A. *State Practices and Zionist Images: Shaping Economic Development in Arab Towns in Israel*. Berghahn Books, 2013.

Yaffe, Aharon. *Lines for the Redemption Process of the Bet Shean Valley*. Jewish National Fund, 1992. https://www.kkl.org.il/files/karka/35/karka-35-1992-10.pdf. [Hebrew.]

Yahav, Nir. "The Wound Opens Anew Every Day: The War in Which Israeli Arabs Also Paid in Blood." *Walla*, July 23, 2016. https://news.walla.co.il/item/2976317. [Hebrew.]

Zakaria, Fareed. "What in the World: Turkey's Transition into an Illiberal Democracy." CNN, April 17, 2015. https://edition.cnn.com/videos/tv/2015/04/17/what-in-the-world-turkeys-transition-into-an-illiberal-democracy.cnn.

Zureik, Elia T. *The Palestinians in Israel: A Study in Internal Colonialism*. Routledge and Kegan Paul, 1979.

Index

Abbas, Mansour, 100, 102, 128
Adelson, Sheldon, 66
Aghbaria, Hasan, 116
Aghbaria, Raja, 116
Agudat Yisrael, 46, 53
Ahad Ha'am, 21, 22, 74
Ahdut HaAvoda (Unity of Labor), 36, 74
Al-Aqsa Intifada, 62
Al-Ard movement, 82, 107–108, 113–115
Alkalai, Yehuda ben Shlomo Chai, 32
Alon, Yigal, 78
Amir, Yigal, 59
Ariel, Uri, 65
Arlozorov, Haim, 25

Bahrain, viii
Balad party, 91, 110, 118–120
Balfour Declaration, 74
Barak, Aharon, 56
Barak, Ehud, 61
Basic Laws, 45, 56, 67, 97
Bastuni, Rostam, 108
Battle of Tel Hai, 26
Begin, Menachem, 37, 39, 52–53, 85, 133
Beit Hadassah, 31
Ben-Gurion, David, 27, 28, 30, 48, 49, 74–75, 78, 114
Ben-Gvir Itamar, 50

Bennett, Naftali, 102, 128
Bishara, Azmi, 91, 118
Bivas, Yehuda Aryeh Leon, 23, 43
Bond, 26
Borochov, Dov, 25, 26
Bosnia and Herzegovina, 8
Brazil, 30
Brooks, Clem, 10
Brubaker, Roger, 3

Canada, 56
Communist party (Rakah, Hadash), 82–83, 108, 110, 112–113
Cooper, Frederick, 3

Darawshe, Abdulwahab, 109
Darwish, Abdullah Nimer, 117
Dayan, Moshe, 30, 31
Deryi, Aryeh, 16, 17
Druckman, Haim, 50
Duterte, Rodrigo, 69

East Jerusalem, 51
Erdoğan, Recep Tayyip, 69
Eshkol, Levi, 30, 31, 82–83

Finkelstein, Arthur, 61
France, 5, 15, 16, 36–38

Galili, Yisrael, 49
Gantz, Benny, 68

Gaza Strip, viii, xi, 9, 51, 54, 70, 83, 87
García-Canclini, Nestor, 6
Germany, 17, 56
Ghattas, Basel, 123–124
Gordon, Aharon David, 26, 27
Goern, Shlomo, 34, 35
Golan Heights, 51
Gottholf, Yehuda, 16
Guttmacher, Eliyahu, 32, 33

Habibi, Emile, 113
Halacha, 41, 57–58, 132
Hamas, xi, 58, 61, 117, 132
Hapoel Hatzair (The Young Worker), 26
Hatnua (political party), 65
Hazan, Ya'akov, 27
Hebron, 7, 31, 34–35, 40, 47, 115
Hebron Agreement, 52
Herzl, Binyamin Ze'ev, 23–25, 33, 43, 74
Hess, Moshe, 25, 26
Histadrut, 32, 35, 80–82
Hovevei Zion (Lovers of Zion), 43

Iliberal democracy, 41–42, 69
Iqrit and Bir'am, 78
Islamic Movement, 90, 110, 116–117
Italy, 56

Jabotinsky, Ze'ev, 25, 27, 35, 44, 50, 74, 76
Jarjoura, Amin, 113
Joint Arab List, 105, 112, 118, 120–125
Judea and Samaria, 31, 37, 51, 54, 65, 87

Kadima (political party), 64
Kahana, Meir, 94
Kalischer, Zvi Hirsch, 32, 33

Kaminitz Law, 97
Kardoush, Mansour, 113
Katznelson, Berl, 25
Khamis, Yosef, 108
Khaougi, Habib, 113–114
Khazan, Shukri, 114
Khoury, Amir, 73
King Hussein, 58
Kiryat Arba, 31
Kook, Yitzhak HaCohen, 44, 49–50
Kook, Zvi Yehuda, 34

Lapid, Yair, 102–103, 128
Law of Return, 45
Leavy, Patricia, 6
Lebanon, 2
Levin, Yariv, 71
Levinger, Moshe, 58
Liberalism, 18
Lieberman, Avigdor, ix, 68, 94
Likud party, 31, 44, 53, 61–62, 64, 87, 95
Lior, Dov, 50, 65
Lipset, Seymour, 9, 10, 106
Lenin, Vladimir, 19
Louis XVI, 15

Mafdal (National Religious Party), 48
Makhool, Na'im, 114
Mandelblit, Avichai, 67
Manza, Jeff, 10
Mapai, 27, 29, 31, 48, 74, 80
Marcos, Ferdinand Jr., 69
Meir, Golda, 27
Melamed, Eliezer, 60
Military government, 30, 77, 79, 82
Mizrachi movement, 33
Mohliever, Shmuel, 33
Morocco, viii

Nablus, 31
Nakara, Hana, 113

Nakba, 77, 97, 114
Netanyahu, Benjamin, 32, 41, 52, 58, 61–62, 65, 67, 89, 94–96, 99–100, 133
Nettl, John P., 43
Nieuwbeerta, Paul, 10

Odeh, Ayman, 100, 123–124
Olmert, Ehud, 64, 67, 92, 95
Operation Defensive Shield, 62
Orbach, Ori, 65
Orbán, Victor, 69
Orr Commission, 91, 93–94
Oslo Accords, xi, 34, 52, 56–59, 61, 133
Ovadia, Yosef, 39

Palestinian Islamic Jihad, 61
Papastergiadis, Nikos, 6
Papo, Eliezer, 33
Peel Commission, 28, 29, 75
Peres, Shimon, 41, 64, 88
Poale Zion (Workers of Zion), 27
Porat, Hanan, 50
Progressive List for Peace (Ramal), 108–109

Ra'am party, 100, 102, 105, 126–128
Rabin, Yitzhak, viii, 59, 88–89, 133
Rhodes Agreements, 47
Rivlin, Reuven, ix, 11, 66
Rokkan, Stein, 9, 10
Rooksby, Ed, 19
Rothman, Simcha, 67, 132
Rupin, Arthur, 28, 29
Russia, 17
Rwanda, 8

Salah, Raed, 90
Sarsour, Ibrahim, 90
Sasson, Eliyahu, 30
Shamir, Yitzhak, 53, 87

Shapira, Haim-Moshe, 30
Sharf, Ze'ev, 30
Sharon, Ariel, 31, 53, 64, 93
Shas, 39–40, 53, 62
Simon, Bernd, 3, 4
Slomiansky, Nissan, 50
Smith, Keri Iyall, 6
Smotrich, Bezalel, 50
Socialism, 18
South Africa, 56
Stalin, Joseph, 19
Sudan, viii

Tabenkin Yitzhak, 27
Tchernichovsky, Shaul, 1
Temple Mount, 93, 124
Tibi, Ahmad, 125–127
Tilly, Charles, 3
Tikva Hadasha (political party), 68
Toubi, Tawfik, 113
Trotsky, Leon, 19
Tunisia, 2

United Arab Emirates, viii
United States, 3, 8, 56
Uziel, Ben-Zion Meir Hay, 44

Weber, Max, 42
Weizmann, Chaim, 35, 44
West Bank, viii, 52, 70, 83
Wye River Memorandum

Yahadut Ha-Torah (political party), 62
Yahalom, Shaul, 50
Yesh Atid (political party), 65
Yisrael Beiteinu (political party), 62, 68, 121
Yogev, Moti, 65

Ziad, Tawfiq, 113
Zionist Congress, 23, 27, 33
Zion Youth Movement, 26

www.ingramcontent.com/pod-product-compliance
Lightning Source LLC
Chambersburg PA
CBHW030345240426
43661CB00052B/1743